S0-DNL-440

Microsoft
WORD 97
The Cram Sheet

This Cram Sheet contains the distilled, key tasks in Microsoft Word 97. Review this information last thing before you enter the test room, paying special attention to those areas where you feel you need the most review. You can transfer any of the tasks from this sheet onto a blank piece of paper before beginning the exam. This side of the Cram Sheet lists tasks important to master in order to pass the Proficiency level Word exam, the flip side covers tasks for experts.

Proficiency Level Tasks

FILE MANAGEMENT

1. Click the Open button on the Standard toolbar to open a file.

2. Select File|Save As to save a document with a different name or to a different folder.

3. Select File|Close to close a document.

4. Remember how to browse for files and folders from the Open and Save As dialog boxes when opening and saving documents!

5. To save a document as a template, select File|Save As. Then select Document Template from the Save As Type box.

IMPORTANT TOOLBARS

6. To save, open, print, and spellcheck documents; or copy, cut, and paste text, use the Standard toolbar.

7. To apply styles; pick fonts and font sizes; align text; create bullet and number lists; and assign text colors and basic text styles, use the Formatting toolbar.

8. To edit tables, display the Tables And Borders toolbar by clicking the Tables And Borders button on the Standard toolbar.

9. To draw and edit lines, ovals, rectangles, AutoShapes, and callouts, display the Drawing toolbar by clicking the Drawing button on the Standard toolbar.

TEXT EDITING

10. Select Edit|Find to locate words and Edit|GoTo to locate headings, sections, bookmarks, tables, and graphics.

11. Use Edit|Replace to locate and replace words throughout a document.

12. To check spelling and grammar, click the Spelling And Grammar button on the Standard toolbar.

AUTOTEXT AND AUTOCORRECT

13. To create AutoText Entries, select the text, then select Insert|AutoText|New.

14. To create an AutoCorrect entry, select Tools|AutoCorrect.

DOCUMENT MAP

15. To display a Document Map, select View|Document Map.

16. To jump to items listed in a document map, click the item.

option on the Browse button on the vertical scroll bar.

BORDERS AND SHADING

27. When you open the Borders and Shading dialog box, you must reapply the formatting in the Apply to list box prior to closing the dialog box. The Apply to list box always defaults back to the Whole Document option whenever the dialog box is displayed.

28. Use the Tables and Borders toolbar to shade a paragraph or page.

29. Click Insert|Break and then select a section break to add a different border to a page or section of your document.

MACROS

30. Remember that a macro name can contain up to 80 letters and numbers, but the name must begin with a letter.

31. You cannot use spaces or symbols in a macro name. However, you can use the underscore character to separate words.

32. The easiest place to put a button that runs a macro is on the menu bar, to the right of the Help menu. Don't bother taking the time to give the button a picture (unless you're directed to)—just place it, record the macro, and then use it.

33. Run macros from the Macro dialog box by clicking Tools|Macro|Macros.

34. To delete a macro, click Tools|Macro| Macros, select a macro, and then click the Delete button.

35. Click Tools|Macros|Macro to delete a macro.

WORKGROUP EDITING

36. You can double-click the Versions icon on the bottom-right side of the status bar to quickly take you to the Versions dialog box.

37. Unless you need to change the viewing or printing options for tracked changes, you can use the Reviewing toolbar to enable the Track Changes feature.

38. You can start the Track Changes feature by double-clicking the TRK button in the status bar.

39. You can use the Track Changes dialog box to accept or reject each change individually, or you can accept or reject all changes collectively by clicking either the Accept All or Reject All button.

40. You can't convert a document with file versions to a master document. You must delete all versions before you can convert the document.

41. When you get to the end of a table, pressing the Tab key will add another row for you.

LISTS, FORMS, AND MAIL MERGES

42. You can press the Control+A keys to select all the text in a document.

43. When you are viewing a data source you can click the Manage Fields button on the Database toolbar to add a column header.

44. You can use the Insert Table button on the Standard toolbar to create up to a 4×5 table.

45. You can press the Enter key twice to deselect the bullet option and create a blank line.

46. An online form must be created and saved as a template. The user will open the template, fill it in, and then save the current form as a document.

SORTING

47. You can sort paragraphs by first numbering each paragraph.

48. You can sort records prior to a mail merge using the Mail Merge Helper.

ADVANCED FILE MANAGEMENT

49. When a document is protected, you cannot accept or reject changes, but you can continue to edit the document.

50. You can easily locate a document with a particular property by typing or selecting the property information in the Text or property list box in the Open dialog box.

Certification Insider™ Press

EXAM
CRAM™

Microsoft
WORD 97

MICROSOFT
OFFICE
USER
SPECIALIST

Deborah Alyne Christy
Elisabeth Parker

Microsoft Word 97 Exam Cram

Copyright © The Coriolis Group, 1999

Limits of Liability and Disclaimer of Warranty

Trademarks

The Coriolis Group, Inc.
An International Thomson Publishing Company
14455 N. Hayden Road, Suite 220
Scottsdale, Arizona 85260

602/483-0192
FAX 602/483-0193
http://www.coriolis.com

Library of Congress Cataloging-in-Publication Data
Christy, Deborah Alyne
    Microsoft Word 97 exam cram / by Deborah Alyne Christy and
Elisabeth Parker
        p. cm.
    Includes index.
    ISBN 1-57610-222-X
    1. Microsoft Word. 2. Word processing. I. Parker, Elisabeth.
II. Title.
Z52.5.M52C483 1999
652.5'5369--DC21   98-4560
                                                    CIP

Printed in the United States of America
10 9 8 7 6 5 4 3 2 1

Publisher
Keith Weiskamp

Acquisitions Editor
Shari Jo Hehr

Marketing Specialist
Cynthia Caldwell

Project Editor
Michelle Stroup

Technical Reviewer
Theresa Brown

Production Coordinator
Kim Eoff

Cover Design
Anthony Stock

Layout Design
April Nielsen

CD-ROM Developer
Robert Clarfield

an International Thomson Publishing company

Albany, NY • Belmont, CA • Bonn • Boston • Cincinnati • Detroit • Johannesburg • London • Madrid
Melbourne • Mexico City • New York • Paris • Singapore • Tokyo • Toronto • Washington

CORIOLIS

14455 North Hayden, Suite 220 • Scottsdale, Arizona 85260

The Smart Way To Get Certified ™

Thank you for purchasing one of our innovative certification study guides, just one of the many members of the Coriolis family of certification products.

Certification Insider Press™ was created in late 1997 by The Coriolis Group to help professionals like you obtain certification and advance your career. Achieving certification involves a major commitment and a great deal of hard work. To help you reach your goals, we've listened to others like you and have designed our entire product line around you and the way you like to study, learn, and master challenging subjects. Our approach is the *Smart Way to Get Certified.*

In less than a year, Coriolis has published over one million copies of our highly popular *Exam Cram, Exam Prep,* and *On Site* guides. Our *Exam Cram* series, specifically written to help you pass an exam, is the number one certification self-study guide in the industry. *Exam Crams* are the perfect complement to any study plan you have, as well as to the rest of the Certification Insider Press series: *Exam Prep,* comprehensive study guides designed to help you thoroughly learn and master certification topics, and *On Site,* guides that really show you how to apply your skills and knowledge on the job.

Our commitment to you is to ensure that all of the certification study guides we develop help you save time and frustration. Each one provides unique study tips and techniques, memory joggers, custom quizzes, insight about test taking, practical problems to solve, real-world examples, and much more.

We'd like to hear from you. Help us continue to provide the very best certification study materials possible. Write us or email us at **craminfo@coriolis.com** and let us know how our books have helped you study, or tell us about new features that you'd like us to add. If you send us a story about how an *Exam Cram, Exam Prep, or On Site* guide has helped you and we use it in one of our books, we'll send you an official Coriolis shirt for your efforts.

Good luck with your certification exam and your career. Thank you for allowing us to help you achieve your goals.

Keith Weiskamp
Publisher, Certification Insider Press

This book is for my parents, and all those like them, who entered the brave new world of computers with trepidation and survived.

—*Deborah Alyne Christy*

To my grandmother Lola M. Hoffman and the memory of my grandfather, Edward N. Hoffman.

—*Elisabeth Parker*

❧

About The Authors

Deborah Alyne Christy

Deborah Alyne Christy specializes in Microsoft Office. Within one year of starting out as a technical reviewer and copyeditor, Deborah was creating test banks, writing Instructor Solutions manuals, and working as a contributing author.

Elisabeth Parker

Elisabeth Parker is author of *Home Page Improvement, Build A Home Page In A Day*, and *Netscape Communicator: A Jumpstart Tutorial*. She lives in San Francisco with her husband (and fellow computer book author) Rich Grace, and Puddy, their cat. You can visit her Web site at **http://www.byteit.com/**.

Acknowledgments

I would like to thank Don Barker for his incredible knowledge and friendship. It is largely due to Don's assistance, encouragement, and influence that I am an author today (Don, should I thank you or beat you?). I would also like to thank all of the divisions of ITP (Course Technology, Shelley Cashman, and Coriolis) for the opportunities to work on your projects (Thanks Jim for all the work you shot my way). I would also like to thank my daughter for her endless patience during my book deadlines and the insanity that usually ensues.

—*Deborah Alyne Christy*

I want to thank the hard-working people at Coriolis, my co-author Deborah, the people at the A+ Computer School/Testing Center for squeezing me into their busy testing schedule so I could finally finish my part of the book, and my husband Richard Grace and Puddy the fat lazy cat for putting up with my whining.

—*Elisabeth Parker*

Contents At A Glance

Table Of Contents

Proficiency Level

Introduction

Welcome to the *Microsoft Word 97 Exam Cram*. This book aims to help you get ready to take—and pass—the Microsoft Word Proficient Specialist and the Microsoft Word Expert Specialist exams. In this introduction we explain the Microsoft Office User Specialist program in general and talk about how the *Exam Cram* series can help you prepare for the Microsoft Office User Specialist exams.

Exam Cram books help you understand and appreciate the subjects and skills you need to pass Microsoft Office User Specialist exams. The books are aimed strictly at test preparation and review. They do not teach you everything you need to know about an application. Instead, we (the authors) present and dissect the questions and problems that you're likely to encounter on a test. We've worked from Microsoft's proficiency guidelines, the exams , and third-party test preparation tools. Our aim is to bring together as much information as possible about the Microsoft Office User Specialist exams.

Nevertheless, to completely prepare yourself for any Microsoft test, we recommend that you begin your studies with some classroom training or that you pick up and read one of the many study guides available. We recommend *Exam Preps* from Certification Insider Press—a complete learning and test preparation system when used in conjunction with the Exam Cram you have in hand. Exam Preps feature a practice environment that simulates the application you are learning on the companion CD. If you choose another study guide, we strongly recommend that you install, configure, and fool around with the software or environment that you'll be tested on, because nothing beats hands-on experience and familiarity when it comes to understanding the questions you're likely to encounter on a certification test. Book learning is essential, but hands-on experience is the best teacher of all. The tests are designed to validate your skill level for a specific Microsoft Office application. They accomplish this by testing you on real-world problems within the application on which you are being tested. The Microsoft Office User Specialist certification sets you apart from candidates with whom you are competing for job openings in all areas of business and industry. It proves to a potential employer that you have the skills that are in demand.

The Microsoft Office User Specialist program currently offers certification for Word, Excel, PowerPoint, Access, FrontPage, and Outlook. Exams are available for all Windows 95 versions of Word 97, Excel 97, and PowerPoint 97. The Access 97 exam is due shortly. FrontPage, Outlook, and Office Integration Expert tests will follow over the next several months. If you're already running Windows 98, that's OK. Your Microsoft Office programs should work the same way as they do on Windows 95.

There are two certification skill levels for Word and Excel: Proficient and Expert. Only the Expert level is offered for all other applications at this time. Proficient Specialists are able to perform a wide range of daily tasks. Expert Specialists are able to handle more complex tasks in addition to the daily tasks.

The most prestigious certification is that of the Microsoft Office Expert. In order to obtain the Microsoft Office Expert certification, users must obtain Expert Specialist status on all five Office applications and then pass the Office 97 Integration Exam. Passing this exam guarantees that you are not only skilled in each application, but also that you possess integration skills between the Office 97 applications.

Taking A Certification Exam

All Microsoft Office User Specialist exams are offered by Authorized Client Testing (ACT) Centers. Although exams are currently available only in English, exams in Japanese and other languages will be offered as soon as courseware exists. Each computer-based exam costs from $50 to $65, and if you do not pass, you may retest for an additional $50 or $65 each time. Although most centers require that you pre-register, you may be able to walk in and test. Don't be afraid to ask. You may register by calling 800-933-4493, or contact a local ACT Center directly. If you dial the 800 number, you will be asked for your ZIP code. You will then be given the contact information for one or more centers located near you. Each ACT Center has policies that cover canceling an appointment, missing a scheduled appointment, and arriving late (e.g., you may not be able to get a refund for a missed appointment). Be sure to find out about your responsibilities and your options. Visit one of these Web sites for more information about the program, the exams, and what people are saying about their test experience before you schedule your exam: **www.officecert.com** or **www.microsoft.com/office/train_cert**.

All exams are timed; you will have 30 to 60 minutes for each one, depending on the application. The tests measure productivity and efficiency; that means that both speed and accuracy are important in order to pass! You will be asked to perform 6 to 10 tasks on 3 to 4 actual files, which translates into approximately 30-43 tasks within about 60 minutes.

Microsoft Office User Specialist Program

Application	Proficiency	Expert
Microsoft Word 97	Proves your ability to handle a wide range of everyday tasks. This exam will not qualify for Office Integration Expert.	Proves your ability to do all everyday tasks, plus more complex assignments.
Microsoft Excel 97	Proves your ability to handle a wide range of everyday tasks. This exam will not qualify you for Office Integration Expert.	Proves your ability to do all everyday tasks, plus more complex assignments.
Microsoft Access 97	There will be no Proficiency exam.	Proves your ability to do all everyday tasks, plus more complex assignments.
Microsoft Outlook 97	There will be no Proficiency exam.	Proves your ability to do all everyday tasks, plus more complex assignments.
Microsoft PowerPoint 97	There will be no Proficiency exam.	Proves your ability to do all everyday tasks, plus more complex assignments.
Microsoft Office Integration	There will be no Proficiency exam.	Has attained Expert status in each of the 5 core Office 97 applications. Demonstrates an ability to synthesize the various applications within the Office Suite.

The **Microsoft Office User Specialist** program will be expanded to include Microsoft applications outside the Office Suite, such as Microsoft FrontPage 97 and Microsoft Project.

Proficiency and Expert level tests are also available for Microsoft Word 7 and Microsoft Excel 7 (Office 95).

Be sure to arrive early enough to complete the registration that you began on the phone. Many centers require you to appear within a specific time interval before the test begins. For example, you might have to arrive 30 minutes prior to your test appointment time. When you call to schedule your exam, ask when you need to be there. You must provide two valid forms of identification at the test center. The tests are monitored and you may not use any test aids (books, notes, etc.). A blank sheet of paper and pencil or a wipe-off board and marker will be provided on which you can take notes. You may read all of the questions before the clock starts ticking. Plan to write down the sequence you will follow in completing the questions. If there is a task with which you are unfamiliar or one that will take more time than you feel you have to complete it, you may wish to leave it until last. You do not have to answer the questions in any specific order, but some are multi-part questions. You must complete all parts of a question if you are to receive credit for any of it. Office Help screens and ToolTips are available to you, but you won't have time to use them *and* complete the exam within the time allowed. You must surrender the paper or wipe-off board on which your notes are written when you leave the test room.

Test results are on shown on the computer screen when the exam ends, so you will know immediately if you passed or failed. You will pass if you perform all but two tasks correctly on several exams, so there's not much room for error. If you do not pass, the screen will display a wide range of skill areas that you need to practice before you attempt to take the test again.

Tracking MSOUS Status

If you pass your exam, a certificate will be sent to you by mail within one to two weeks. Exam results are reported only to you and to Microsoft. If you pass the Word 97 Proficient level exam, your certificate will affirm that you are a "Microsoft Word 97 Proficient Specialist." If you pass the Word Expert level exam, your certificate will affirm that you are a "Microsoft Word 97 Expert Specialist." The certificate gives you the proof you need to substantiate the level of expertise you include on your resume.

How To Prepare For An Exam

At a minimum, preparing for a Word 97 test requires that you obtain and study the following materials:

We highly recommend the *Word 97 Exam Prep*, also from Certification Insider Press. This comprehensive, Microsoft-approved study guide provides step-by-step coverage of all of the topics included on the exam. There's a lot of practice, too—end-of-chapter review questions and projects-in the book, plus the award-winning Word 97 tutorial simulator on the companion CD-ROM. This interactive tutorial guides you every step of the way through all of the Word 97 basics and then tests your skill mastery. The CD-ROM also includes the practice documents you'll need in order to perform all of the exercises in the book, saving you hours of valuable study time.

If you can't find the *Word 97 Exam Prep* on the shelf at your favorite bookstore, please refer to the ordering information in the back of this book or ask your local bookstore to order a copy for you.

If you know that you need more practice or if you like to study by using a variety of resources, then refer to the "Need To Know More" sections at the end of each chapter. These Web sites also offer suggestions for further study: **www.officecert.com, www.mous.net,** or **www.microsoft.com/office/train_cert.**

About This Book

Each topical *Exam Cram* chapter follows a similar structure, along with graphical cues about especially important or useful material. Here's the structure of a typical chapter:

➤ **Opening hotlists** Each chapter begins with lists of the terms, tools, and skills that you must learn and understand before you can be fully conversant with the chapter's subject matter.

➤ **Tasks** After the opening hotlists, each chapter gives you a series of tasks to complete related to the topics. We will highlight information helpful for the test using a special Study Alert layout, like this:

This is what a Study Alert looks like. Normally, a Study Alert stresses concepts, terms, software, or activities that will most likely appear in one or more certification test questions. For that reason, we think any information found offset in Study Alert format is worthy of unusual attentiveness on your part. Indeed, most of the facts appearing in The Cram Sheet (inside the front cover of this book) appear as Study Alerts within the text.

We have also provided tips, notes, and alerts that will help build a better foundation of knowledge about the Office application on which you'll test. Although the information may not be on the exam, it is highly relevant and will help you become a better test taker.

This is how tips are formatted. Keep your eyes open for these, and you'll become a test guru in no time.

HOLD That Skill!

Look for Hold That Skill as something for you to practice so you can ace the test. They are essential for you to know to pass the exam.

➤ **Practice Projects** This section presents a series of mock test projects and solutions.

➤ **Details and resources** Every chapter ends with a section titled "Need To Know More?" That section provides direct pointers to Microsoft and third-party resources that offer further details on the chapter's subject. In addition, this section tries to rate the quality and thoroughness of the topic's coverage by each resource. If you find a resource you like in this collection, use it, but don't feel compelled to use all the resources. On the other hand, we recommend only resources we use on a regular basis, so none of our recommendations will be a waste of your time or money.

The bulk of the book follows this chapter structure slavishly, but there are a few other elements that we'd like to point out: the answer keys to the sample tests that appear in Chapters 12 and 24 and a reasonably exhaustive glossary of terms. Finally, look for The Cram Sheet, which appears inside the front cover of this *Exam Cram* book. It is a valuable tool that represents a condensed and compiled collection of facts, figures, and tips that we think you should memorize before taking the test. Because you can dump this information out of your head and onto a piece of paper before answering any exam questions, you can master this information by brute force—you need to remember it only long enough to write it down when you walk into the test room. You might even want to look at it in the car or in the lobby of the testing center just before you walk in to take the test.

How To Use This Book

This book is designed to be read in sequence and the tasks and skills practice questions allow you to build on what you've learned. We encourage you to do yourself a favor and go for a complete review. However, if you already know Word 97 and are just brushing up before the exam or if you have taken the exam and failed, you can take the practice exam at the end of the book to reveal any skill weaknesses you need to work on. You can then focus on practicing the skills that you need to work on (the one challenge in this approach is that the practice documents that are provided on the companion diskette may build on earlier practice questions).

We'd like to hear from you! If you have comments about our Microsoft Office User Specialist Exam Crams, please email us at **craminfo@coriolis.com** or email them directly to Elisabeth Parker at **eparker@byteit.com** (for questions related to the Proficiency exam) or Deborah Alyne Christy at **author4life@unforgettable.com** (for questions related to the Expert exam).

Thanks, and enjoy the book!

Proficiency Level

If you can do the following Word tasks, then you should take the Proficiency Word exam:

➤ Identify elements in the Word application window
➤ Create and open documents
➤ Enter text
➤ Format characters and paragraphs
➤ Save and close documents
➤ Create and edit tables
➤ Create styles and apply them to text
➤ Work with outlines
➤ Print documents, envelopes, and labels
➤ Use the drawing tools
➤ Format text in columns
➤ Create headers and footers
➤ Apply indents and tabs to text
➤ Create Internet and intranet documents

Microsoft Office User Specialist Tests

Terms you'll need to understand:

√ Document

√ Task

√ Testing strategy

√ Testing environment

√ Careful reading

√ Process of elimination

Skills you'll need to master:

√ Preparing to take an MOUS exam

√ Practicing (to make perfect)

√ Making the best use of the testing software

√ Budgeting your time

√ Saving the hardest tasks until last

√ Guessing (as a last resort)

You've probably taken literally hundreds of tests in your life by now: multiple-choice, essay questions, fill-ins, and the kind where you have to show your work. Microsoft Office User Specialist (MOUS) tests focus on accomplishing real-world requirements through the use of documents and tasks. In each document (an overall scenario), there are tasks to complete (a step-by-step progression to fulfilling the objectives of the document). You've probably already performed many of these tasks during your training or day-to-day work, so your job is to learn how they are formatted for the test.

The concept behind testing is that if you pass, you know the material and are proficient at it. However, as we all know some folks are better test-takers than others. This leads to the notion that someone who is very good at doing the actual work could still fail the test, while someone who is only mediocre could pass the exam with flying colors.

In fact, even the most carefully designed test cannot perfectly predict on-the-job performance. Be that as it may, most people would agree that a well-constructed test is better than no test at all. What other objective measure can employers use to tell the difference between those who claim they're knowledgeable and those who really are? Therefore, it's up to you to learn the skills and strategies you need to do well on the test.

Understanding the exam-taking particulars (how much time to spend on questions, the setting you'll be in, and so on) and the testing software will help you concentrate on the material rather than on the environment. Likewise, mastering a few basic test-taking skills should help you recognize—and hopefully overcome—the tricks and gotchas you're bound to find in the Microsoft test exercises.

In this chapter, we'll explain the testing environment and software, as well as describe some proven test-taking strategies you can use to your advantage. The entire Exam-Cram Team has compiled this information based on the many Microsoft Office User Specialist and other Microsoft certification exams we have taken ourselves, and we've also drawn on the advice of our friends and colleagues, some of whom have taken quite a number of Microsoft tests!

The Testing Situation

Think of your Word exam as a challenging (and very temporary) new job assignment, with the test providing instructions as a supervisor or co-worker normally would. The MOUS Word Proficient level test takes you through a series of common tasks in the workplace, like editing text and tables, moving text, formatting text, applying character and paragraph styles, and spell checking. Chapters 2 through 13 cover what you'll need to know in order to ace the Proficient level exam.

The MOUS Word Expert level test is an intensive and challenging series of tasks for the experienced Word user, such as using macros, performing mail merges, using master documents, advanced page layout and formatting, and much more. This test isn't designed for those who only use Word as a word processor; it covers advanced techniques that enable you to get the most out of Microsoft Word's vast tools and formatting options.

When you arrive at the Marketshare Corp. ACT Center where you scheduled your test, you'll need to sign in with a test coordinator. He or she will ask you to produce two forms of identification, one of which must be a photo ID. Once you've signed in and your time slot arrives, you'll be asked to deposit any books, bags, or other items you brought with you, and you'll be escorted into a closed room. Typically, that room will be furnished with anywhere from one to half a dozen computers, and each workstation is separated from the others by dividers designed to keep you from seeing what's happening on someone else's computer.

You'll be given a pen or pencil and a blank sheet of paper, or in some cases, an erasable plastic sheet and an erasable felt-tip pen. You're allowed to write down any information you want, and you can write stuff on both sides of the page. We suggest that you memorize as much as possible of the material that appears on The Cram Sheet (inside the front cover of this book), and then write that information down on the blank sheet as soon as you sit down in front of the test machine. You can refer to it anytime you like during the test, but you'll have to surrender the sheet when you leave the room.

There are several techniques you can use to memorize important facts for the exam. One is to associate lists of features with an easily remembered phrase. For example, the Word Proficient level test requires you to use four toolbars: Standard, Format, Tables And Borders, and Drawing. You can make up a phrase to remember them, like "Some Forget To Be Dedicated." Sounds corny, but it works!

Most test rooms feature a wall with a large picture window. This is to permit the test coordinator to monitor the room, to prevent test-takers from talking to one another, and to observe anything out of the ordinary that might go on. The test coordinator will have preloaded the Microsoft certification test you've signed up for—for this book, that's Microsoft Word 97 Proficient or Microsoft Word 97 Expert—and you'll be permitted to start as soon as you're seated in front of the machine.

All Microsoft Office User Specialist exams permit you to take up to a certain maximum amount of time to complete the test. Microsoft Word 97 Proficiency and Microsoft Word 97 Expert tests randomly select 30 to 43 tasks, and asks you to work with certain documents in different ways. You can take up to 60 minutes to complete the exam.

All Microsoft Office User Specialist exams are computer generated and use a document (exercise) format. The exercise format means that you will work with 3 or 4 files, divided into roughly 10 tasks each. The test asks you to perform document-specific tasks that grow progressively more complex. Although this might sound easy, the exercises are constructed not just to check your mastery of basic facts and figures about Microsoft Word 97, but they also require you to evaluate one or more sets of circumstances or requirements. There will probably be several technically correct ways to accomplish the objective, but you need to use the most efficient method, or the best or most effective solution to a problem. It's quite an adventure, and it involves real thinking. This book will show you what to expect and how to deal with the problems, puzzles, and predicaments you're likely to find on the test.

Test Layout And Design

When the test begins, the testing software launches Microsoft Word, loads a document, and displays a dialog box with a list of changes for you to make to the document. When you click your mouse button anywhere on the document to begin working, the dialog box minimizes so you can work more easily. The list of tasks then appears on the testing software's status bar, located below the Word application window. This way, you don't have to worry about remembering all of the tasks before you begin working.

A typical test exercise and the first two tasks for the Word 97 Proficient exam are depicted in Document 1. It's an exercise that requires you to change the text formatting and layout in a document.

Document 2 contains a sample test question from the Word 97 Expert exam, and it requires that you add a footer and then change its numbering format.

Document 1

Make the following changes to Letter.doc.

- O a. Task 1 – Change the text colored in red to Arial 24 point bold.
- O b. Task 2 – Format the paragraphs colored in blue as a bulleted list.
- O c. Task 3 – Save the document as "MyLetter.doc".

The correct way to make changes to the letter is to select the text colored in red, and to select Arial from the Font box and 24 from the Font Size box on the Format toolbar.

Next, select the blue paragraphs and click the Bullets button on the Format toolbar.

Save the document with a different name by selecting Save As from the File menu and then enter the new document name in the Save As dialog box's File Name box. This exercise requires you to know how to select text and apply different text formats using the Format toolbar buttons, and how to save a file with a different name.

Document 2

Copy the file Ch15Designs to your hard drive from the Chapter 15 folder on the disk. Rename the file Sample.doc. Make the following changes to Sample.doc:

○ a. Task 1 – Insert a footnote at the end of the following sentence: "…There are a variety of sizes and designs available." Type the following text as the footer: We now offer FIVE NEW SIZES: 12", 24", 30", 36", and 72".

○ b. Task 2 – Change the numbering format to uppercase roman numerals.

Click to the right of the sentence that ends, "…There are a variety of sizes and designs available" and then select Insert|Footnote. Click OK. Type the text *We now offer FIVE NEW SIZES: 12", 24", 30", 36", and 72"* into the footnote pane, and then close the footnote pane.

Select Insert|Footnote, click the Options button, and then click the All Footnotes tab. Click the list arrow in the Number format box, click the uppercase roman numeral (I, II, III) option, and then click OK.

These sample exercises correspond closely to those you'll see on Microsoft Office User Specialist tests. To correctly complete the tasks during the test, read the list of tasks, perform each task in order according to the instructions, and indicate when you are done as instructed by the test software (this usually means clicking the Next button at the bottom of the testing software's screen). The only difference between the MOUS exam and these exercises is that the real exercises don't come with the answers!

You may often find more than one technically correct way to accomplish a particular task. That's fine. But with the clock ticking away, you should know how to do things in the fastest, most efficient way possible. Always keep in mind that the test wants you to demonstrate knowledge of Word's many features, even though it won't explicitly tell you to use them. For example, if an exercise asks you to apply identical complex formatting to several nonconsecutive paragraphs, you can lose points if you don't use the Format Painter. The best way to prepare for the test is to read this book, to keep practicing, and to start applying what you learn to your daily work so you can get more comfortable with using different features.

Note also, that in cases in which one or more solutions to a given task may exist, as far as we can tell (and Microsoft won't comment), such exercises are scored as wrong unless the best solution is chosen. In other words, a technically correct but less than optimum answer does not result in partial credit when the test is scored. In addition, if you make the wrong choice when you solve the first task, it will lead you in the wrong direction on the following tasks, because each task builds upon previous tasks.

Using Microsoft's Test Software Effectively

Once the test begins, you will have an hour to complete all of the tasks. You can use the Help function, but it can seriously rob you of precious test-taking time. You must complete each task before moving on to the next one, and you can't skip any questions with the hope of returning to them later. Take a few seconds before moving on to make sure you have done everything correctly.

Keep working on the tasks until you are absolutely sure of all your answers or until you know you'll run out of time. If there are still unsolved tasks, you'll want to zip through them and guess. Not attempting the task guarantees no credit for it, and a guess has at least a chance of being correct. This strategy only works because Microsoft counts blank answers and incorrect answers as equally wrong.

 At the very end of your test period, you're better off guessing than leaving tasks blank or unsolved.

Taking Testing Seriously

The most important advice we can give you about taking any Microsoft exam is this: Read each exercise carefully! Follow each step within a task in order and know that the test won't try to trick you. But you still need to do exactly what the test tells you to, and nothing else. For example, we've all been taught to save documents frequently. But on the test, you should never save a document unless an exercise tells you to do so. In addition, the test expects you to know when it is appropriate to use certain features like OverType, the Format Painter, and the Tables And Borders toolbar. We've taken numerous practice exams and real exams, and in nearly every test we've gotten at least one task wrong because we didn't read it closely or carefully enough.

Here are some suggestions on how to deal with the tendency to skim over the instructions too quickly:

➤ Make sure you read every word in the task. If you find yourself jumping ahead impatiently, go back and start over.

➤ As you read, try to restate the tasks in your own terms. If you can do this, you should be able to pick the correct solution much more easily.

➤ Take a hint, and remember that the test wants you to know when to use certain features. For example, if a task asks you to replace text at the end of a line or paragraph, it wants you to switch to OverType mode.

➤ It is uncertain if using the shortcut menus (right-clicking) results in an incorrect response. Use the menus and toolbars unless the test instructions tell you that shortcut menus are acceptable.

➤ Don't feel rushed. If you read this book, do all the practice exercises until you get them right, and start applying what you learn to your daily work, then you can easily get through the test in the allotted 60 minutes. Remember that the test tries to simulate an office environment and gives you enough time to do your work carefully and accurately—if only our co-workers always treated us with the same consideration!

Above all, try to deal with each question by thinking through what you know about the Microsoft Office application utilities, characteristics, behaviors, facts, and figures involved. By reviewing what you know (and what you've written down on your information sheet), you'll often recall or understand things sufficiently to determine the best solution to the task.

Task-Handling Strategies

Numerous tasks assume that the default behavior of a particular Office application is in effect. It's essential, therefore, to know and understand the default settings for Microsoft Office applications. If you know the defaults and understand what they mean, this knowledge will help you untangle many complex situations.

Likewise, when dealing with tasks that require multiple steps, you must know and perform all the correct steps to get credit. This, too, qualifies as an example of why "careful reading" is so important.

As you work your way through the test, another counter that Microsoft thankfully provides will come in handy—the number of tasks completed and tasks outstanding. Budget your time by making sure that you've completed one-fourth of the tasks one-quarter of the way through the test period (or between 10 and 11 tasks in the first 15 minutes).Check again three-quarters of the way through (you should have at least 30 to 35 questions completed after 45 minutes).

If you're not through with the test after 50 minutes, use the last 10 minutes to guess your way through the remaining tasks. Remember, guesses are potentially more valuable than incomplete or skipped tasks, because blanks are always wrong, but a guess might turn out to be right.

Strategies For Success

The most important single factor in passing the test is a thorough understanding of the material coupled with extensive practice. As the saying goes, practice makes perfect, and practicing the demonstration of knowledge on simulated exams is just the ticket. If you study the materials in this book carefully and review all of the Exam Prep questions at the end of each chapter, you shouldn't have any trouble identifying those areas where additional preparation and practice is required.

Next, follow up by reading some or all of the materials recommended in the "Need To Know More?" section at the end of each chapter. The idea is to become familiar enough with the concepts and situations you find in the sample tasks to be able to reason your way through similar situations on a real exam. If you know the material and have practiced extensively, you have every right to be confident that you can pass the test.

Once you've worked your way through the book, take the practice tests. The Proficient level test practice test is in Chapter 12, and the Expert level practice test is in Chapter 24. This provides a reality check and additional help in identifying areas that need more work. Make sure you follow up and review materials related to the questions you miss before scheduling a real test. Only when you've covered all the ground and feel comfortable with the whole scope of the practice test, should you take a real test.

If you take our practice test and don't score at least 75 correct, you'll want to practice further. At a minimum, che if there are Personal Exam Prep (PEP) tests and the self-assessment tests available at the Microsoft Training And Certification Web site's download page (its location appears in the next section). If you're more ambitious or better funded, you might want to purchase a practice test from one of the third-party vendors that offers them. Transcender Corporation and Self Test Software (the vendors who supply the PEP tests) should have practice tests available by the time you read this. See the next section in this chapter for contact information.

Armed with the information in this book and with the determination to augment your knowledge, you should be able to pass the Microsoft Office User Specialist exam. Considering the fee for taking the test (pass or fail) each time may be from $50 to $100, it's definitely worth the effort to work hard at preparation. If you prepare seriously, the exam should go flawlessly. Good luck!

Additional Resources

A good source of information about Microsoft certification exams comes from Microsoft itself. Because its products and technologies—and the exams that go with them—change frequently, the best place to go for exam-related information is online.

If you haven't already visited the Microsoft Certified Professional site, do so right now. The MCP home page resides at **www.microsoft.com/mcp/**, (see Figure 1.1). You can also visit the Microsoft Office User Specialist home page at **www.mous.net/**.

Note: This page might not be there by the time you read this, or it might have been replaced by something new and different, because things change regularly on the Microsoft site. Should this happen, please read the sidebar titled "Coping With Change On The Web."

The menu options in the left column of the home page point to the most important sources of information in the MCP pages. Here's what to check out:

➤ **Certification Choices**   Use this menu entry to read about the various certification programs that Microsoft offers.

➤ **Search/Find An Exam**   Use this menu entry to pull up a search tool that lets you list all Microsoft exams, and to locate all exams relevant to any

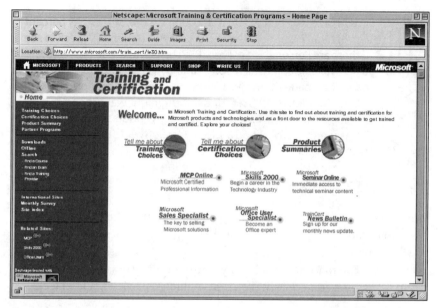

Figure 1.1   The Microsoft Certified Professional home page.

Microsoft certification (MCPS, MCSE, MCT, and so on) or those exams that cover a particular product. This tool is quite useful not only to examine the options but also to obtain specific exam preparation information, because each exam has its own associated preparation guide.

➤ **Downloads**   Use this menu entry to find a list of the files and practice exams that Microsoft makes available to the public. These include several items worth downloading, especially the Certification Update, the Personal Exam Prep (PEP) exams, various assessment exams, and a general exam study guide. Try to make time to peruse these materials before taking your first exam.

These are just the high points of what's available in the Microsoft Certified Professional pages. As you browse through them—and we strongly recommend that you do—you'll probably find other informational tidbits mentioned that are every bit as interesting and compelling.

Coping With Change On The Web

Sooner or later, all the information we've shared with you about the Microsoft Certified Professional pages and the other Web-based resources mentioned throughout the rest of this book will go stale or be replaced by newer information. In some cases, the URLs you find here might lead you to their replacements; in other cases, the URLs will go nowhere, leaving you with the dreaded "404 File not found" error message. When that happens, don't give up.

There's always a way to find what you want on the Web if you're willing to invest some time and energy. Most large or complex Web sites—and Microsoft's qualifies on both counts—offer a search engine. Looking back at Figure 1.1, you can see that a Search button appears along the top edge of the page. As long as you can get to Microsoft's site (it should stay at **www.microsoft.com** for a long while yet), you can use this tool to help you find what you need.

The more focused you can make a search request, the more likely the results will include information you can use. For example, you can search for the string "training and certification" to produce a lot of data about the subject in general, but if you're looking for the preparation guide for Exam 70-079, "Implementing and Supporting Microsoft Internet Explorer 4.0 by Using the Internet Explorer Administration Kit," you'll be more likely to get there quickly if you use a search string similar to the following:

```
"Exam 70-079" AND "preparation guide"
```

Finally, feel free to use general search tools—such as **www.search.com**, **www.altavista.com**, and **www.excite.com**—to search for related information. Although Microsoft offers the best information about its certification exams online, there are plenty of third-party sources of information, training, and assistance in this area that need not follow Microsoft's party line. The bottom line is this: If you can't find something where the book says it lives, start looking around. If worse comes to worst, you can always email us. We just might have a clue.

Using The Practice Disk

To help you prepare for your exam, we've included practice projects at the end of each chapter; a sample Word Proficient level test in Chapter 12 along with the answers in Chapter 13; a sample Word Expert level test in Chapter 24 along with answers in Chapter 25; and a practice disk with Word documents to work on. The Proficient level practice documents are located in the Proficiency folder on the practice disk, and the Expert level practice documents are located in the Expert folder on the practice disk.

Although we can't simulate the test environment for you, and our practice files won't automatically load and save themselves (as they do on the test), we have done our best to develop exercises that approximate what you'll find on the test.

We *strongly* suggest that you copy the practice disk folders over to your computer, rather than work with documents straight from the disk. First of all, working with documents on a disk can be infuriatingly slow. More importantly, you should keep the original files intact so you can keep practicing with them. The practice projects in the book build on the changes you make to documents in previous chapters. If you make mistakes (and we all do), you may have trouble with some of the exercises. That's why it is a good idea to change the name of the document to reflect the new information it contains. For example, you might open TempFiles14 in Chapter 14, and then use the file again in Chapter 15. Save the new document as TempFiles15. You get the idea. That way, you can also keep track of tasks that were done incorrectly.

If you're taking the Proficient level test and you somehow lose your files, never fear. You can visit Elisabeth Parker's Web site at **http://www.byteit.com/ WordExam/** and download the practice files again. We will also provide links and updated information on this Web site.

Word Basics, File Management

2

Terms you'll need to understand:

- √ File management
- √ Document
- √ Current document
- √ Document window
- √ Folder

- √ Subfolder
- √ Save vs. Save As
- √ Template
- √ Find
- √ Go To

Skills you'll need to master:

- √ Finding a document
- √ Opening a document in the same folder
- √ Opening a document in a subfolder
- √ Saving a document with the same file name
- √ Saving a document with a different file name
- √ Saving a new document
- √ Saving a document to a new folder

- √ Creating a new document from the Normal template
- √ Creating a new document and choosing a template
- √ Closing a document
- √ Locating text with the Find command
- √ Locating document elements with the Go To command
- √ Navigating a document with keyboard commands

If you're like most people, you probably don't like taking tests very much. Luckily, a good part of the Microsoft Word Proficiency exam focuses on simple tasks that you already know how to do—such as opening and saving files, and moving around your document. This chapter helps you brush up on the basics so you can start your test off on the right foot.

Microsoft Word Overview

Microsoft Word 97 enjoys great popularity as a word processing program, but that's not all. Microsoft has tightly integrated Word with a suite of Office productivity applications that includes Excel for spreadsheets, PowerPoint for presentations, and Access for databases. You can also use Word to format documents as Web pages for an office intranet or the Internet.

Brushing Up On Word Basics

You may be a Word whiz. But like all of us, you may have forgotten some things. As you prepare for the test, you should re-familiarize yourself with Word basics. This includes displaying toolbars that you may not use often, saving files to other directories, and other tasks that the test will probably require you to perform.

Document Window

When you create or open a document, it appears in the *document window*. The file displayed in your document window is often referred to as the *current document*.

Title Bar

The Title bar appears at the top of the application window. On the left side, it displays the Word icon and the title of the current document. On the right side, the title bar features a row of buttons. The first button minimizes the application window, the second button resizes the application window, and the third button (with the x) exits the application.

Menu Bar

The menu bar appears at the top of the application window, where you can select commands from the pull-down lists. Although you can perform most tasks faster by using key combinations or clicking toolbar buttons, some tasks—such as saving a document with a different name—require you to select items from the menu bar. On the far right side, the menu bar features a row of buttons.

The first button minimizes the current document window, the second button resizes the current document window, and the third button (with the x) closes the document.

Ruler

The test will ask you to reformat margins and to set up tab stops for selected text. The ruler gives you an easy, intuitive way to do this.

Status Bar

The Status Bar is located at the bottom of the application window. The section on the left tells you the page number, section number, and number of pages. The section in the middle reveals the current position of your cursor in relation to the current page. The section on the right provides a list of abbreviations for common word tasks (such as OVR for switching back and forth between Overtype mode, as discussed in Chapter 3).

Toolbars

Toolbars consist of rows of buttons that you can click to quickly perform tasks. The Standard and Formatting toolbars contain most of the toolbar buttons you need to get through the test. However, you'll also need to use the Tables And Borders toolbar and the Drawing toolbar.

 The testing program may have only the menu bar, ruler, and Standard and Formatting toolbars displayed. The "Displaying Toolbars And Docking A Floating Toolbar" section of this chapter tells you how to display other toolbars.

Standard

The Standard toolbar contains buttons for basic functions, such as opening and saving documents, checking spelling and grammar, displaying other toolbars, getting help, and zooming in and out of documents. When you take your test, the Standard toolbar will already be displayed.

Formatting

You can select text and apply styles, fonts, bullets, colors, and attributes with the Formatting toolbar. When you take your test, the Standard toolbar will already be displayed.

Tables And Borders

The Tables And Borders toolbar contains buttons for creating and formatting tables, as well as for adding borders to selected objects. When the test asks you to perform tasks that involve tables and borders for tables, you may have to click the Tables And Borders button on the Standard toolbar to display the Tables And Borders toolbar.

Drawing

If the test asks you to create or edit simple graphics, the Drawing toolbar has everything you need. When the test asks you to perform tasks that involve pictures, you may need to click the Drawing button on the Standard toolbar to display the Drawing toolbar.

Displaying Toolbars And Docking A Floating Toolbar

Microsoft Word has customizable toolbars that you can display and move to different parts of the application window, which means that the testing center's toolbars might look different than they do at home or at work. That's okay. If you need a toolbar to perform a task, you can easily display it. Some toolbars (such as the Tables And Borders and Drawing toolbars) are *floating toolbars*, which means they appear in the middle of the application window when you first display them. You can *dock* a floating toolbar to get it out of the way. Docking a toolbar means anchoring it to the top, bottom, or left edge of the document window.

Task 1   Displaying a toolbar.

1. Select Customize from the Tools menu.

2. When the Customize dialog box appears, as shown in Figure 2.1, select the toolbar that you want to display.

3. Click the Close button.

HOLD That Skill!

You can display the Tables And Borders or Drawing toolbar more quickly by selecting the Tables And Borders or Drawing toolbar buttons from the Standard toolbar. You can also select Toolbars from the View menu; then select a toolbar from the cascading list—or you can right-click any toolbar to display a list of other toolbars to select from.

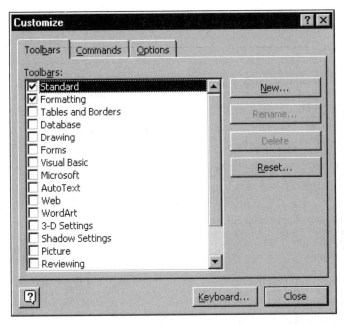

Figure 2.1   Selecting a toolbar from the Customize dialog box.

Task 2   *Docking a floating toolbar.*

1. Click and hold the floating toolbar's title bar.

2. Drag the toolbar toward the top, left, or bottom of the application window.

3. When the toolbar anchors itself, release the mouse button.

You can also dock a toolbar by double-clicking it.

File Management

Yikes! File management. Sounds pretty scary. Not to worry, though. If you use Microsoft Word regularly (or even just occasionally), you already know how to manage files. *File management* is just a fancy term for finding, opening, saving, and creating word processing documents. The test will tell you to locate, open, and save files. You also may be asked to save a document with a different name or to save it to a new folder.

Opening Documents

The test will ask you to open documents. When you select Open from the File menu, the Open dialog box appears with a list of files and folders within the *current folder* (the folder that contains the current document). You can open files and folders in the current folder, or browse for files located in other directories.

Task 3 Opening a document in the current folder.

Locating and opening documents in the current folder is easy. You don't have to browse for them, because they appear on the list of files as soon as you display the Open dialog box.

1. Select Open from the File menu.

 You can also display the Open dialog box by pressing Ctrl+O key combination.

2. When the Open dialog box appears, as shown in Figure 2.2, select a document from the list of files.

3. Click the Open button.

 You should know how to open a document in the current folder.

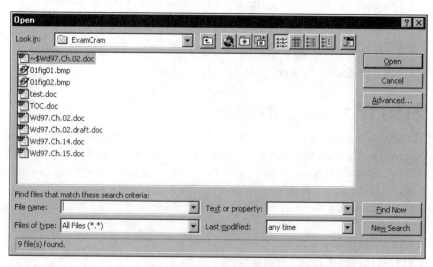

Figure 2.2 Opening a document from the Open dialog box.

Task 4   *Opening a document in a subfolder.*

A *subfolder* is a folder located within the current folder. To open a document in a subfolder, you first have to open the subfolder.

1. Select Open from the File menu.

2. When the Open dialog box appears with the list of files and folders, select a folder.

3. Click the Open button.

4. When the subfolder's file list appears, select a document.

5. Click the Open button.

Task 5   *Opening a document in a different folder.*

Opening a document in a different directory requires *browsing* for the file. Browsing means moving to different levels in the folder hierarchy and viewing the contents of folders to locate your document.

1. Select Open from the File menu.

2. When the Open dialog box appears with the list of files and folders, click the Up One Level button to display the contents of the folder or drive that the current folder is located in.

3. When the files and folders appear on the files list, select a folder and click the Open button.

4. When the list of files and folders appears on the files list, select a document, and click the Open button.

Creating New Documents

The test may ask you to open a new document by loading the Normal template, or to create one from a template. The *Normal template* is that blank document that loads automatically in the document window when you launch Microsoft Word. It comes in handy when you need to create a document from scratch. A *template* is a preformatted document with styles, headers and footers, boilerplate text, sections, graphics, and other page elements.

Task 6   *Creating a new document with the Normal template.*

1. Click the New button.

You can also create a new document with the default Normal template by pressing Ctrl+N key combination.

Task 7   Creating a new document from a template.

1. Select New from the File menu.

2. When the New dialog box appears, as shown in Figure 2.3, click the tabs to locate the template you are asked to use.

3. Select a template and click OK.

Saving Documents

The test may ask you to save documents in different ways. With Microsoft Word, you can save a document with the same file name, save a document with a different file name, name and save a new document, and save a document to a new folder.

 You should know how to save documents in several ways.

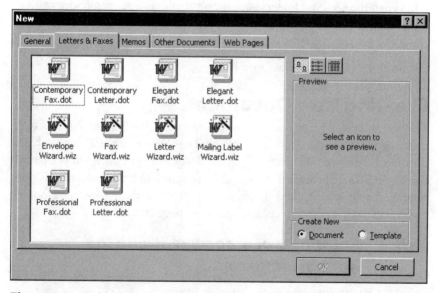

Figure 2.3   Selecting a template from the New dialog box.

Task 8   *Saving a document with the same name.*

1. Select Save from the File menu, click the Save toolbar button.

 You can also save the current document with the same name by pressing Ctrl+S key combination.

Task 9   *Saving a document with a different name.*

1. Select Save As from the File menu.

2. When the Save As dialog box appears, as shown in Figure 2.4, enter the new file name in the File name text field.

3. Click the Save button.

 Smart Microsoft Word users (like you) always save their files...but *not* necessarily during the proficiency test! Don't save any files unless the test tells you to do so.

 If you need to save a document with the same name to a different folder, use Save As.

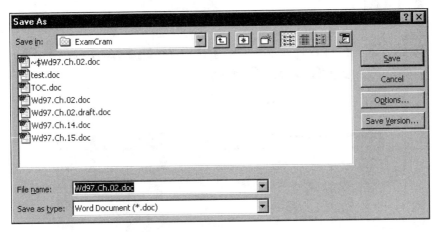

Figure 2.4   The Save As dialog box.

Task 10 Naming and saving a new document.

1. Select Save from the File menu, click the Save toolbar button, or use the Ctrl+S key combination.

2. When the Save As dialog box appears (refer to Figure 2.4), enter a file name in the File Name text field and make sure that Word Document (*.doc) is selected from the Files Of Type list.

3. Click the Save button.

Task 11 Saving a document to a new folder.

1. From the current document, select Save As from the File menu.

2. When the Save As dialog box appears (refer to Figure 2.4), click the Create New Folder button.

3. When the New Folder dialog box appears, as shown in Figure 2.5, enter a name for your folder.

4. When the new folder appears, select it, and click the Open button.

5. Enter a file name in the File Name text field and make sure that Word Document (*.doc) is selected from the Files Of Type list.

6. Click the Save button.

 Remember how to save a document with a different name and how to save a document to a new folder.

Task 12 Saving a document with the same name to a different folder.

1. From the current document, select Save As from the File menu.

New Folder		? ⊠
Current Folder:		OK
C:\Books\ExamCram		Cancel
Name:	New Folder	

Figure 2.5 The New Folder dialog box.

2. When the Save As dialog box appears (refer to Figure 2.4), browse for the folder the same way as you would when opening a document (refer to Tasks 4 and 5).

3. Make sure the document name appears in the File Name box.

4. Click the Save button.

Closing Documents

The test may (or it may *not*) ask you to close the current document.

Task 13   *Closing a document.*

1. Select Close from the File menu.

 You can also close documents by clicking the document window's Close box to the far right of the menu bar.

Navigating Documents

Finding your way around Microsoft Word documents quickly and efficiently is the key to passing your exam. Although the test questions don't always tell you specifically to demonstrate document navigation skills, you'll be asked to find text, tables, pages, sections, paragraphs, and graphics so that you can modify them. Because you have only a limited amount of time to complete the test, the faster you can find document elements, the more time you have for more challenging tasks.

Find

The test will ask you to find a word or group of words and to reformat them— or the paragraph where they appear. You can find a word or group of words quickly and easily with the Find command.

 To edit or change the formatting for a particular word, you should use the Find command.

To use Find:

➤ Select Find from the Edit menu, or use the Ctrl+F key combination.

➤ When the Find dialog box appears (with the Find tab selected, as shown in Figure 2.6), enter the text in the Find What text field, and click the Find Next button.

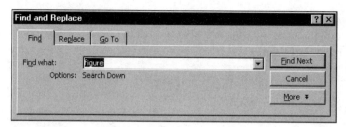

Figure 2.6 The Find dialog box.

➤ To find another instance in which the text appears, click the Find Next button again.

Microsoft Word also automatically selects the text so that you can edit or reformat it.

 Remember the Find command! You may need to locate specific words.

Go To

Word documents can have many elements besides text—including pages, sections, tables, bookmarks, and graphics. When the test asks you to work with these elements, you can find them fast with the Go To command.

➤ Select Go To from the Edit menu, or use the Ctrl+G key combination.

➤ When the Find And Replace dialog box appears with the Go To tab selected, as shown in Figure 2.7, select a page element from the Go To What list.

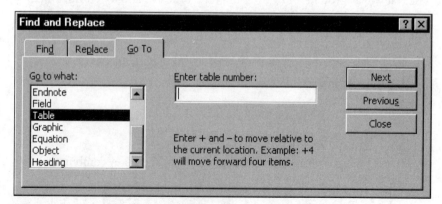

Figure 2.7 The Go To dialog box.

➤ Depending on your selection, enter either a number or a name for the page element in the text field. A line of text appears above the text field and prompts you for information, and instructions appear below the text field.

➤ Click the Next button.

➤ When Go To locates the page element, click the Close button.

Microsoft Word also automatically selects the page element so that you can make changes to it.

 Remember the Go To command! The test will ask you to locate headings, sections, graphics, bookmarks, and tables.

Practice Projects

Complete the following projects based on the material in this chapter. All of the documents mentioned in the Microsoft Word Proficiency exam section are located in the Proficiency folder of the practice floppy disk attached to this book. You should move the documents to your computer now, so you can re-use the practice documents for the practice test in Chapter 12.

When you take the test, the documents you work with are located in a default folder (the folder that Word automatically opens documents from or saves documents to). In order to best simulate the test environment, you should move the practice documents from your floppy disk to your current default folder. In most cases, this is the My Documents folder.

Project 1   Open a document.

1. Open Memorandum.doc.

Answer to Project 1

To open a document, select Open from the File menu. When the Open dialog box appears, select the drive or folder that contains the document from the Look In pull-down list. Double-click folders in the Folder list until you locate the folder that contains the document. Select the document and click the Open button.

Follow the test instructions exactly. If the document is located in an upper-level folder or subfolder, the test will tell you so. In most cases, the document will be located in the default folder.

Project 2   Save a document with a different file name to a new folder.

1. Open Memorandum.doc (it is located on the floppy disk in the Proficiency folder).

2. Save Memorandum.doc to a new folder within the current folder and name the new folder "Practice".

3. Name the document "Memorandumch02.doc".

We all know that Word adds the .doc file name extension automatically. Nonetheless, you should name your files *exactly* the way the test asks you to.

Answer to Project 2

Select Open from the File menu. Browse to find Memorandum.doc. To save a document with a different file name to a new folder, select Save As from the File menu. When the Save As dialog box appears, click the Create New Folder icon. When the New Folder dialog box appears, enter a name for the new folder (in this case, Practice). Select the new folder and click the Open button.

From within the new folder, enter a new name (in this case, Memorandumch02.doc) for your document in the File Name text field. Click the Save button.

 If the test asks you to create a new folder, do not attempt to do so from Windows Explorer. The test *only* asks you to perform tasks from within the Word application.

Project 3   Create a new document from a template and then save and close the document.

1. Create a new business letter with the template called Professional Letter (this template comes with Microsoft Word 97).

2. Save it to the current directory as "MyLetterch02.doc."

3. Close the document.

Answer to Project 3

To create a new document from a template, select New from the File menu. When the New dialog box appears, click the tabs until you find the template you want (in this case, it's called Professional Letter and is located in Letters And Faxes). Select the template and click OK.

To save and name the new document, select Save from the File menu. When the Save As dialog box appears, enter a name (in this case, MyLetterch02.doc) for your document in the File Name text field, and click the Save button.

To close the document, select Close from the File menu or click the document window's Close button.

 Do not close a document unless the test specifically tells you to do so.

Need To Know More?

 Leonhard, Woody, Lee Hudspeth, and T.J. Lee: *Word 97 Annoy-ances*. O'Reilly and Associates, Inc. Sebastopol, CA, 1997. ISBN 1-56592-308-1. Chapters 2 and 3 explain how to customize your Word 97 environment for efficiency and effectiveness.

 Quick Course in Microsoft Word 97. Microsoft Press. Redmond, WA, 1997. ISBN 0-57231-725-6. Chapter 1 contains informa-tion about Word 97 basics and file management.

Entering And Processing Text

3

Terms you'll need to understand:

√ Overtype Mode

√ Font styles

√ Character effects

√ Undo/Repeat

√ AutoText

√ AutoCorrect entries and AutoCorrect exceptions

Skills you'll need to master:

√ Entering text

√ Entering text in Overtype Mode

√ Entering a date and time

√ Formatting characters

√ Undoing and redoing actions

√ Creating and applying AutoText entries

√ Setting up AutoCorrect exceptions

√ Creating and using AutoCorrections

Entering and processing text is at the heart of any word processing program—and Word 97 is no exception. You will be expected to enter text, format characters, and use Word's features for entering a date or time automatically. In addition, the Undo/Redo commands come in handy when you make mistakes or want to repeat your last actions.

Entering Text

The test will frequently ask you to enter text. You can type text in a variety of ways, depending on the task at hand.

Task 1 Inserting text.

You can insert text in the current paragraph.

1. Place your cursor where you want to enter your text (this is called the *insertion point*).

2. Begin typing.

Task 2 Entering text in Overtype Mode.

You can replace existing text in the current paragraph while you're typing.

1. Select Options from the Tools menu.

2. When the Options dialog box appears, click the Edit tab.

3. When the Edit options appear, as shown in Figure 3.1, select the Overtype Mode checkbox.

4. Click OK.

5. Place your cursor at the insertion point and begin typing

HOLD That Skill!

Switching to Overtype Mode seems like more effort than simply selecting text and typing over it! Never fear. There's an easier way. To switch between regular and Overtype Mode, double-click the OVR item on the status bar at the bottom of the application window.

Learn to use Overtype Mode when appropriate. The test may never even mention Overtype Mode. But your test score will reflect whether or not you use it.

Figure 3.1   The Options dialog box with the Edit tab displayed.

If the test asks you to type over a sentence (especially when it's at the end of a paragraph), and you generally do this by selecting the text and then typing, use Overtype Mode instead.

Task 3   *Finding text and replacing it by typing over it.*

If the test asks you to find a line of text, replace the text, and continue typing, use the Find command.

1. Select Find from the Edit menu.

You can also display the Find And Replace dialog box by pressing Ctrl+F key combination.

2. When the Find And Replace dialog box appears, as shown in Figure 3.2, enter a word or group of words.

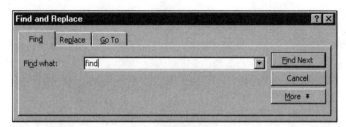

Figure 3.2 The Find And Replace dialog box.

3. Click the Find Next button.

4. When Find locates and selects the text for you, click the Cancel button to return to the document window, or press the Escape key.

5. Begin typing the new text.

 If the test asks you to locate a word or a couple of words, the Find command can help you do it quickly.

 If the test asks you to find an entire sentence and change it, enter the first couple of words in the Find dialog box, find the sentence, and use Overtype Mode to replace the rest of the sentence.

Entering The Current Date And Time

The exam may ask you to enter the current date and time. Word's Date And Time feature makes it easy.

Task 4 Entering the current date and time.

1. Place your cursor where you want to insert the date and time.

2. Select Date And Time from the Insert menu, or use the Alt+I, and then T key combination.

3. When the Date And Time dialog box appears, as shown in Figure 3.3, select an option from the Available Formats list.

4. Click OK.

When you return to the document window, the date and time appear at the insertion point of your document.

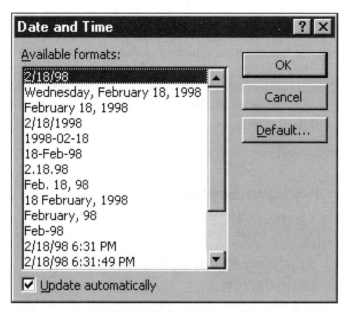

Figure 3.3   The Date And Time dialog box.

Task 5   *Entering a date and time that automatically updates.*

You can also enter a date and time that automatically changes to the current date and time whenever you open the document.

1. Place your cursor where you want to insert an automatically updating date and time.

2. Select Date And Time from the Insert menu, or use the Alt+I, and then T key combination.

3. When the Date And Time dialog box appears (refer to Figure 3.3), select your preferred option from the Available Formats list.

4. Select the Update Automatically checkbox.

5. Click OK.

 If the test asks you to insert a date and time, pay close attention to the instructions and make sure you select the correct format. You also need to make sure the Update Automatically checkbox is selected or deselected, depending on what the test tells you to do.

Formatting Characters

You can make documents more attractive and easier to read with Word's formatting features. Formatting characters means selecting text and changing the font, font style, size, color, or effect. Although Word has a wide variety of text formatting capabilities, you don't have to worry about whether you remember them all. The Font dialog box, as shown in Figure 3.4, has everything you need. To view the Font dialog box's font options, select Font from the Format menu and then click the Font tab.

Applying Font Styles

Applying font styles means making text bold, italic, or underlined. You can do that, right? Table 3.1 explains basic font styles.

Task 6 Applying a font style (bold, italic, or underline).

1. Select the text you want to apply a font style to.

2. Click the Bold, Italic, or Underline button on the Formatting toolbar.

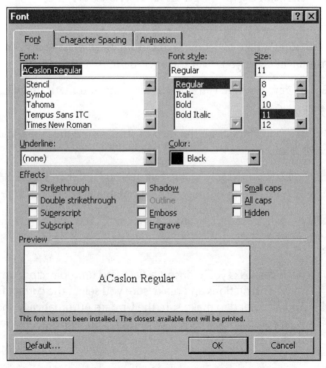

Figure 3.4 The Font dialog box with Font tab selected.

Table 3.1 Font styles.	
Font Style	**Result**
Bold	Makes text bold
Italic	Italicizes text
<u>Underline</u>	Underlines text

HOLD That Skill!

Key combinations can help you work faster.

- Ctrl+B   Bolds selected text
- Ctrl+I   Italicizes selected text
- Ctrl+U   Underlines selected text

Changing Fonts And Font Sizes

Fonts are fun. Most of us collect lots of fonts and wind up with mile-long menus that make it hard to find anything. Fortunately, the people at the testing center aren't as creative as we are. They have nice short font lists that help you change fonts and font sizes quickly and easily.

Task 7   Applying a new font and font size.

1. Select the text you want to apply a new font and font size to.

2. Select a font from the Font box on the Formatting toolbar.

3. Enter a font size in the Font Size box on the Formatting toolbar.

 Know how to apply fonts, font sizes, and font styles.

Task 8   Applying a new font and font size to an entire document.

1. Choose Select All from the Edit menu.

 You can also select an entire document by pressing Ctrl+A.

2. Select a font from the Font box on the Formatting toolbar.

3. Enter a font size in the Font Size box on the Formatting toolbar.

Choosing Underline Options

Do you enjoy underlining text? Oh, good. Word offers a lot of underlining options, and the test may ask you to apply one or two of them. Table 3.2 shows Word 97's underlining options.

 If the test asks you to underline text with a plain, single line, you don't need to display the Font dialog box. You can simply use the Underline toolbar button as explained in the "Applying Font Styles" section of this chapter.

Task 9   Applying an underline option to text.

1. Select the text you want to underline.

2. Select Font from the Format menu.

HOLD That Skill!

You can also display the Format menu by using the Alt+O, and then F key combination.

Table 3.2 Underline options.	
Option	**Result**
Single	Underlines words and spaces between words with a single line
Words only	Underlines words with a single line, but not the spaces between the words
Double	Underlines words with a double underline
Dotted	Underlines words with dots
Thick	Underlines words with a thick underline
Dash	Underlines words with dashes
Dot dash	Underlines words with alternating dots and dashes
Dot dot dash	Underlines words with two dots alternating with single dashes
Wave	Underlines words with a wavy line

3. When the Font dialog box appears with the Font tab selected, select an option from the Underline box.

4. Click OK to apply the underline, and return to the document window.

 Remember how to apply different underline options.

Applying Character Effects

The test may ask you to apply a character effect. You may get to do something fun like making your text look like an engraved invitation. Or, you may have to format the 2 in h20 in superscript so it reads as $h^2 0$, the formula for water. Table 3.3 explains the Character effects options.

 Know how to apply a Superscript, Subscript, Small Caps, or All Caps to selected text.

Table 3.3   Character effects options.

Option	Result
~~Strikethrough~~	Draws a line through the middle of the text
~~Double strikethrough~~	Draws a double line through the middle of the text
Superscript	Applies superscript formatting to the text
Subscript	Applies subscript formatting to the text
Shadow	Applies a shadow to text
Outline	Applies an outline to text
Engrave	Applies an embossed effect to text
Emboss	Applies an engraved effect to text
SMALL CAPS	Capitalizes all letters and formats lowercase letters as a smaller size
ALL CAPS	Capitalizes all letters
Hidden	Hides text so it neither appears nor prints unless you choose to display or print hidden text through the Options dialog box

Task 10 Applying a character effect.

1. Select the text you want to apply an effect to.

2. Select Font from the Format menu, or use the Alt+O, and then F key combination.

3. When the Font dialog box appears with the Font tab selected, select a checkbox from the Effects list.

4. Click OK to apply the effect, and return to the document window.

Applying Colors To Text

If you have a color printer or distribute documents online, you can add a dash of color to your text.

Task 11 Applying a color to text.

1. Select the text you want to apply a color to.

2. Select Font from the Format menu.

3. When the Font dialog box appears with the Font tab selected, select a color from the Color box.

4. Click OK to apply the color, and return to the document window.

 If you're asked to apply a color to text, make sure to select the correct color. The test will specify any colors they want you to apply by name. When you select colors from the Font dialog box, the color names appear on the list. When you select colors by clicking the arrow next to the Font Color toolbar button to display the color palette, the color names appear as tooltips.

Displaying Hidden Text

You might be asked to display or edit hidden text. Hidden text only appears and prints if you tell it to. It comes in handy when you can't quite muster the courage to say what you *really* think in that memo to your managers (but only if they don't know about this feature). Hidden text is a character effect that you can apply, as explained in the "Applying Character Effects" section in this chapter.

Task 12 Displaying hidden text.

1. Select Options from the Tools menu.

2. When the Options dialog box appears, select the View tab.

You can also display the Options dialog box by using the Alt+T+O key combination.

3. When the View options appear, as shown in Figure 3.5, select the Hidden Text checkbox from the Nonprinting Characters options list.

4. Click OK to display nonprinting characters, and return to the document window.

Once you display hidden text, you can edit it like any other text. Hidden text displays with a gray, dotted line underneath it. You can hide the text again by repeating the steps in Task 12 and deselecting the checkbox.

Undo/Redo

The Undo and Redo features come in handy when you need to quickly cancel a mistake you just made or repeat something you just did.

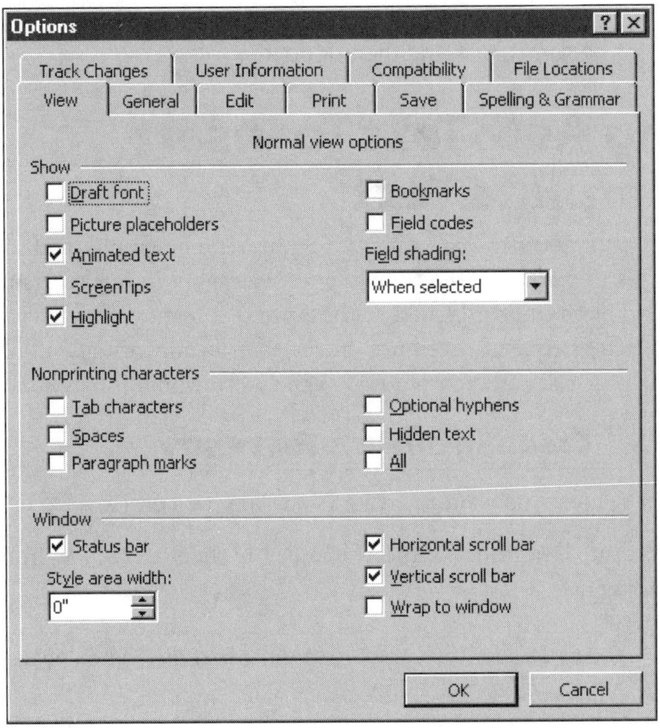

Figure 3.5   The Options dialog box with the View tab selected.

Task 13   Undoing an action.

1. Select Undo from the Edit menu, click the Undo button on the Stand-ard toolbar.

You can also undo an action by using the Ctrl+Z key combination.

Task 14   Redoing an action.

1. Click the Redo toolbar button on the Standard toolbar. You can also redo an action by using the Ctrl+Y key combination.

The Undo and Redo features work for most actions, but not all of them. When you can't undo or repeat an action, the option appears grayed out on the Standard toolbar and on the Edit menu.

If you make a mistake during the test and catch it on time, you can Undo it without losing points. The test also may ask you to perform a task and then Undo it.

Using AutoText To Insert Boilerplate Text

Just about everyone uses *boilerplate* text—phrases, paragraphs, and sometimes entire pages of text that we use over and over again in our correspondence, reports, and publications. Thanks to the AutoText feature, you'll never have to copy and paste frequently used text from other documents again. Word even comes with a list of common phrases, such as "To whom it may concern."

Task 15   Creating an AutoText entry.

1. Select the text you want to create as an AutoText entry.

2. Select AutoText from the Insert menu, and then select New from the cascading list.

You can also display the Create AutoText dialog box by using the Alt+F3 key combination.

3. When the Create AutoText dialog box appears, as shown in Figure 3.6, you can either enter a name for your AutoText entry in the text field or keep the one that Word suggests.

4. Click OK.

Task 16   Creating an AutoText entry with style sheet formatting.

1. Click the Show/Hide Paragraphs button on the Standard toolbar.

2. Select the text you want to create as an AutoText entry, including the paragraph mark (¶) following it (as shown in Figure 3.7).

3. Select AutoText from the Insert menu, and then select New from the cascading list.

4. When the Create AutoText dialog box appears (refer to Figure 3.6), you can either enter a name for your AutoText entry in the text field or keep the one that Word suggests.

5. Click OK.

Task 17   Applying AutoText.

1. Place your cursor where you want to place your AutoText.

2. Select AutoText from the Insert menu.

3. Select an AutoText entry from the cascading list.

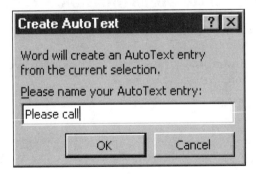

Figure 3.6   The Create AutoText dialog box.

Figure 3.7   Selecting text with a paragraph mark.

The AutoText feature also activates when you begin typing an AutoText phrase. When the tooltip appears with the AutoText entry, press the Enter key to insert the entry.

If you don't see the AutoText entry required by the test, don't panic. Look at the directions again. It will probably mention the paragraph style associated with the AutoText entry, such as a Subject Line, Normal, or Signature style. Select the paragraph style from the cascading list, and your AutoText entry will appear.

Don't confuse AutoText with AutoCorrect! They are similar because both features allow you to create entries and automatically insert text. But the test expects you to use AutoText and AutoCorrect in different ways. For more about AutoCorrect entries, see the "Creating And Entering AutoCorrect Entries" at the end of this chapter.

Specifying AutoCorrect Exceptions

Word 97 automatically corrects text while you type. When we type "teh" instead of "the," we love AutoCorrect. However, AutoCorrect can get annoying when it changes words like "SOFTwareCO, Inc." to "SoftwareCo, Inc." For this reason, you can specify AutoCorrect exceptions to keep Word from making unwanted corrections.

Task 18   Setting up Word so it will not automatically capitalize words that follow abbreviations.

1. Select AutoCorrect from the Tools menu.

You can also display the AutoCorrect dialog box by using the Alt+T, and then A key combination.

2. When the AutoCorrect dialog box appears, make sure the AutoCorrect tab is selected, as shown in Figure 3.8, and then click the Exceptions button.

3. When the AutoCorrect Exceptions dialog box appears, select the First Letter tab, as shown in Figure 3.9.

4. Type the abbreviation (with a period at the end) in the Don't Capitalize After box; then click the Add button.

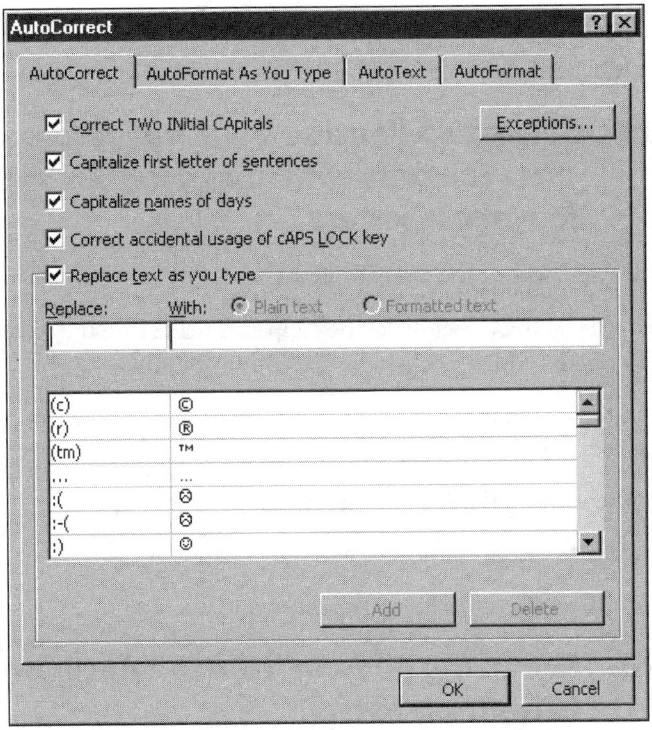

Figure 3.8   The AutoCorrect dialog box.

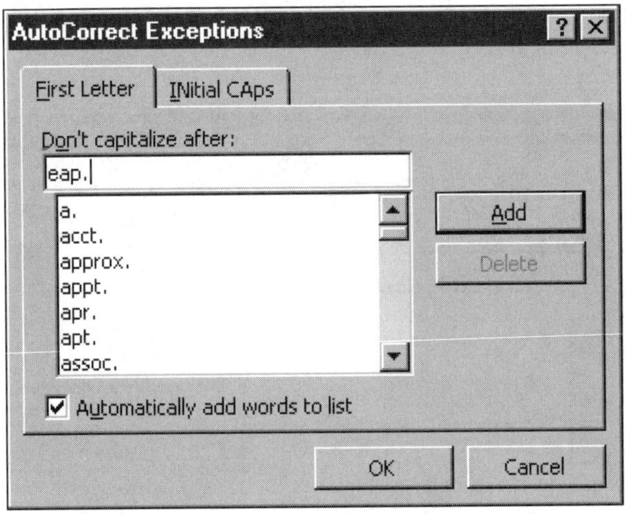

Figure 3.9   The AutoCorrect Exceptions dialog box with the First Letter
tab selected.

5. Click OK to return to the AutoCorrect dialog box.

6. Click OK to return to the document window.

Task 19 Setting up Word so it will not automatically correct words with mixed uppercase and lowercase letters.

1. Select AutoCorrect from the Tools menu.

2. When the AutoCorrect dialog box appears, make sure the AutoCorrect tab is selected and then click the Exceptions button.

3. When the AutoCorrect Exceptions dialog box appears, select the INitial CAps tab, as shown in Figure 3.10.

4. Type the word in the Don't Correct box.

5. Click OK to return to the AutoCorrect dialog box.

6. Click OK to return to the document window.

Task 20 Removing an item from the AutoCorrect Exceptions lists.

1. Select AutoCorrect from the Tools menu.

2. When the AutoCorrect dialog box appears, make sure the AutoCorrect tab is selected and then click the Exceptions button.

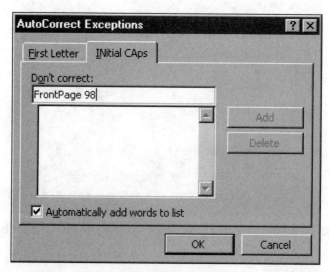

Figure 3.10 The AutoCorrect Exceptions dialog box with the INitial CAps tab selected.

3. When the AutoCorrect Exceptions dialog box appears, select the First Letter tab or the INitial CAps tab.

4. When the First Letter or INitial CAps list appears, select an item from the list and click the Delete button.

5. Click OK to return to the AutoCorrect dialog box.

6. Click OK to return to the document window.

Creating And Entering AutoCorrect Entries

The AutoText feature works great for inserting sentences and long, boilerplate phrases. But what about all those full personal names and company names you have to type all the time? For example, typing out the company name "The Law Firm of Dewey, Cheatham, and Howe Associates" all the time can get rather tiresome. Wouldn't it be nice if you could simply type "DCH" and have word enter the entire name for you? You can do this by specifying an AutoCorrect entry.

Task 21   Creating an AutoCorrect entry.

1. Select AutoCorrect from the Tools menu.

2. When the AutoCorrect dialog box appears, as shown in Figure 3.11, make sure the AutoCorrect tab is selected.

3. Enter the initials or short phrase that you want Word to automatically replace in the Replace box.

4. Type the entire phrase in the With box.

5. Click the Add button (which becomes enabled when you enter information in the Replace and With boxes).

6. Click OK to return to the document window.

Task 22   Entering an AutoCorrect entry.

Once an AutoCorrect entry has been created, all you have to do is to enter the abbreviated text, and Word automatically replaces it.

1. Type the abbreviated text AutoCorrect entry.

If you still feel confused about the difference between AutoCorrect and AutoText entries, not to worry. Just remember that these are two different things, follow the test instructions *exactly*, and you'll do fine.

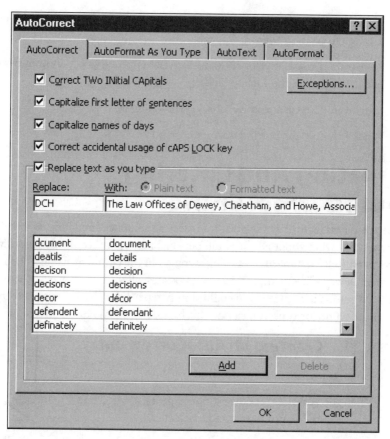

Figure 3.11   The AutoCorrect Exceptions dialog box with the
AutoCorrect tab selected.

Practice Projects

Perform the following projects based on this chapter.

Project 1   Locate and enter text.

1. Open BusinessLetter.doc.

2. Find the text that reads "To Whom It May Concern:".

3. Replace it with "Dear Mr. Abercrombie Peterson:".

Answer to Project 1

Select Open from the File menu and browse to find BusinessLetter.doc. Display the Find dialog box from the Edit menu. When the Find dialog box appears, enter "To Whom" in the Find what box, and then click the Find button. When Word locates and selects "To Whom", click the Cancel box or press the Escape key to close the Find dialog box and return to the document.

Switch to Overtype Mode by selecting Options from the Tools menu, clicking the Edit tab and selecting the Overtype Mode checkbox, or simply double-click the OVR item on the status bar. Type "Dear Mr. Abercrombie Peterson:"

Notice that these instructions do *not* ask you to close the document!

Project 2   Insert the Date and Time.

1. In the current document, insert today's date at the bookmark named "Date."

2. Use the Thursday, January 1, 1998 format.

Answer to Project 2

Select Go To from the Edit menu. When the Go To dialog box appears, select Bookmark from the Go To What list and select "Date" from the Enter Bookmark Name box, then click Go To. When the Cursor moves to the bookmark, click the Close box to return to the document. Select Date and Time from the Insert menu, select the desired format from the list, and click OK.

When the test asks you to locate an item by line number or page element (such as a bookmark, section, or table), it wants you to use the Go To command.

Project 3   Format text.

1. Locate and select the text at the beginning of the letter that reads "Dewey, Cheatham, & Howe, Associates."

2. Change the text to 24-point Arial and make it bold.

3. Format it in Small Caps and apply a dotted underline.

Answer to Project 3

Display the Find dialog box from the Edit menu and search for "Dewey, Cheatham, & Howe Associates".

When Word locates and selects "Dewey, Cheatham, & Howe, Associates," click the Close box to return to the document window. From the Formatting toolbar, select the number 24 in the Font Size box. From the Font box, select Arial, and then click the Bold toolbar button. Display the Font options from the Format menu by selecting Font and clicking the Font tab.

Select the Small Caps checkbox in the Effects list. Select Wave from the Underline box and click OK.

 You can also simply enter "Dewey" in the Find dialog box to locate the line of text. When you return to the document, you can place your cursor anywhere on the line and click three times quickly (triple-click) to select the entire line.

Project 4   Add a character effect.

1. Locate "Abercrombie Peterson, III".

2. Replace "III." with "the 3d".

3. Format the "d" in 3d as superscript text.

Answer to Project 4

Locate "III".

Replace it with "3d".

Select the text "d". Select Font from the Format menu. Select the Superscript checkbox from the Effects list. Click OK.

Project 5   Create and apply an AutoText entry.

1. Locate and select the text at the top of the document that reads "Dewey, Cheatham, & Howe, Associates".

2. Create the line that reads "Dewey, Cheatham, & Howe Associates" as an AutoText entry, name it "Dewey, Cheatham", and include the style formatting.

3. Open a new document and insert the Dewey, Cheatham AutoText Entry.

4. Close the new document without saving it and return to BusinessLetter.doc.

Answer to Project 5

Click the Show/Hide Paragraphs toolbar button to display paragraph marks. Select "Dewey, Cheatham, & Howe, Associates," and include the paragraph (¶) mark that follows it.

From the Insert menu select AutoText, then select New from the cascading list. When the Create AutoText dialog box appears, name the AutoText entry "Dewey, Cheatham".

Open a new document by selecting New from the File menu and choosing a template. Place your cursor in the document, then insert the "Dewey, Cheatham" AutoText entry by selecting AutoText from the Insert menu and selecting "Dewey, Cheatham" from the cascading list (if you don't see it, select Company Name to display the "Dewey, Cheatham" option).

When Word inserts the AutoText entry, select Close from the File menu. When the dialog box appears and asks if you want to close without saving the document, click OK.

You can also apply an AutoText entry by typing it. When you start typing, an AutoText entry tooltip appears and displays the entry. Press the Enter key to apply the entire entry.

HOLD That Skill!

Try typing an AutoText entry right now, with one of the entries that comes with Word. Start typing: "To Whom It May Concern". When the tooltip appears, press the Enter key.

Project 6   Create and apply an AutoCorrect entry.

1. Create a new AutoCorrect entry for "The Law Offices of Dewey, Cheatham, & Howe Associates" and name the AutoCorrect entry "DCH".

2. At the bottom of page 2, create a new line and enter the "DCH" AutoCorrect entry.

3. Save the current document as BusinessLetterch03.doc.

4. Close the new document.

Answer to Project 6

To create an AutoCorrect entry for "The Law Offices of Dewey, Cheatham, & Howe, Associates" named "DCH," select AutoCorrect from the Tools menu. When the AutoCorrect dialog box appears, select the AutoCorrect tab, enter "DCH" in the Replace box, and "The Law Offices of Dewey, Cheatham, & Howe, Associates" in the With box. Click the Add button and click OK.

Find page 2 by selecting Go To from the Edit menu or using the Ctrl+G key combination. When the Go To dialog box displays, select Page from the Go To What list and enter "2" in the Enter Page Number box. When you locate page 2, close the Go To window by clicking the Close button. To create a new line at the bottom of the page, scroll down to the bottom of the page, place your cursor at the end of the last line, and press the Enter key. To insert your AutoCorrect entry, type "DCH". When Word inserts the AutoCorrect entry, select Close from the File menu. When the dialog box appears and asks if you want to close without saving the document, click OK.

To save BusinessLetter.doc with a new name, select Save As from the File menu. When the Save As dialog box appears, enter BusinessLetterch03.doc in the File name box and click Save.

To close the document, select Close from the File menu, or click the Close box on the far right of the menu bar.

 If you close a document using the Close box make sure you don't click the Close box on the title bar and exit the Word application by mistake! The test won't like that.

HOLD That Skill!

Try AutoCorrect right now with one of the entries that comes with Word. Type: "should of been" (a common error) and watch Word change it to "should have been."

Need To Know More?

 Leonhard, Woody, Lee Hudspeth, and T.J. Lee: *Word 97 Annoyances*. O'Reilly and Associates, Inc, Sebastopol, CA, 1997. ISBN 1-56592-308-1. Chapter 3 discusses the formatting toolbar.

 Microsoft Word 97 Step by Step. Microsoft Press, Redmond, WA, 1997. ISBN 1-57231-313-7. Lesson 1 talks about entering text and using the Undo/Redo features. Lesson 3 explains how to format characters.

Formatting Paragraphs, Numbering, And Bullets

Terms you'll need to understand:

√ Aligning paragraphs

√ Spacing

√ Line spacing

√ Left and right indent

√ First line indent

√ Hanging indent

√ Tabs and tab stops

√ Tab alignment

√ Tab leader

√ Bulleted list and bullet style

√ Numbered list and number style

Skills you'll need to master:

√ Aligning a paragraph

√ Applying spacing options to a paragraph

√ Applying line spacing options to a paragraph

√ Setting left, right, first line, and hanging indents

√ Entering and resetting tab stop positions

√ Setting left, center, right, decimal, and bar tabs

√ Applying a tab leader

√ Formatting bulleted lists and choosing bullet styles

√ Formatting numbered lists and choosing number styles

Formatting paragraphs is a major part of a Word user's daily work. The test will expect you to apply alignment, spacing, line spacing, and indenting options with confidence. In addition, you also need to know how to work with tabs, bulleted lists, and numbered lists.

Formatting Paragraphs

If your memory works more like a sieve than like a steel trap, you'll do just fine when it comes to formatting paragraphs. Select Paragraph from the Format menu and then select the Indents and Spacing tab to display the dialog box shown in Figure 4.1. This dialog box has most of the functions you need to modify paragraphs for the test (including the Tabs button, which you can click to display Tab options).

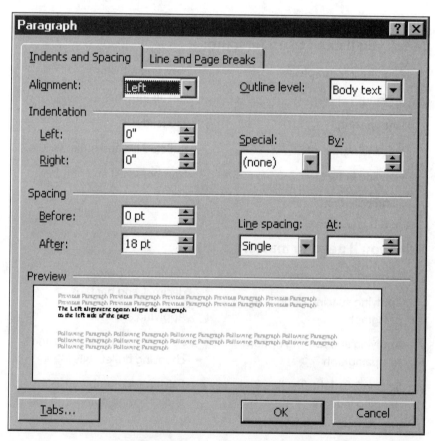

Figure 4.1 The Paragraph dialog box with the Indents And Spacing tab selected.

Any line of text followed by the Enter key counts as a paragraph—even if it consists of only a single line or word.

Task 1   Aligning a paragraph.

You can align a paragraph to the left, right, or center of the page. You can also justify the text. When you justify a paragraph, the words in each line spread out evenly across the page, with equal space between each word.

1. Place your cursor in a paragraph.

2. Select Paragraph from the Format menu.

HOLD That Skill!

You can also access the Paragraph dialog box with the key combination Alt+O, and then P. Or you can right click-the mouse anywhere within the paragraph, and select Paragraph from the drop-down list.

3. Select the Indents And Spacing tab.

4. When the Indents And Spacing options appear, select an option from the Alignment box.

5. Click OK.

 You can align paragraphs quickly and easily by placing your cursor anywhere on the paragraph and clicking the Align Left, Center, Align Right, or Justify toolbar buttons on the Formatting toolbar.

Applying Spacing And Line Spacing Options To Paragraphs

You can apply spacing options to determine the amount of space between paragraphs, and you can also choose whether to insert the space above or below each paragraph. The test may ask you to select paragraphs and specify the amount of space between lines within a paragraph—such as single, single and a half, or double spaced. You can do this with Word's Line Spacing options.

Word measures font sizes as well as the space between lines and paragraphs in *points*.

Task 2 Inserting space above paragraphs.

1. Select a paragraph or paragraphs to which you want to apply spacing options.

2. Open the Paragraph dialog box.

3. Select the Indents And Spacing tab.

4. When the Indents And Spacing options appear, enter a number of points in the Spacing Before box.

5. Click OK.

Task 3 Inserting space below paragraphs.

1. Select a paragraph or paragraphs to which you want to apply spacing options.

2. Open the Paragraph dialog box.

3. Select the Indents And Spacing tab.

4. When the Indents And Spacing options appear, enter a number of points in the Spacing After box.

5. Click OK.

Task 4 Applying line spacing options to a paragraph.

1. Select a paragraph or paragraphs to which you want to apply spacing options.

2. Open the Paragraph dialog box.

3. Select the Indents And Spacing tab.

4. When the Indents And Spacing options appear, select an option from the Line Spacing box.

5. Click OK.

HOLD That Skill!

If the test asks you to change a paragraph or paragraphs to single, single-and-a-half (1.5 Lines), or double spacing (Double), select an option from the Paragraph dialog box's Line Spacing box. If the test asks you to change the amount of space above or below a paragraph, select a value from the Spacing Before or Spacing After box in the Paragraph dialog box.

Indenting Paragraphs

When you take the test, you need to know how to set indents. When you indent paragraphs, you increase the margin around the text so it stands out from the rest of the text. You can indent the left side, the right side, or both. In addition, you can set first line indents (the first line of text indents further in than the rest of the paragraph) or hanging indents (the first line begins further to the left than the rest of the paragraph).

Task 5   Applying a left indent.

The test may ask you to format a paragraph or two with a left indent and to specify a measurement (such as 0.5 inches).

Word measures indents and tabs in *inches*. A half inch is 0.5 inches. A quarter inch is 0.25 inches.

1. Select a paragraph or paragraphs to which you want to apply a left indent.

2. Open the Paragraph dialog box.

3. Select the Indents And Spacing tab.

4. When the Indents And Spacing options appear, select a number of inches from the Left box, located on the Indentation list.

5. Click OK.

If the test tells you to indent an entire paragraph and specifies a measurement, it wants you to apply a left indent.

Task 6   Setting a right indent.

The test may ask you to format a paragraph or several paragraphs with a right indent and to specify a measurement (such as 0.5 inches).

1. Select a paragraph or paragraphs to which you want to apply a right indent.

2. Open the Paragraph dialog box.

3. Select the Indents And Spacing tab.

4. When the Indents And Spacing options appear, select a number of inches from the Indentation Right box.

5. Click OK.

Task 7   Setting a first line indent.

The test may ask you to add a first line indent to some paragraphs and to specify a number of inches (such as 0.5) for the indent.

1. Select a paragraph or paragraphs to which you want to apply a first line indent.

2. Open the Paragraph dialog box.

3. Select the Indents And Spacing tab.

4. When the Indents And Spacing options appear, select First Line from the Special box and then enter or select a value (such as 0.5) from the By box.

5. Click OK.

If the test asks you to indent the first line of a paragraph, or several paragraphs, you should apply a first line indent.

Don't confuse first line indents with left indents.

Task 8   Setting a hanging indent.

The test may ask you to add a hanging indent to some paragraphs and to specify a number of inches (such as 0.5) for the indent.

1. Select a paragraph or paragraphs to which you want to apply a hanging indent.

2. Open the Paragraph dialog box.

3. Select the Indents And Spacing tab.

4. When the Indents And Spacing options appear, select Hanging from the Special box and then enter or select a value from the By box.

5. Click OK.

 In most cases, hanging indents are used for bulleted and numbered lists. As you'll see later in this chapter, when you set up numbered and bulleted lists, Word automatically formats the hanging indents for you. Nonetheless, you may be tested on whether you can format a hanging indent from scratch.

Setting And Formatting Tabs

You also may need to create or modify tabs in a document. You can work with tabs quickly and easily by selecting Tabs from the Format menu to display the Tabs dialog box, shown in Figure 4.2.

 Experienced Word users may prefer to use the ruler when working with indents and tabs. Resist that temptation during the test. You're better off using the Tabs dialog box to enter exact numbers. If the test asks you to create a decimal tab at 3.5 inches and you set it up for 3.6 inches, that fraction of an inch will cost you. You need to follow instructions *exactly* to pass the test.

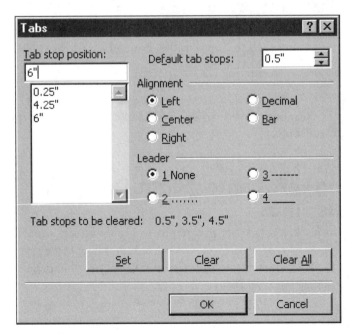

Figure 4.2   The Tabs dialog box.

Task 9   Tabbing text with the Tab key.

You can tab text with the Tab key. When you press the Tab key, the text in front of the cursor jumps to the next tab stop.

1. Place your cursor in front of the text you want to tab.

2. Press the Tab key.

Entering Tab Stop Positions

The Tabs dialog box makes it easy for you to enter and edit tab stop positions. Tab stop positions determine where text moves to when you press the Tab key.

Task 10   Entering tab stop positions.

1. Select Tabs from the Format menu.

 You can also access the Tabs dialog box with the key combination Alt+O, and then T.

2. When the Tabs dialog box appears, enter a tab stop position (in inches) in the Tab Stop Position box, and then click the Set button.

3. When the new tab stop appears on the list, you can enter another tab stop position in the Tab Stop Position box and click the Set button.

4. When you finish entering tab stop positions, click OK.

 If you make a mistake, select the item from the list and click the Clear button. You can also clear all the tabs by clicking the Clear All button.

Setting Left, Center, Right, Decimal, And Bar Tabs

The test may ask you to select paragraphs and to set up left, center, right, or decimal tabs. The type of tab you select determines how text aligns with the tab stop. Table 4.1 explains the structure of different tab alignment options.

 By default, tab stops align to the left.

Table 4.1	Tab alignment options and functions.
Alignment	**Function**
Left	Text aligns to the left beginning at the tab stop
Center	Text aligns to the center of the tab stop
Right	Text is right justified at the tab stop
Decimal	Decimal points in numbers align at the tab stop
Bar	Places a vertical line at the tab stop

Task 11   Choosing a tab stop alignment option.

1. Open the Tabs dialog box.

2. When the Tabs dialog box appears, select a tab stop from the Tab Stop Position list.

3. Select an option from the Alignment list, and then click the Set button.

4. Repeat steps 2 and 3 for any other tab stops that require realigning.

5. Click OK.

Applying Tab Leaders

A leader is a dotted, dashed, or straight line that connects text at the previous tab stop with the text at the current tab stop.

Task 12   Applying a tab leader.

1. Select Tabs from the Format menu, or use the Alt+O, and then T key combination to open the Tabs dialog box.

2. When the Tabs dialog box appears, select a tab stop from the Tab Stop Position list.

3. Select an option from the Leaders list.

4. Repeat steps 2 and 3 for any other tab stops that require leaders.

5. Click OK.

The default for tab leader characters is None.

Editing Tab Stop Options

The test may require you to edit existing tab stops for part of a document.

Task 13   Editing a tab stop.

1. Open the Tabs dialog box.

2. When the Tabs dialog box appears, select a tab stop from the Tab Stop Position list.

3. Select an option from the Alignment or Leaders list.

4. Repeat steps 2 and 3 for any other tab stops that require changes.

5. Click OK.

HOLD That Skill!

You can also display the Tabs dialog box with the tab stop you want to edit selected by double-clicking the tab stop on the ruler. Just make sure you don't accidentally move the tab stop when double-clicking it!

Formatting Numbered And Bulleted Lists

Proficient Word users know how to format paragraphs as numbered and bulleted lists. Simply select a series of paragraphs (remember that even a single line followed by pressing the Enter key counts as a paragraph), click the Numbering List or Bullets button on the Formatting toolbar, and voilà! You can even customize how your bullets or numbers look.

Task 14   Formatting text as a bulleted list with the default bullet style.

1. Select the paragraphs or lines you want to format as a bulleted list.

2. Click the Bullets button on the Formatting toolbar.

Task 15   Formatting text as a bulleted list and choosing a bullet style.

1. Select the paragraphs or lines you want to format as a bulleted list.

2. Select Bullets And Numbering from the Format menu.

You can also access the Bullets And Numbering dialog box with the key combination Alt+O, and then N.

3. When the Bullets And Numbering dialog box appears, select the Bulleted tab.

4. When the Bulleted options appear, as shown in Figure 4.3, select a bullet style.

5. If the bullet style indicated by the test does not appear, select a bullet style, click the Customize button to display the Customize Bulleted List dialog box (as shown in Figure 4.4), select a bullet style, and then click OK to return to the Bullets And Numbering dialog box.

6. Click OK to apply the bullets, and return to the document window.

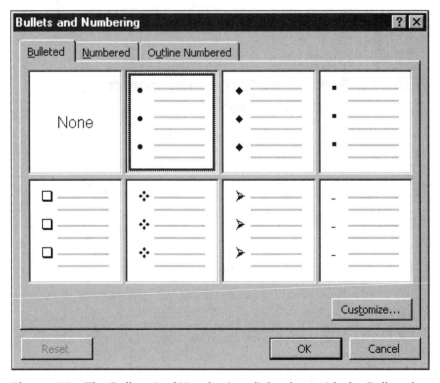

Figure 4.3 The Bullets And Numbering dialog box with the Bulleted tab selected.

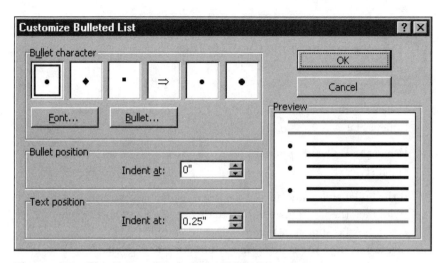

Figure 4.4 The Customize Bulleted List dialog box.

 You can pretty much count on being asked to apply bulleted or numbered lists to text when you take the test.

Task 16 Formatting text as a numbered list with the default number style.

1. Select the paragraphs or lines you want to format as a numbered list.

2. Click the Numbering button on the Standard toolbar.

Task 17 Formatting text as a numbered list and choosing a number style.

1. Select the paragraphs or lines you want to format as a numbered list.

2. Select Bullets And Numbering from the Format menu.

3. When the Bullets And Numbering dialog box appears, select the Numbers tab.

4. When the Numbered options appear, as shown in Figure 4.5, select a number style.

5. If the number style indicated by the test does not appear, select a number style, click the Customize button to display the Customize Numbered List dialog box (shown in Figure 4.6), select a number style, and then click OK to return to the Bullets And Numbering dialog box.

6. Click OK to apply the numbers, and return to the document window.

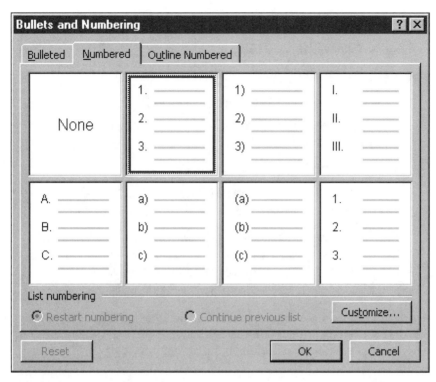

Figure 4.5 The Bullets And Numbering dialog box with the Numbered tab selected.

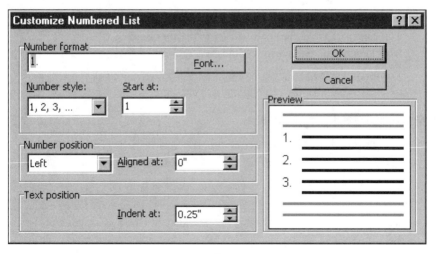

Figure 4.6 The Customize Numbered List dialog box.

Practice Projects

Perform the following projects based on this chapter.

Project 1   Align a paragraph.

1. Open BusinessLetterch03.doc (which you saved in Chapter 3).

2. Select Dewey, Cheatham, & Howe, Associates at the top of the page and center the text.

Answer to Project 1

To open the document, select Open from the File menu to display the Open dialog box; then select BusinessLetterch03.doc and click OK.

To center the text, select "Dewey, Cheatham, & Howe, Associates"; display the Indents And Spacing options by selecting Paragraph from the Format menu, clicking the Indents And Spacing tab when the Paragraph dialog box appears, and selecting Center from the Alignment list. Click OK to apply the formatting and return to the document.

> If you're asked to align text with no other modifications, you can accomplish this faster by selecting the text and clicking the Center toolbar button on the Formatting toolbar.

Project 2   Apply spacing and line spacing options to paragraphs.

1. Open BusinessLetterch03.doc.

2. Select all the text starting with "Dear Mr. Abercrombie Peterson" and ending with "Sincerely,".

3. Format it as single-and-a-half-spaced text with 0 point line spacing before, and 14 point line spacing after.

Answer to Project 2

Select Open from the File menu and select BusinessLetterch03.doc. To select text beginning with "Dear Mr. Abercrombie Peterson," select all paragraphs including "Sincerely,".

To display the Paragraph dialog box with the Indents And Spacing tab selected, select Paragraph from the Format menu, then click the Indents And Spacing Tab. When the Indents And Spacing options appear, select 1.5" from the Line Spacing box and then select 14 points from the Spacing After box. Click OK to return to the document. With the changes you've made so far, BusinessLetter.doc should now look like the document shown in Figure 4.7.

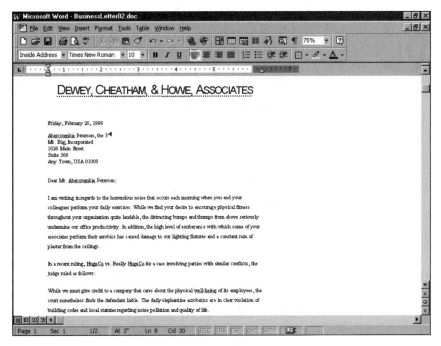

Figure 4.7   BusinessLetterch03.doc after Projects 1 and 2.

 You can also hold down Ctrl+Shift while pressing the down-arrow key to select each paragraph.

 The test may have you select some paragraphs and not others, in which case, you would have to select and apply formatting to one paragraph at a time.

Project 3   Apply left, right, and first line indents to a paragraph.

1. Select the paragraph beginning "While we must give credit to" and indent it one inch on the left and right.

2. Format a first line indent for the paragraph and set it to 0.5 inches.

Answer to Project 3

To locate the paragraph beginning with "While we must give credit to," use the Find feature. To select the paragraph, drag your cursor across it downwards and diagonally.

You can select an entire paragraph by placing your cursor any-where in the paragraph and quickly clicking the mouse button three times.

To begin formatting a first line indent, select Paragraph from the Format menu, then select the Indents And Spacing tab.

HOLD That Skill!

You can also display the Paragraphs dialog box by pressing the Alt+O, and then P key combination.

When the Indents And Spacing options appear, select or enter 1 from the Indentation Left box and 1 from the Indentation Right box to format the indents.

To format the First Line indent, select First Line from the Special box and then enter 0.5" in the By box. Click OK.

Project 4   Reposition and align tab stops.

1. Locate the tabbed list beneath the first heading in the document.

2. For the lines highlighted in red, set the first tab stop at 3" and align it to the center.

3. Position the second tab stop at 5" and make it a decimal tab.

Answer to Project 4

To locate the first heading in the document, select Go To from the Edit menu, choose Heading from the Go To What list when the Go To dialog box appears, enter 1 in the Heading Number box, click the Go To button, and then click the Close button when Word jumps you to the heading.

Select the lines highlighted in red, beginning with "Item" and ending with "Hospital bills." To begin formatting your tabs, display the Tabs dialog box by selecting Tabs from the Format menu. When the Tabs dialog box appears, click the Clear All button to remove the current tab settings. To create and format the first tab, enter 3" in the Tab Stop Posi-tion box and click the Set button. Now, select the item from the list of tab stop positions, click the Center radio button from the Alignment list, then click the Set button again.

To create and format the second tab enter 5" in the Tab Stop Position box, and click the Set button. Now, select the second item from the list of tab stop positions (it should be

5"), click the Decimal radio button from the Alignment list, and then click the Set button. Click OK to apply your settings and return to the document.

 If the test asks you to change a tab stop alignment or leader, you can do so by selecting the tab stop from the Tab Stop Position list and then clicking an Alignment or Leader option. If the test asks you to change a position for a tab stop, then you need to first clear the tab stop that needs to be changed.

Project 5   Set a tab leader.

1. Select the line from the list of tabbed items that is highlighted in blue.

2. Format the line with a decimal tab and a dotted-line leader.

3. Save the document to your Practice folder as BusinessLetterch04.doc and close the document.

Answer to Project 5

To begin applying a dotted-line leader to a tab, select the line that is highlighted in blue, then select Tabs from the Format menu.

When the Tabs dialog box appears, apply a dotted-line leader to the tab stop by selecting the tab stop from the Tab Stop position list and clicking the second radio button (with the dotted line) from the Leaders list. Format the tab stop as a decimal tab by selecting the Decimal radio button from the Alignment list.

To apply the new tab settings and return to the document, click the Set button and then click OK. The list of tabbed items should now appear as shown in Figure 4.8. To save the document with a different name, select Save As from the File menu, browse for the Practice folder you created, and enter BusinessLetterch04.doc in the File Name box.

Project 6   Format a bullet list with a bullet style.

1. Open Memorandumch02.doc from your practice folder. You created this document in Chapter 2.

We respectfully request compensation for the following damages|

Item	Description	Amount
Ceiling	Required massive repairs	$2,000.00
Chandelier	Fell down	$4,000.00
Hospital bills	Injuries from falling plaster	$10,000.00
Total..		$16,000.00

Figure 4.8   List of tabbed items as formatted in Projects 4 and 5.

2. Format the lines highlighted in red as a bulleted list, using the ❖ bullet style.

Answer to Project 6

Select Open from the File menu and open Memorandumch02.doc. To apply bullets to the lines highlighted in red, select the three lines, then select Bullets And Numbering from the Format menu and click the Bulleted tab. Select the style shown from the Bulleted List options and then click OK to return to the document. Your document should now look like Figure 4.9.

Project 7 Format a numbered list with the default style.

1. Format the three lines highlighted in blue as a numbered list with the default number style.

2. Save the document to your Practice folder as Memorandumch04.doc.

Answer to Project 7

To apply a numbered list with the default style, select the lines that are highlighted in blue and click the Numbering toolbar button on the Formatting toolbar.

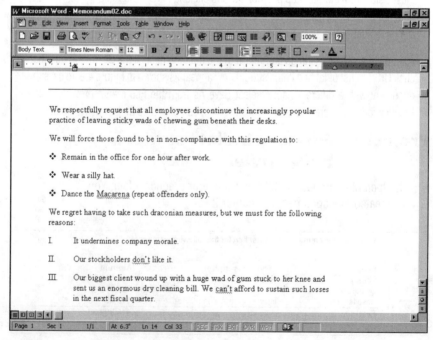

Figure 4.9 Memorandumch04.doc document with bulleted and numbered lists applied.

To save the document with a different name, select Save As from the File menu. When the Save As dialog box appears, enter Memorandumch04.doc in the File Name box and click the Save button. To close the document, select Close from the File menu.

Project 8   Apply hanging indents.

1. Open Declaration.doc from the practice disk.

2. Locate the list of signatures on page 4, and apply a 0.1" hanging indent to the entire list of signatures starting with "Georgia."

3. Save the document to the Practice folder on your hard drive as Declarationch04.doc.

Answer to Project 8

Select Open from the File menu and open Declaration.doc.

To find the list of signatures, use the Find command to locate the word "Georgia", or use the Go To command to locate page 4. Select the entire list of names. To format the list of signatures with a hanging indent, select Paragraphs from the Format menu. When the Paragraphs dialog box appears with the Indents And Spacing tab selected, choose the Hanging option from the Special box and enter 0.1" in the By box. Click OK to return to the document. You will not notice the new formatting. However, when you format the text into columns in the next chapter, names that take up more than one line will indent on the second line.

To save the document with a different name, select Save As from the File menu. When the Save As dialog box appears, enter Declarationch04.doc in the File Name box, and click the Save button.

Need To Know More?

 Leonhard, Woody, Lee Hudspeth, and T. J. Lee: *Word 97 Annoyances*. O'Reilly and Associates, Inc, Sebastopol, CA, 1997. ISBN 1-56592-308-1. Chapter 6 covers Word's formatting idiosyncrasies.

 Microsoft Word 97 Step by Step. Microsoft Press, Redmond, WA, 1997. ISBN 1-57231-313-7. Lesson 3 tells you how to format paragraphs, create bulleted and numbered lists, and use indents and tabs.

Tables
And Columns

Terms you'll need to understand:

- √ Normal view
- √ Page Layout view
- √ Columns
- √ Column spacing and width
- √ Table
- √ Table row, column, and cell
- √ Row height and column width
- √ Borders
- √ Shading
- √ Changing text direction
- √ Sort ascending/ sort descending

Skills you'll need to master:

- √ Switching between Normal and Page Layout views
- √ Locating text with columns
- √ Typing and editing text in columns
- √ Formatting and editing columns
- √ Changing column numbers, width, and spacing
- √ Creating tables
- √ Formatting tables automatically
- √ Adding rows and columns
- √ Merging and splitting cells
- √ Applying borders and shading to tables and table cells
- √ Rotating text
- √ Sorting alphabetically/ numerically

Word's Columns and Tables features help you present information more effectively. For example, you can create tables to display sales figures for your department, or you can format long lists as columns. The Word Proficiency test will ask you to demonstrate your ability to edit and insert text in existing tables and columns, as well as to format simple tables and columns on your own.

Typing And Editing Text In Columns

Have you ever created or edited documents with columns before? Not to worry. Columns are easy to format and work with. Word even automatically flows text from the bottom of a column to the top of the next column.

Views

Before you can view or edit text laid out in columns, you need to understand the difference between the *Normal* and *Page Layout* views. Most of the time, documents are viewed in Normal mode. When you work in the Normal view, nontext elements such as headers, footers, columns, and graphics do not display. In order to view columns so you can work with them, you first have to switch to Page Layout view. To practice switching views, you can open one of the sample documents included on the practice disk.

Task 1   *Switching to Page Layout view.*

1. Open a document.

2. Select Page Layout from the View menu.

 You can also access Page Layout view with the key combination Alt+V, and then P.

Figure 5.1 shows how text with column formatting will appear when displayed in Page Layout view.

 Don't confuse Page Layout view with Online Layout view. Chapter 11 talks about working with documents online.

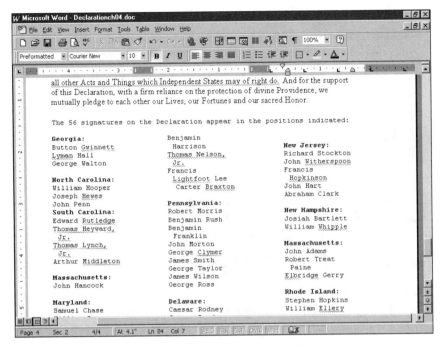

Figure 5.1   Columns shown in Page Layout view.

Task 2   *Switching to Normal view.*

1. Select Normal from the View menu.

You can also access Normal view with the key combination Alt+V, and then N.

Uh oh! Where did the columns go? Don't worry. They're still there. The Normal view displays the text but not the column formatting.

Task 3   *Locating column-formatted text.*

To edit or type text in columns, you first need to locate column-formatted text in a document. Because columns always follow a section break (for more about breaks, see Chapter 9), you can jump from section to section with the Go To command.

1. Go to Page Layout view.

2. Select Go To from the Edit menu, or use the Ctrl+G key combination.

3. When the Find And Replace dialog box appears with the Go To tab selected, as shown in Figure 5.2, select Section from the Go To What list; then click the Next button until you locate the section break followed by columned text.

 The dotted lines indicating section breaks do not display in the Page Layout view. Section breaks only display in the Normal view.

 The test may not specifically tell you to use the Go To feature, but you will be expected to know when it is appropriate to do so. If the test asks you to locate or modify a table, graphic, section, heading, or page, you can save time with Go To.

Task 4   *Editing and typing text in columns.*

You can edit and type text in columns the same way you edit any other text. When making edits or quick additions, it's easier to make changes in the Page Layout view so you can make sure the text flows properly.

1. Go to Page Layout view.

2. Select the text you want to edit, or place your cursor where you want to enter new text.

3. Begin typing.

Applying And Reformatting Columns

The test will ask you to either select text and apply column formatting, or reformat existing columns. Columns consist of the columns themselves, as well as *spacing* between the columns.

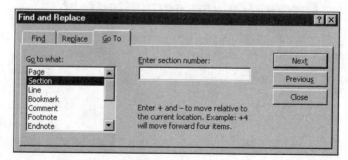

Figure 5.2   Find And Replace dialog box with the Go To tab selected.

Task 5   *Applying simple columns.*

1. Select the text you want to format into columns.

2. Click the Columns toolbar button.

3. When the pop-up box appears, as shown in Figure 5.3, select the number of columns you want by dragging the cursor across them to the right.

4. Release the mouse button.

 If you select text in Normal view and click the Columns toolbar button, Word will automatically switch to the Page Layout view.

Task 6   *Applying columns with specific attributes.*

The test may ask you to format columns with more specific attributes, such as two columns with .5 inch spacing.

1. Select the text you want to format into columns.

2. Select Columns from the Format menu, or use the key combination Alt+O, and then C.

3. When the Columns dialog box appears, as shown in Figure 5.4, enter or select a number of columns in the Number Of Columns box.

4. Select the Equal Column Width checkbox to apply the same attributes to the columns, or deselect the checkbox to apply different widths to different columns.

5. Select or enter a value in the Width box to determine the column width.

6. Select or enter a value in the Spacing box to determine the column spacing (if you select the Equal Column Width checkbox, only the first column's boxes will be enabled).

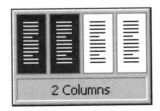

Figure 5.3   The pop-up box for selecting a number of columns.

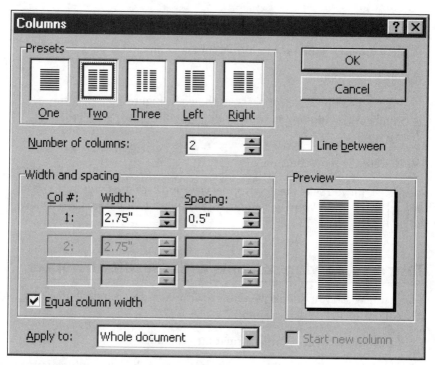

Figure 5.4   The Columns dialog box.

7. Select an option from the Apply To box. If the test asks you to apply columns to the entire document, select Whole document. If the test asks you to apply columns to only part of the text, choose Selected Text (if you have not already selected your text, this option will not be available).

When you select text and apply columns, Word inserts two section breaks. The first section break begins the column formatting, and the second section break ends the column formatting. When you apply columns without selecting text, Word inserts a section break that applies columns to the entire section. Chapter 9 talks more about section breaks.

The test probably will not ask you to apply complex column formatting—such as columns with different widths and spacing.

Task 7   Removing column formatting.

Because column formatting is indicated by section breaks, you can remove columns by deleting the section breaks. Section breaks display only in Normal view.

1. Go to Page Layout view.

2. Select Go To.

3. When the Find And Replace dialog box appears, select the Go To tab (if needed), and then choose Section from the Go To What list. Then, click the Next button until you locate the section break followed by the columned text.

4. Display the document in Normal view so you can see the section breaks.

5. When Word switches to Normal view, select the section break by placing your cursor on it, and then press the Delete key.

6. If the columns were applied to the entire document or document section, then you're finished. If the columns were applied to only part of the document, locate the next section break with the Go To command.

7. Select the second section break by placing your cursor on it and then press the Delete key.

Task 8   *Changing the number of columns.*

1. Go to Page Layout view.

2. Locate and select the columned text.

3. Go to the Columns dialog box, and select or enter a number of columns in the Number Of Columns box.

HOLD That Skill!

You can also change the number of columns by selecting the columned text, clicking the Columns toolbar button, and selecting the new number of columns from the pop-up box.

Task 9   *Changing the column width.*

The column width settings determine how wide the columns are.

1. Go to Page Layout view.

2. Locate and select the columned text.

3. Go to the Columns dialog box, and select or enter a measurement in the Width box for the column you want to change.

Task 10   *Changing the column spacing.*

You may also be asked to change the amount of space in between columns.

1. Go to Page Layout view.

2. Locate and select the columned text.

3. Go to the Columns dialog box, and select or enter a measurement in the Spacing box for the column you want to change.

Working With Tables

Managers and co-workers just love tables. Take a look at the documents that pass through your office every day. People use tables for everything ranging from calendars to status reports and product comparisons. The test will definitely ask you to work with tables a bit. You won't have to do anything fancy, but you should be comfortable with creating and editing simple tables.

Task 11   Displaying the Tables And Borders toolbar.

Creating tables is fairly simple. But in order to edit tables, you'll often need to access features that are only available from the Tables And Borders toolbar.

1. Click the Tables And Borders toolbar button on the Standard toolbar. When you display the Tables And Borders toolbar, Word switches to the Page Layout view.

Task 12   Creating a table.

If the test asks you to create a simple table with no special formatting, you can use the Insert Table toolbar button on the standard toolbar.

1. Place your cursor where you want to insert the table.

2. Click the Insert Table toolbar button on the Standard toolbar.

3. When the pop-up box appears, as shown in Figure 5.5, select a number of columns and rows by dragging your cursor diagonally toward the lower right.

Figure 5.5   The Table pop-up box.

4. Release the mouse button.

 You can expand the number of possible columns and rows available in the Insert Table pop-up box by clicking the mouse arrow on any border and dragging it horizontally or vertically.

Task 13   *Formatting a table automatically.*

If the test asks you to automatically format a table, that means it wants you to use the Table AutoFormat feature.

1. Place your cursor anywhere on the table.

2. Select Table AutoFormat from the Table menu, or use the key combination Alt+A, and then F.

3. When the Table AutoFormat dialog box appears, as shown in Figure 5.6, select a format from the Formats list.

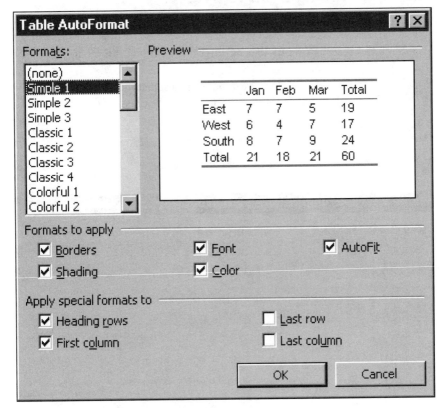

Figure 5.6   The Table AutoFormat dialog box.

4. Select formats to apply by selecting or deselecting the checkboxes (you can view the results in the Preview box).

5. Click OK.

 You can also display the Table AutoFormat dialog box by clicking the Table AutoFormat button on the Tables And Borders toolbar.

Task 14   Navigating a table and entering text.

You can enter or edit text in tables as you normally would. You can also move around within a table by using the key combinations listed in Table 5.1.

1. Place your cursor in a table cell.

2. Begin typing or select the text you want to edit, and then begin typing.

Task 15   Adding a row to a table.

1. Select the row below where you want to add the new row.

2. Click the Insert Rows toolbar button on the Standard toolbar.

 You can also use key combinations to select rows, columns, or entire tables. Simply press the Shift key while pressing the other keys.

Word adds a row above the currently selected row.

Table 5.1 Key combinations for moving around in a table.	
Key Combination	**Function**
Tab	Go to the next cell (from left to right)
Shift+Tab	Go back one cell
Up Arrow	Go up one row
Down Arrow	Go down one row
Alt+Home	Go to the first cell in the row
Alt+End	Go to the last cell in the row
Alt+PgUp	Go to the top of the column
Alt+PgDn	Go to the bottom of the column

The Add Row toolbar button appears only when you select a table row.

You can also select a table row by placing the cursor in the "selection bar" alongside the row you want to select. The selection bar is an invisible area in the left margin of the screen. When the cursor turns into an arrow pointed at the row, click once and the row is selected. You can also try this trick to select a line of ordinary text.

Task 16   *Adding a row to the bottom of a table.*

If the test asks you to add a row to the bottom of a table, you can do it with the Tab key.

1. Place your cursor in the last table cell at the bottom row, right column.

2. Press the Tab key.

Task 17   *Adding a column.*

You can add a new column to a table.

1. Select the column to the left of where you want the new column to appear.

2. Click the Add Column toolbar button on the Standard toolbar.

HOLD That Skill!

You can select a column by placing your cursor in the upper-most cell and using the Alt+PgDn key combination. Or, you can aim the mouse pointer downward at the column and click once. The Add Column toolbar button appears only when you select a table column.

The Add Row and Add Column toolbar buttons are really the same button. They change depending on whether a row or a column is selected. The Add Row button is the default button.

Task 18   *Splitting a table cell.*

You can divide a table cell in half.

1. Select the cell you want to split.

2. Select the Split Cells button from the Tables And Borders toolbar.

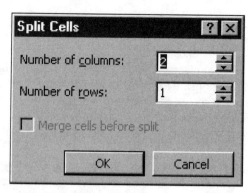

Figure 5.7 The Split Cells dialog box.

3. When the Split Cells dialog box appears, as shown in Figure 5.7, enter or select a number of columns (to divide a table cell horizontally) and/or a number of rows (to divide a table cell vertically).

4. Click OK.

Task 19   Merging cells.

You can combine adjacent table cells by merging them.

1. Select the cells that you want to merge.

2. Click the Merge Cells button on the Tables And Borders toolbar.

Task 20   Adjusting row height and column width.

You can control your table layout by specifying height settings for rows and width settings for columns. Word applies height settings to all cells in the same row and width settings to all cells in the same column.

1. Select a table cell.

2. Select Cell Height And Width from the Table menu.

3. When the Cell Height And Width dialog box appears, as shown in Figure 5.8, select the Row tab.

4. From the Height Of Rows box, select the Exactly option to specify a precise height measurement or the At Least option to specify a minimum height; then enter a measurement (in points) in the At box.

5. You can also specify settings for adjacent rows by clicking the Next Row or Previous Row button.

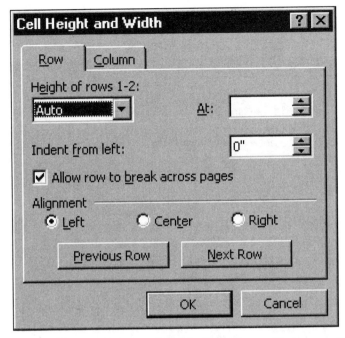

Figure 5.8 The Cell Height And Width dialog box with Row options.

6. Select the Column tab, as shown in Figure 5.9. Enter or select a measurement in the Width Of Columns box and a measurement in the Space Between Columns box (the space between columns pads the table cells so text and other table cell elements don't run together).

7. You can also specify settings for adjacent columns by clicking the Next Column or Previous Column button.

You can apply height and width settings to an entire table by selecting the table first. To select the entire table, choose the Select Table command from the Table menu.

Task 21   *Applying borders to a table.*

The test may ask you to add or reformat table borders.

1. Select a table or the rows, columns, or cells to which you want to apply borders.

2. Select Borders And Shading from the Format menu, or use the key combination Alt+O, and then B.

3. When the Borders And Shading dialog box appears, select the Borders tab, as shown in Figure 5.10.

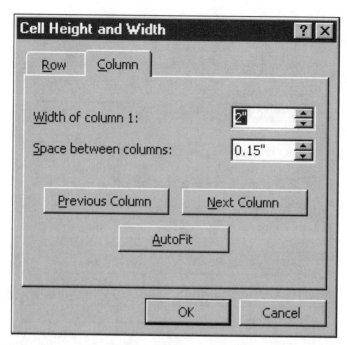

Figure 5.9 The Cell Height And Width dialog box with Column options.

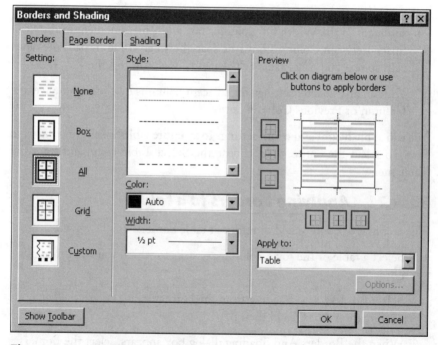

Figure 5.10 The Borders And Shading dialog box with Borders options displayed.

4. Select Box to create a box around the table or All to apply borders to all the table's cells.

5. Select a line style, width, and color from the Style, Width, and Color boxes.

6. You can also click the buttons alongside the Preview diagram box, or click directly on the borders displayed in the Preview diagram box, to apply borders specifically to the top, bottom, or sides, or to remove or add lines.

7. Select Table from the Apply To box to apply the borders to the entire table, or you can select Cell to apply the borders to the selected cells.

8. Click OK.

You may also be asked to apply borders to individual cells, columns, or rows. To do this, select the cells, columns, or rows to which you want to apply a border, and then perform steps 2 through 6 from the above task. You can then select Cell from the Apply To box and click OK.

 When applying borders and shading to cells, make sure you select the *end cell markers* as well as the cells. You can display the end cell markers by clicking the Show Paragraph Marks toolbar button on the Standard toolbar.

 You can also apply Border styles, line weight, and colors, as well as apply borders to parts of the table from the Tables And Borders toolbar. But if tables aren't your forte, you may find it easier to use the Borders And Shading dialog box.

Task 22   *Applying shading.*

The test may also ask you to apply shading to a table, row, column, or cell.

1. Select a table or the rows, columns, or cells to which you want to apply shading.

2. Select Borders And Shading from the Format menu to display the Borders And Shading dialog box, and select the Shading tab, as shown in Figure 5.11.

3. Select a fill from the color palette or from the Color box.

4. Select a shading or pattern option from the Style box.

5. Select Table from the Apply To box to apply the shading to the entire table, or you can select Cell to apply the shading to the selected table cells.

6. Click OK.

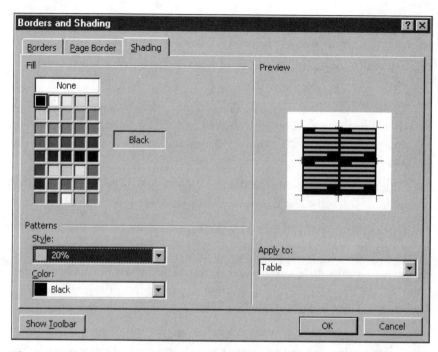

Figure 5.11 Borders And Shading dialog box with Shading tab selected.

You may also be asked to apply shading to individual cells, columns, or rows. To do this, select the cells, columns, or rows to which you want to apply shading to, and then perform steps 2 through 6 from the previous task. You can then select Cell from the Apply To box and click OK.

Task 23 Rotating text in a table cell.

You can also rotate text in a table cell with the Change Text Direction button on the Tables And Borders toolbar. Each click rotates the text in 90 degree increments.

1. Click on the cell that contains the text you want to rotate.

2. Click the Change Text Direction button on the Tables And Borders toolbar.

You can also rotate text in a table cell by selecting Text Direction from the Format menu. But it's easier to do it with the Tables And Borders toolbar.

Task 24   *Sorting table items in alphabetical and numerical order.*

The test may also display a table with a list of items and ask you to sort them by column in alphabetical or numerical order. Never fear. This is easy.

1. Select the column with the heading for the category that you want to sort by.

2. Click the Sort Ascending or Sort Descending button on the Tables And Borders toolbar.

In most cases, you should click the Sort Ascending button. This sorts items from A-Z or 1-100.

Practice Projects

Perform the following projects based on this chapter.

Project 1   Apply columns and edit text.

1. Open Declarationch04.doc, which you created in the Chapter 4.

2. Locate the list of signatures beginning with "Georgia." on page 4.

3. Format the entire list of states and names into three columns that are each 1.83" wide with 0.4" gutters between the columns.

4. Type the name Samuel Adams above the name John Adams.

5. Save the document as Declarationch05.doc, and close it.

The spaces in between columns are often referred to as "gutters". If the test asks you to specify gutters, you can do so by entering a value in the "Spacing" box in the Columns dialog box.

Answer to Project 1

Open Declarationch04.doc using the Open command from the File menu.

To locate the list of signatures, use the Find command and search for the word "Georgia." Or you can use the Go To command to find page 4.

To begin formatting the list into columns, select the entire list of states and names; then select Columns from the Format menu. When the Columns dialog box appears, enter the number 3 in the Number Of Columns box. Because you were instructed to make the columns of equal width, select the Equal Column Width checkbox. Enter 1.9 in the Width box to reset the column width. Enter .4 in the Spacing box to determine the column spacing. Choose Selected Text from the Apply To box and click OK. When you return to the document, it will display in the Page Layout view and look like the document shown in Figure 5.1 at the beginning of this chapter.

To add the name Samuel Adams above the name John Adams, use the Find command to find the name John Adams. Place your cursor to the left of the J, type the name Samuel Adams, and then press the Enter key.

To save the document with another name, select Save As from the File menu to save the document with a different file name. When the Save As dialog box displays, enter "Declarationch05.doc" in the File Name box and click the Save button. To close the document, select Close from the File menu.

Project 2   Create and format a table.

1. Open a new document from the Blank Document template.
2. Create a table with three columns and three rows.

Answer to Project 2

To create a new document, select FilelNew and choose the Blank template when the New dialog box appears.

To create a table, place your cursor in the new document, click the Insert Table toolbar button, and then drag your cursor across three columns and down three rows in the pop-up table box.

Project 3   Merge cells in a table and enter text in a table cell.

1. Merge all the cells in the top row.
2. Type "My Table" in the top row.

Answer to Project 3

To merge all the cells in the top row, select the entire top row, display the Tables And Borders toolbar, and click the Merge Cells button.

Place your cursor anywhere in the newly merged cell and type "My Table."

Project 4   Enter text in table cells and navigate tables.

1. In the second row of the table, type "One" in the first cell, "Two" in the second cell, and "Three" in the third cell.
2. In the bottom row of the table, type "Four" in the first cell, "Five" in the second cell, and "Six" in the third cell.

Answer to Project 4

Press the Tab key to move to the next cell, enter the text.

Press the Tab key again to move to the next cell.

Project 5   Add borders and shading to a table.

1. Add a black, 1.5 point, solid line border to the entire table and all the cells.
2. Add 25% black shading to the top row of the table.

Answer to Project 5

Select Borders And Shading from the Format menu and click the Borders tab. When the border options display, select the All button, choose a solid line from the Style box, choose Black from the Color box, and then choose 1 1/2 pt. from the Width box. Select Table from the Apply To box and click OK.

Select the top row cell (which you recently merged) by placing your cursor in it and then choose Borders And Shading from the Format menu. When the Borders and Shading dialog box appears, select the Shading tab. Select 25% from the Style box and Black from the Color box. Select Cell from the Apply To box and click OK to return to the document.

Project 6   Add a row to the bottom of a table.

1. Add a row to the bottom of the table.
2. Save the file as MyTable.doc.

Answer to Project 6

To add a row to the bottom of the table, tab to the last cell and press the Tab key again.

To save the table, select Save from the File menu and enter MyTable.doc in the Save dialog box's File Name box. The table should now look like the example shown in Figure 5.12.

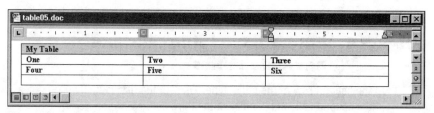

Figure 5.12   The Project 6 table.

Need To Know More?

 Microsoft Word 97 Step by Step. Microsoft Press, Redmond, WA, 1997. ISBN 1-57231-313-7. Go to Lesson 8 to learn how to create a table and Lesson 12 for more on columns.

Drawing Tools

Terms you'll need to understand:

√ AutoShapes

√ Line styles

√ Dashed line styles

√ Arrow styles

√ Borders and fills

√ Shadows and 3-D Effects

√ Callouts

√ Rotate and flip

Skills you'll need to master:

√ Displaying the Drawing toolbar

√ Drawing lines and arrows

√ Applying colors to lines and arrows

√ Applying line styles, dash styles, and arrow styles

√ Resizing lines

√ Drawing shapes such as rectangles, ovals, and AutoShapes

√ Resizing shapes

√ Editing borders and applying fills

√ Applying shadows and 3-D effects

√ Rotating and flipping objects

√ Creating callouts

Word 97 comes with a variety of fairly sophisticated drawing features for jazzing up documents, creating flow charts, and more. Nobody expects you to be the next Michelangelo, but the test does require you to be comfortable with the basics. The Drawing toolbar provides options for creating shapes, lines, 3-D shapes, and arrows in a variety of colors and styles. In addition, you can apply borders, fills, and shadows to shapes, as well as rotate text. As is the case with columns, drawings only appear when you switch to the Page Layout view.

Task 1   Displaying the Drawing toolbar.

Before you can draw, you'll need to display the Drawing toolbar.

1. Click the Drawing toolbar button on the Standard toolbar. Word will automatically display your document in the Page Layout view.

2. If the Drawing toolbar appears as a floating toolbar in the middle of the document window, you can dock it. Just select the toolbar and drag it toward the top, left, or bottom of the document window to anchor it; then release your mouse button.

 Familiarize yourself with the drawing toolbar! Not only will you do better on the test, you'll also be able to jazz up your documents.

Drawing And Editing Lines

You can draw lines, apply colors and line styles, and create arrows. Figure 6.1 shows a solid line, a dashed line, and an arrow.

Task 2   Drawing a line.

1. Click the Line toolbar button on the Drawing toolbar. This switches you to the Page Layout view if you're in the Normal view.

2. Place your cursor where you want to begin the line, and hold down the mouse key. When the cursor appears as a cross hair on the screen, drag the mouse to the right, left, or at an angle to position your line.

3. Release the mouse key.

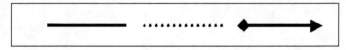

Figure 6.1   A solid line, a dashed line, and an arrow.

HOLD That Skill!

Remember that whenever you click a button from the Drawing toolbar, Word automatically switches you to the Page Layout view. You can also switch to Page Layout view by selecting Page Layout from the View menu, or use the Alt+V, and then P key combination.

Task 3   Drawing an arrow.

1. Click the Drawing toolbar button on the Standard toolbar to display the Drawing toolbar. Word automatically changes to the Page Layout view.

2. Click the Arrow toolbar button on the Drawing toolbar.

3. Place your cursor where you want to begin the arrow, and hold down the mouse key. When the cursor appears as a cross hair on the screen, drag the mouse to the right, left, or at an angle to position your line.

4. Release the mouse key.

Task 4   Applying a color to a line or arrow.

1. Select the line or arrow to which you want to apply a color.

2. Click the down arrow to the right of the Line Color button on the Drawing toolbar.

3. When the Line Color box appears, select a color and release the mouse button.

When you pass your mouse over a color, a ToolTip appears and tells you the name of the color. If the test asks you to apply a color to a line, it will tell you the name of the color. Make sure you select the correct one.

Task 5   Applying a line style.

The line style determines the width of the line or arrow. Word measures line widths in points (pt).

1. Select a line.

2. Click the Line Style toolbar button on the Drawing toolbar to display the drop-down list of line style options.

3. Select a line style option.

If the test asks you to create a line with a specific width, such as a 1/2 pt line, then it wants you to apply a line style.

 Do you find dialog boxes less confusing than toolbars? You can also edit a line or shape by double-clicking it to display the Format AutoShape dialog box.

Task 6   Applying a dash style.

You can also apply a dash style to a line or arrow.

1. Select a line.

2. Click the Dash Style toolbar button on the Drawing toolbar to display the drop-down list of dash style options.

3. Select a dash style option.

 When you pass your mouse over a dash style, a ToolTip appears and tells you the name of the dash style. If the test asks you to apply a dash style to a line, it will tell you the name of the dash style. Make sure you select the correct one.

Task 7   Applying an arrow style.

You can use the Arrow Style options to turn the current line into an arrow, to change the arrow style, or to change an arrow into a straight line.

1. Select a line.

2. Click the Arrow Style toolbar button on the Drawing toolbar to display the drop-down list of arrow style options.

3. Select an arrow style option.

 When you pass your mouse over an arrow style, a ToolTip appears and tells you the name of the arrow style. If the test asks you to apply an arrow style to a line, it will tell you the name of the arrow style. Make sure you select the correct one.

Task 8   Resizing a line.

The test may ask you to create a line with a specific length.

1. Select a line.

2. Display the Format AutoShape dialog box by selecting AutoShape from the Format menu.

3. When the Format AutoShape dialog box appears, as shown in Figure 6.2, select the Size tab.

4. Enter a measurement in the Width box.

5. Click OK.

 Remember that you can also display the Format AutoShape dialog box by double-clicking a line or any other AutoShape.

Drawing Shapes

The test may ask you to draw rectangles, squares, ovals, circles, and AutoShapes, such as the ones shown in Figure 6.3.

 When you click a button to create a shape, Word switches automatically to the Page Layout view.

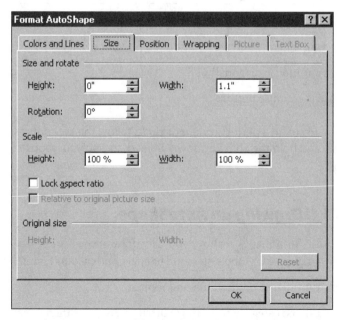

Figure 6.2 The Format AutoShape dialog box with Size options displayed.

Figure 6.3   A rectangle, an oval, and a few AutoShapes. The shape on the far right is a callout with text inserted.

Task 9   Drawing a rectangle.

1. Click the Rectangle button on the Drawing toolbar.

2. Place your cursor where you want to begin your rectangle.

3. Drag your mouse diagonally.

4. Release the mouse button.

 To create a perfect square, hold the Shift key while dragging your mouse.

Task 10   Drawing an oval.

1. Click the Oval button on the Drawing toolbar.

2. Place your cursor where you want to begin your oval.

3. Drag your mouse diagonally.

4. Release the mouse button.

 To create a perfect square or circle, follow the procedures above, and hold the Shift key down while dragging your mouse.

Task 11   Drawing an AutoShape.

With Word's AutoShapes feature, you can draw special lines, basic shapes, block arrows, flowchart symbols, stars and banners, and callouts (comic balloons).

1. Click AutoShapes on the Drawing toolbar.

2. Select a shape category from the shortcut menu, and then select a shape from the cascading menu, as shown in Figure 6.4.

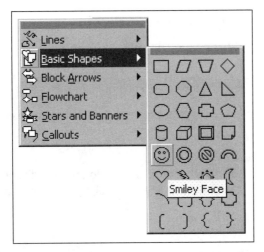

Figure 6.4   Selecting an AutoShape.

3. Place your cursor where you want to draw your AutoShape.

4. Drag your mouse diagonally.

5. Release the mouse button.

 When you pass your mouse over an AutoShape option, a ToolTip appears and tells you the name of the AutoShape option. If the test asks you to apply an AutoShape, be sure to select the shape by the name specified.

HOLD That Skill!

Familiarize yourself with the different types of AutoShapes (such as Basic Shapes, Callouts, and Stars And Banners). Callouts are a type of autoshape that lets you point to a place in a picture and enter explanatory text.

Editing Shapes

Once you create shapes, you can resize them, apply borders, and even change the object to a different shape.

Task 12   Resizing a shape.

The test may ask you to create a shape with specific height and width dimensions. You can first draw the shape and then specify a height and width in the Format AutoShape dialog box.

1. Select a shape that has already been drawn.

2. Display the Format AutoShape dialog box by selecting AutoShape from the Format menu.

3. When the Format AutoShape dialog box appears, select the Size tab.

4. Enter your measurements in the Width and Height boxes.

5. Click OK.

 You can display the AutoShape dialog box to edit lines and shapes by double-clicking on the line or shape you want to edit.

Task 13   *Editing a border and applying a fill.*

Once you create a shape, you can apply a line style, dash style, and color to the border as you would when editing a line. You can also fill in the shape with a color.

1. Select a shape.

2. Display the Format AutoShape dialog box by selecting AutoShape from the Format menu.

3. When the Format AutoShape dialog box appears, select the Colors And Lines tab, as shown in Figure 6.5.

4. To fill in the shape with a color, select a color from the Color box in the Fill area.

5. To choose a border color, select a color from the Color box in the Line area.

6. To choose a line style, select an option from the Style box in the Line area (this option is not available for some shapes).

7. To choose a dash style, select an option from the Dashed box in the Line area.

8. If you prefer a line thickness that doesn't appear in the Style options, you can enter a custom line weight (such as 1.75 pt) in the Weight box.

9. Click OK.

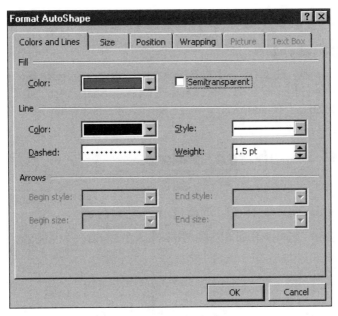

Figure 6.5 The Format AutoShape dialog box with Colors And Lines
options displayed.

  You can also change lines and colors by clicking the buttons on
the Drawing Toolbar.

Task 14 *Changing an AutoShape.*

You can change any shape into a different shape.

1. Select a shape.

2. Select Change AutoShape from the Draw button drop-down menu.

3. Select a shape category from the cascading menu.

4. When the next cascading menu appears that contains the new shape you
   want, select it and release the mouse button.

Word changes the current shape to the new shape you select.

  Rectangles and ovals are AutoShapes, too. You can select them
from the Basic Shapes options on the AutoShapes menu.

Applying Special Effects To Shapes

You can apply shadows and 3-D effects to shapes. Figure 6.6 shows an AutoShape with no special effect applied, an AutoShape with a shadow, and a 3-D AutoShape. In addition, you can rotate objects and flip them vertically and horizontally.

Task 15   Applying a shadow.

1. Select a shape.

2. Click the Shadow button on the Drawing toolbar.

3. When the list of shadow styles appears, select a style and release the mouse button.

The Shadow option is not available for some shapes. In these cases, the option is disabled.

To apply a different shadow effect, select a shadowed object, click the Shadow button on the Drawing toolbar, and then select a new shadow style.

When you pass your mouse over a shadow option, a ToolTip appears and tells you the name of the shadow option. If the test asks you to apply a shadow option to a line or shape, it will tell you the name of the shadow option. Make sure you select the correct one.

Task 16   Removing a shadow.

1. Select a shape with a shadow.

2. Click the Shadow button on the Drawing toolbar.

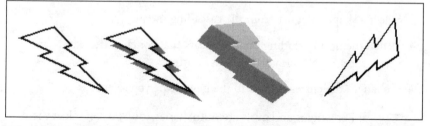

Figure 6.6   From left to right, an AutoShape with no special effect applied, an AutoShape with a shadow, a 3-D AutoShape, and a rotated and flipped AutoShape.

3. When the list of shadow styles appears, choose No Shadow.

 Notice that shadowing and 3-D options are not available from the Format AutoShape dialog box.

Task 17   *Applying a 3-D effect.*

1. Select a shape.

2. Click the 3-D button on the Drawing toolbar.

3. When the list of 3-D styles appears, select a style and release the mouse button.

The 3-D option is not available for every shape. When this is the case, the 3-D option is disabled.

 You can change a 3-D shape's 3-D effect. To apply a different 3-D effect, select a 3-D object, click the 3-D button on the Drawing toolbar, and then select a new 3-D style.

 When you pass your mouse over a 3-D effect, a ToolTip appears and tells you the name of the 3-D effect. If the test asks you to apply a 3-D effect to a shape, it will tell you the name of the 3-D effect. Make sure you select the correct one.

Task 18   *Removing a 3-D effect.*

1. Select a shape.

2. Click the 3-D button on the Drawing toolbar.

3. When the list of 3-D styles appears, select No 3-D and release the mouse button.

Task 19   *Rotating a shape.*

1. Select a shape.

2. Display the Format AutoShape dialog box by selecting AutoShape from the Format menu.

3. When the Format AutoShape dialog box appears, select the Size tab.

4. Enter a number of degrees in the Rotation box.

5. Click OK.

You can also rotate a shape by selecting a shape, clicking the Free Rotate toolbar button on the Drawing toolbar, placing the cursor on one of the green circular handles, and then dragging in the desired direction. However, the test is more likely to ask you to rotate the shape by a specified number of degrees—which requires displaying the Format AutoShape dialog box.

Task 20   Rotating a shape 90 degrees to the right or left.

You can rotate a shape 90 degrees to the right or left without going through so many steps.

1. Select a shape.

2. Click the Draw button on the Drawing toolbar, and then select Rotate or Flip.

3. When the cascading menu appears, select Rotate Right or Rotate Left; then release the mouse button.

Task 21   Flipping a shape vertically or horizontally.

You can also flip a shape vertically or horizontally so it mirrors itself across a vertical or horizontal axis.

1. Select a shape.

2. Click the Draw button on the Drawing toolbar, and then select Rotate or Flip.

3. When the cascading menu appears, select Flip Right or Flip Left; then release the mouse button.

Task 22   Positioning a line or shape.

You may also be asked to position a line in relation to the page, left margin, nearest column, or text.

1. Select a line or shape.

2. Display the Format AutoShape dialog box by selecting AutoShape from the Format menu.

3. When the Format AutoShape dialog box appears, select the Position tab, as shown in Figure 6.7.

4. To specify where the left edge of the object is positioned in relation to the left edge of the page, margin, or column, enter a value in the Horizontal box, and select an option from the From box.

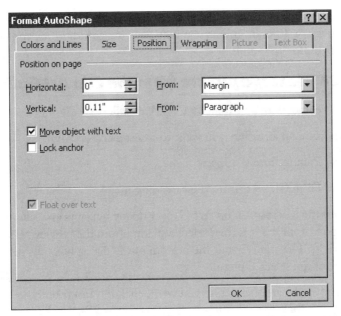

Figure 6.7   The Format AutoShape dialog box with Position tab selected.

5. To specify where the top edge of the object is positioned in relation to the top of the page, top margin, or bottom of the previous paragraph, enter a value in the Vertical box, and select an option from the From box.

6. Click OK.

Working With Pictures

The test may also ask you to work with pictures. No, you don't need to take a graphic design class. (Wait till you take the Microsoft Word expert test for that!) But you may be asked to insert a picture or to edit a picture's border.

Task 23   Insert a picture from a file.

Inserting a picture from a file (such as a photograph stored in a folder on the computer) is similar to opening a document, because you have to browse for a file.

1. Place your cursor where you want to insert the picture.

2. Select Picture from the Insert menu.

3. Select From A File from the cascading menu.

4. When the Insert Picture dialog box appears, select an image file (if it's located in a different folder, you may have to browse for it), and click the Insert button.

Task 24 Insert a picture from the Clip Art Gallery.

Word also comes with an extensive Clip Art Gallery.

1. Place your cursor where you want to insert a clip art item.

2. Select Picture from the Insert menu.

3. Select From Clip Art from the cascading menu.

4. When the Microsoft Clip Art Gallery dialog box appears, select a category from the list, then select a picture from the preview window on the right. The status bar at the bottom of the dialog box tells you the name of the selected picture.

5. When you locate the picture you want, click the Insert button.

Task 25 Adding a border to a picture or clip art item.

You can also add a border to a picture or clip art item, and apply a line style and border color.

1. Switch to the Page layout view.

2. Locate the picture and select it.

3. Click the Line Style button on the Drawing toolbar and select a line style from the list.

4. Apply a line color by clicking the arrow next to the Line Color button on the Drawing toolbar, and select a color from the pop-up color palette.

 If the test asks you to apply a border to a picture, use the drawing toolbar to do so. Double-clicking a picture does not display a helpful dialog box, as it does with lines and AutoShapes. Instead, it displays the picture in Edit mode. Once you're in Edit mode, you can double-click the picture to display editing options. But who needs the extra step?

 Remember that you can use the Go To feature to locate pictures. If you're in the Normal view, Word automatically switches you to the Page Layout view when it locates a picture.

Task 26   *Create a callout for a picture.*

The test may ask you to create a callout for a picture. Callouts are like comic strip balloons. You can use them to point to an area of a picture and enter a quote, or explanatory text. For example, you could have a picture of your street, with a callout pointing to "our house."

1. Click AutoShapes on the Drawing toolbar.

2. Select Callouts from the shortcut menu, then select a callout from the cascading menu.

3. Place your cursor where you want to position the callout and drag it to draw the callout.

4. Release the mouse, then place your cursor inside the callout.

5 Type the text.

Practice Projects

Perform the following projects based on this chapter.

Project 1   Draw and modify a line.

1. Open Declarationch05.doc from the Practice folder.

2. Create a horizontal line underneath the words "A Transcription" and make it 6.5" wide.

3. Make the line red and apply a 3 pt line thickness.

4. Apply the round dot line style.

 Make sure you select the correct colors and styles. ToolTips tell you the name of each color or style when you pass your mouse button over them.

Answer to Project 1

To open Declarationch05.doc, select Open from the File menu, locate and select the document from the Open dialog box, and click the Open button.

To locate the words "A Transcription," use the Find command. To draw a line, display the Drawing toolbar by clicking the Drawing button on the Standard toolbar, and click the Line button on the Drawing toolbar. When Word switches to the Page Layout view, click underneath the words "A Transcription" and drag the mouse horizontally across the page.

To begin editing the line, click the line to select it. To apply the line color, click the arrow to the right of the Line Color button and select Red from the Line Color options. To apply the line style, click the Line Style toolbar button and select the 3 pt line style.

To apply the Dash style, click the Dash Style toolbar button and select the Round Dot dash style.

Project 2   Resize and position a line.

1. Position the line so it lines up directly with the left margin and is .25" down from the line that reads "A Transcription."

Answer to Project 2

To begin positioning the line, display the Format AutoShapes dialog box by double-clicking the line, or by selecting the line and choosing AutoShape from the Format menu. To resize the line, select the Size tab when the Format AutoShapes dialog box appears. When the Size options display, enter 6.5" in the Width box. To begin positioning the line, select the Position tab. To align the line with the left margin of the page, select 0" from the Horizontal box, and select Margin from the corresponding From box. To specify where the line should be positioned in relation to the bottom of the preceding line of text ("A Transcription"), select .25 from the Vertical box, and select Paragraph from the corresponding From box. Click OK to apply the new line formatting. When you return to the document, it should look like Figure 6.8.

Project 3   Modify AutoShapes.

1. Change the two banner AutoShapes to five-point stars.

2. Change the fill for both stars to light blue.

3. Remove the border around the stars.

4. Apply 3-D style 6 to the star on the left and 3-D style 5 to the star on the right.

5. Save the file as Declarationch06.doc and close it.

Answer to Project 3

To locate the banners, use GoTo. To change the banners to five-point stars, select the banners, click the Draw button on the Drawing toolbar, and then select Change AutoShapes. Select Stars And Banners, and then select the five-point star option and release the mouse key.

To change the fill colors (with the stars still selected), click the Fill Color button and select the Light Blue option.

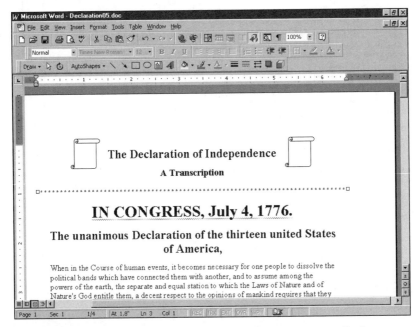

Figure 6.8   Declaration.doc with new line formatting applied.

To edit the borders around the stars, click the Line Color button and select No Line.

 When you need to apply the same changes to two shapes, you can select both of them and modify them simultaneously. Hold down the Shift key and click on both shapes.

To apply the first 3-D style, select the left star, click the 3-D button, and select 3-D style 6. To apply the second 3-D style, select the right star, click the 3-D button, and apply 3-D style 5.

Save the document by selecting Save As from the File menu. When the Save As dialog box appears, enter "Declarationch06.doc" in the File Name dialog box and click the Save button. The document should now look like the one shown in Figure 6.9. Close the Document by selecting Close from the File menu.

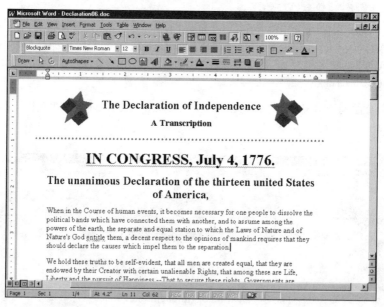

Figure 6.9 Declaration05.doc with AutoShapes modified and applied.

Need To Know More?

Leonhard, Woody, Lee Hudspeth, and T.J. Lee: *Word 97 Annoyances*. O'Reilly and Associates, Inc. Sebastopol, CA, 1997. ISBN 1-56592-308-1. Chapter 6 gives you the real skinny on how the Drawing Layer works.

Microsoft Word 97 Step by Step. Microsoft Press. Redmond, WA, 1997. ISBN 1-57231-313-7. Lesson 12 explains Word's drawing tools and how to arrange graphics within text.

Documents, Headers And Footers, Page Breaks, And Sections

7

Terms you'll need to understand:

√ Page setup

√ Margins

√ Vertical alignment

√ Headers

√ Footers

√ Page numbers

√ Alternating headers and footers

√ Page breaks

√ Section breaks

Skills you'll need to master:

√ Formatting margins

√ Specifying vertical alignment for text

√ Creating and editing headers and footers

√ Moving between headers and footers

√ Creating and formatting page numbers

√ Inserting page breaks

√ Inserting section breaks

√ Creating sections with different formatting from the rest of the document

Most of us spend a good part of our working day creating and processing documents. Office memos and letters are fairly straightforward. However, generating reports, proposals, documentation, and other lengthy documents requires more advanced skills. When you take the test, you'll be expected to format margins, to set up headers and footers with page numbers, and to create sections with different formatting from the rest of a document.

Using Page Setup

You can use Page Setup to format your document's margins and to specify the vertical alignment for pages. Margin settings determine the amount of empty space between the top, bottom, left, and right edges of pages and the contents of the pages. Vertical alignment determines how text and graphics align with the top and bottom of the page.

Task 1   Formatting margins for an entire document.

You can enter measurements for the top, bottom, left, and right margins. Word measures margin widths and heights in inches. The Margin settings are specified in the Margins section of the Page Setup dialog box.

1. Select Page Setup from the File menu, or use the Alt+F, and then U key combination to display the Page Setup dialog box.

2. Click the Margins tab to display the margin options, as shown in Figure 7.1.

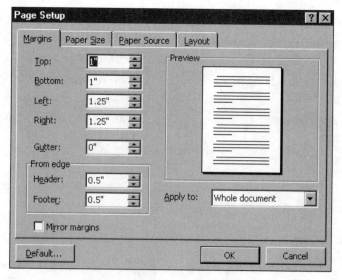

Figure 7.1   The Page Setup dialog box with Margins options displayed.

3. To change the top margin, enter a measurement in the Top box.

4. To change the bottom margin, enter a measurement in the Bottom box.

5. To change the left margin, enter a measurement in the Left box.

6. To change the right margin, enter a measurement in the Right box.

7. Select Whole Document from the Apply To box.

8. Click OK.

Word applies the new margins to the entire document. You can also apply different page settings to a section, as explained in the "Inserting Page Breaks And Creating Section" part of this chapter.

When formatting pages, read the test instructions very carefully to make sure you enter the correct margin settings and select the correct option from the Apply To box.

Task 2   *Specifying a vertical alignment and applying it to the entire document.*

You can align text and other page elements with the top or center of the page. You can also use the Justified option to distribute text and page elements evenly from the top to the bottom of the page. The Justified option only works with full pages. The Vertical Alignment options are specified in the Layout section of the Page Setup dialog box.

1. Select Page Setup from the File menu, or use the Alt+F, and then U key combination to display the Page Setup dialog box.

2. Click the Layout tab to display the layout options, as shown in Figure 7.2.

3. Select Top, Center, or Justify from the Vertical Alignment box.

4. Select Whole Document from the Apply To box.

5. Click OK.

Word applies the new vertical alignment to the entire document. You can also apply different page settings to a section, as explained in the "Inserting Page Breaks And Creating Sections" part of this chapter.

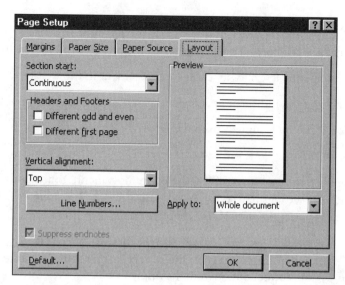

Figure 7.2 The Page Setup dialog box with Layout options displayed.

Working With Headers And Footers

Headers and footers contain information that appears on every page of a document or section, such as the date, title of the document, author, and page number. Headers appear at the top of pages and footers appear at the bottom of pages. As with columns and graphics, headers and footers display in the Page Layout view but not in the Normal view. To create or modify headers and footers, you need to work with them in the Header And Footer view.

Task 3   *Displaying headers and footers in the Header And Footer view.*

In order to add or edit headers and footers, you first need to display them.

1. Select Header And Footer from the View menu, or use the Alt+V, and then H key combination.

When the Header And Footer page view appears with the Header And Footer toolbar, as shown in Figure 7.3, you can begin creating or modifying headers and footers in your document.

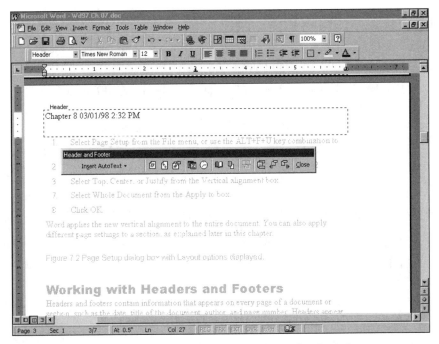

Figure 7.3   Document with Header And Footer displayed.

Task 4   *Switching from the header to the footer.*

You can jump from the header to the footer and back again.

1. Click the Switch Between Header And Footer button on the Header And Footer toolbar.

Task 5   *Moving to different headers and footers within a document.*

If your document has more than one set of headers and footers, you can move to the next or previous header or footer.

1. From within a header or footer, click the Show Next button to move to the next header or footer in the document.

2. From within a header or footer, click the Show Previous button to move to the previous header or footer in the document.

When you've finished with your headers and footers, you can return to the document view you were working in before you switched to the Header And Footer view by clicking the Close button.

Task 6   Adding page numbers to a header or footer.

You can add a page marker to a header or footer that automatically inserts the correct page number on each page.

1. Display the header and footer by selecting Header And Footer from the View menu.

2. From within the header or footer, type the word "Page," press the spacebar, then click the Page Number button on the Header And Footer toolbar.

Word inserts the page number. You can now click the Close button to return to your document, change the page number style, or reformat the text.

 You can format page numbers in many ways. But be sure to follow the test instructions closely.

Task 7   Changing the page number style.

You can choose from different page numbering styles, such as uppercase or lowercase letters or Roman numerals.

1. From the Header And Footer view, click the Page Number Format button on the Header And Footer toolbar.

2. When the Page Number Format dialog box appears, as shown in Figure 7.4, select a format from the Number Format box.

3. To number pages continuously throughout the document, select the Continue From Previous Section radio button from the Page Numbering list.

4. To begin page numbering from a specific page number, select the Start At radio button from the Page Numbering list and then enter or select a number from the Page Numbering box.

5. Click OK.

Task 8   Creating and formatting a header and footer.

Once you get used to viewing and navigating headers and footers, you can create, format, and edit them as you would any other text. You can access type styles, colors, and alignment options from the Formatting toolbar.

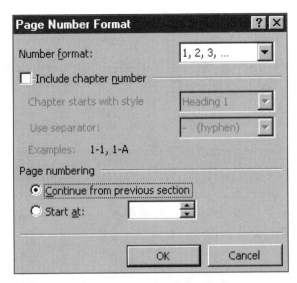

Figure 7.4   The Page Number Format dialog box.

1. From within the header, enter a page number or any text you want to include.

2. Format the text as you would format text within a document.

3. Click the Switch Between Header And Footer button on the Header And Footer toolbar to move to the footer.

4. From within the footer, type text and insert any graphics or other elements you want to include.

5. When you're finished, click the Close button.

Task 9   *Creating a justified header or footer.*

You've probably seen justified headers and footers before. Justified headers and footers feature an item—such as a page number, document title, or date—that lines up with the left margin of the page, and another item that lines up with the right margin of the page, shown in Table 7.1. Sometimes, a justified header or footer also has three items, as with the second item in Table 7.1.

Table 7.1 Justified headers and footers.		
Left Margin Item	**Centered Item**	**Right Margin Item**
Page 1		8/09/98
Page 1	My Document	8/09/98

1. From within the header or footer view, enter the item that you want to appear on the left side of the page and press the Tab key.

2. If you want to create a justified header or footer with three items, enter the item that you want to appear in the center of the page, and press the Tab key.

3. Enter the item that you want to appear on the right side of the page.

4. Click the Justified button on the Formatting toolbar to justify the text.

 If the test asks you to create a header or footer with one item lining up with the left margin and one item lining up with the right margin, you should create a justified header or footer.

HOLD That Skill!

If you try to format a header and footer with only two items, and find that the second item lines up in the center instead of the right side of the page, check the ruler. If a tab stop appears on the ruler, you can remove it by selecting it and dragging your mouse towards the document.

Task 10   Creating alternating headers and footers.

The test may require you to create alternating headers and footers with different formatting for even and odd pages. Alternating headers and footers come in handy when you plan on laying out a document as a booklet or newsletter. For example, when documents are formatted with facing pages, they look better when elements in the left page header and footer align to the left, and right page header and footer elements align to the right.

1. Go to page 1 in a document and select Header And Footer from the View menu.

2. When Word places you in the header and displays the Header And Footer toolbar, click the Page Setup button.

3. When the Page Setup dialog box appears, click the Layout tab.

4. When the layout options display, select the Different Odd And Even checkbox from the Headers And Footers list.

5. Click OK to return to the Header And Footer view. The header label indicates an odd header page. Enter and format any text you want to include in the odd page header.

6. Click the Show Next button to view and format the even page header. The header label now indicates an even header page. Enter and format any text you want to include in the even page header.

7. To begin formatting the page footers, click the Switch Between Header And Footer button on the Header And Footer toolbar.

8. When the footer with the even footer page label displays, enter and format any text you want to include in the even footer.

9. Click the Previous button on the Header And Footer toolbar to jump to the odd footer. When the footer with the odd footer page label displays, enter and format any text you want to include in the odd page footer.

10. When you finish, click the Close button.

When you apply odd and even headers and footers, Word applies them to the entire document. You can apply different formatting to odd and even footers in different sections, but you can't apply odd and even footers to only part of a document.

Inserting Page Breaks And Creating Sections

The test will also ask you to insert manual page breaks in a document and create sections that have different formatting from the rest of the document. A manual page break ends the current page and continues text on the next page. You can also define sections by inserting section breaks. Once you define a new section within a document, you can apply different margins and vertical alignment settings, as well as headers, footers, and columns to the new section.

What? You've never created a section before? Yes you have—even if you didn't realize it. When you formatted text as columns in Chapter 5, Word automatically created a new section for the column formatting.

Task 11   Inserting a manual page break.

1. Place your cursor where you want to insert the page break.

2. Select Break from the Insert menu or use the Alt+I+B key combination.

3. When the Break dialog box appears, as shown in Figure 7.5, select the Page Break radio button.

4. Click OK.

In the Normal view, Word inserts a dotted line labeled Page Break.

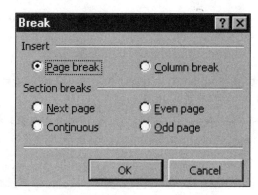

Figure 7.5 The Break dialog box.

 You can also apply a page break without displaying the Break dialog box by using the CTRL+Enter key combination.

Task 12 Inserting a section break.

The first step in creating a section is to insert a section break. There are four types of section breaks: Next page, Continuous, Even page, and Odd page, as explained in Table 7.2.

1. Select Break from the Insert menu.

2. When the Break dialog box appears, select a type of section break from the Section Breaks list.

3. Click OK.

In the Normal view, Word inserts a dotted line labeled Section Break.

Table 7.2 Section break options.	
Option	**Result**
Next page	Begins the section break on the next page
Continuous	Begins the section break on the same page
Even page	Begins the section break on the next even-numbered page
Odd page	Begins the section break on the next odd-numbered page

Task 13　Creating a new section.

1. Place your cursor where you want to begin the new section.

2. Select Break from the Insert menu.

3. When the Break dialog box appears, select a type of section break from the Section Break list and click OK.

4. Place your cursor where you want to end the new section. Then repeat steps 2 and 3.

Task 14　Applying different margin and vertical alignment settings to a section.

1. Create a new section.

2. Place your cursor anywhere within the section.

3. Select Page Setup from the File menu.

4. Select the Margins tab to display the margin options and then enter new margin settings.

5. Select the Layout tab to display the layout options, and then select an option from the Vertical Alignment box.

6. Select the This Section option from the Apply To box.

7. Click OK.

Practice Projects

Perform the following projects based on this chapter.

Project 1   Format margins.

1. Open the Declarationch06.doc.

2. Change the top margin to 1.5 inches and the bottom margin to 1.5 inches.

Answer to Project 1

Open Declarationch06.doc.

To format the margins, select Page Setup from the File menu or use the Alt+F, and then U key combination to display the Page Setup dialog box, and click the Margins tab to display the margin options. To change the left margin, enter 1.25 in the Left box. To change the right margin, enter 1.25 in the Right box. To apply the new margin settings, select Whole Document from the Apply To box, and click OK to return to the document.

Project 2   Create different headers for even and odd pages, and insert page numbers.

1. Create different headers for even and odd pages.

2. Insert page numbers in the even and odd page headers.

3. Align the even page numbers to the left, and the odd page numbers to the right.

Answer to Project 2

To begin creating the headers, go to page 1 in the document and select Header And Footer from the View menu. When Word places you in the Header And Footer view and displays the Header And Footer toolbar, click the Page Setup button. When the Page Setup dialog box appears, click the Layout tab to display the Layout options.

To display different headers on odd and even pages, select the Different Odd And Even checkbox from the Headers And Footers list. To apply the settings to the entire document, select Whole Document from the Apply To list; then click OK to return to the Header And Footer view. The Header label indicates an odd page header. To insert a page number in the odd page header, click the Insert Page Number button on the Header And Footer toolbar. To align the odd page header page number to the right, place your cursor next to the page number and click the Align Right button on the Standard toolbar. To move on to the even page header on the next page, click the Next button. The header label now indicates an even page header.

To insert a page number, click the Insert Page Number button on the Header And Footer toolbar. To align the even page header page number to the left, place the cursor next to the number and click the Align Left toolbar button on the Standard toolbar. If you click the Previous button to return to page 1 and select Two Pages from the Zoom box list on the Standard toolbar, the document should appear as shown in Figure 7.6. Click the Close button on the Header And Footer toolbar, or select Normal from the View menu to return to the document.

Project 3 Create a new section and apply new page settings.

1. In Declarationch06.doc, create a new section starting with the paragraph beginning with "He has refused his Assent to Laws," and ending with the paragraph beginning with "He has excited domestic insurrections amongst us."

2. Begin the section on a new page and end the section with a page break.

3. Change the left and right margins for the new section to 1.5 inches.

4. Save the document as Declarationch07.doc and close the document.

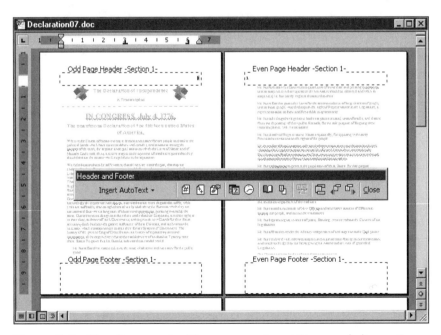

Figure 7.6 The document with new margin settings, and alternating headers and footers.

Answer to Project 3

To locate the place where you need to start the new section, use the Find command to locate the words "He has refused his Assent to Laws."

To insert the section break, place your cursor to the left of the paragraph beginning with "He has refused his Assent to Laws" and then select Break from the Insert menu. When the Break dialog box appears, select Next Page from the Section Breaks list to start the section on a new page. Click OK. To locate the place where you need to end the section, use the Find command to locate the words "He has excited domestic insurrections amongst us." To end the section, place your cursor at the end of the paragraph and then select Break from the Insert menu. When the Break dialog box appears, select Next Page from the Section Breaks list to insert a section break that ends the section and starts a new page. Click OK to return to the document.

To begin resetting the margins, place your cursor anywhere within the new section and then select Page Setup from the File menu. Select the Margins tab to display the margin options. Enter 1.5 in the Left box and 1.5 in the Right box. Select the This Section option from the Apply To box, and click OK to return to the document.

To save the document with a different name, select Save As from the File menu. When the Save As dialog box appears, enter Declarationch07.doc in the File Name box. To close the document, select Close from the File menu.

Need To Know More?

 Leonhard, Woody, Lee Hudspeth, and T.J. Lee: *Word 97 Annoyances*. O'Reilly and Associates, Inc. Sebastopol, CA, 1997. ISBN 1-56592-308-1. Learn more about how Word handles pages and formatting.

 Microsoft Word 97 Step by Step. Microsoft Press, Redmond, WA, 1997. ISBN 1-57231-313-7. Lesson 6 talks about page setup, headers and footers, and working with headers and footers.

Printing

8

Terms you'll need to understand:

√ Print Preview

√ Current page

√ Page range

√ Labels and Envelopes

Skills you'll need to master:

√ Printing documents

√ Previewing documents before printing

√ Printing envelopes

√ Printing labels

√ Adding envelopes to a document

√ Creating labels as a new document

There's no use in creating and formatting documents if you don't know how to print them. The test will have you print a document and an envelope or address label. In addition, you may be asked to view and work with your document in Print Preview.

Printing Documents

Word's Print options let you print an entire document, print the current page, or print pages within a range, such as pages 2 to 4.

Task 1   Printing an entire document.

1. Open a document.

2. Select Print from the File menu, or use the Ctrl+P key combination.

3. When the Print dialog box displays, as shown in Figure 8.1, select the All option button from the Page Range list, and then enter or select the number of copies from the Number Of Copies box.

4. Click OK.

 The printer in the testing center might not actually print your page.

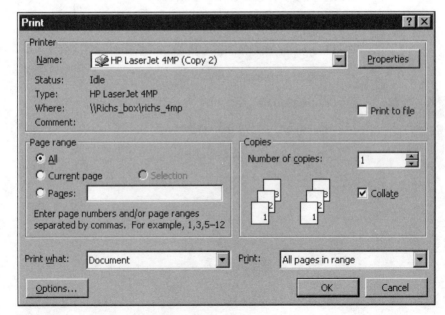

Figure 8.1   The Print dialog box.

Task 2 Printing the current page.

You may be asked to print only the page that is currently displayed in the document window.

1. Place your cursor on the page you wish to print, then select Print from the File menu, or use the Ctrl+P key combination.

2. When the Print dialog box displays, select the Current Page option button from the Page Range list, and then enter or select the number of copies from the Number Of Copies box.

3. Click OK.

Task 3 Printing pages in a range.

The test may ask you to print a range of pages—such as the first two pages—rather than the entire document.

1. Open a document.

2. Select Print from the File menu.

3. When the Print dialog box displays, select the Pages option button from the Page Range list, and then enter the range of page numbers separated by a hyphen (as in 2-4) in the Pages box.

4. Enter or select the number of copies from the Number Of Copies box. Then click OK.

You can also print out nonsequential pages (such as pages 4, 7, and 12) by entering the page numbers and separating them with commas in the Print dialog box's Pages box, as in: 4, 7, 12.

 You can also display the Print dialog box by using the Ctrl+P key combination.

Using Print Preview

How many times have you printed a document only to wind up with a couple of lines straggling onto the final page? You can prevent these annoyances and save yourself a few sheets of paper by using the Print Preview feature. Print Preview allows you to view your pages as they will appear when printed.

When you select Print Preview, it displays the current page or a range of pages that include the current page.

Task 4 Viewing a document in Print Preview.

1. Select Print Preview from the File menu.

2. When the Print Preview window opens, as shown in Figure 8.2, you can preview your document.

The Print Preview toolbar buttons offer the options shown in Table 8.1.

 You can also display the Print Preview window by using the Alt+F, and then V key combination.

Task 5 Moving from page to page.

You move from page to page within the Print Preview display to preview all the pages in your document.

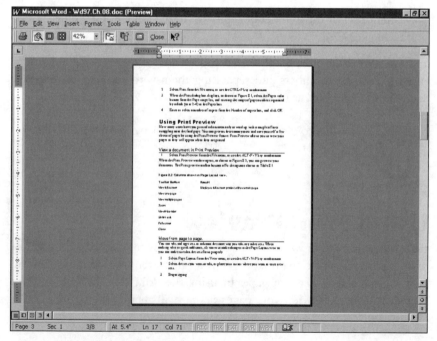

Figure 8.2 Document shown in Print Preview.

Table 8.1	Print Preview toolbar buttons.
Toolbar Button	**Result**
Print	Displays the Print dialog box so you can print the document
Magnifier	Zooms in on the document
One Page	Displays a single page in the preview area
Multiple Pages	Displays a number of page thumbnails simultaneously
Zoom	Provides a pull-down list of magnification options
View/Hide Ruler	Hides or displays the rulers
Shrink to Fit	Reformats the document to prevent lines from straggling onto a new page
Full Screen	Displays a full-screen preview of the current page
Close	Closes the Print Preview window and returns you to the document

1. Click the One Page toolbar button.

2. Click the down scroll bar button to move forward in the document. Click the up scroll bar button to move backward in the document.

Task 6   Using the Shrink To Fit feature.

If your document has a couple of sentences that run onto an extra page, you can use the Shrink To Fit feature to reformat the document.

1. Display the document in Print Preview by selecting Print Preview from the File menu.

2. From within the Print Preview, click the Shrink To Fit button.

Task 7   Editing text in Print Preview.

1. Click the area that contains the text you want to edit.

2. When Word zooms in on the area, click the Magnifier toolbar button.

3. When the cursor changes from a magnifying glass to an I-beam, you can begin editing the text.

You can return to the original page view by clicking the Magnifier toolbar button again and clicking anywhere on the document.

Task 8   *Printing the file from within Print Preview.*

Once you have your pages set up the way you want, you can print the file from the Print Preview window.

1. Select Print Preview from the File menu.

2. Click the Print button.

When you print a document from the Print Preview window, Word prints the entire document and does not display the Print dialog box.

Task 9   *Closing the Print Preview window.*

You can close the Print Preview window and return to your document.

1. Click the Close toolbar button.

Printing Envelopes And Labels

No, the testing center won't have you prepare a big mailing. They'll just have you print a single envelope or mailing label for a letter. Word makes it easy to print envelopes and mailing labels for the current letter.

Task 10   *Printing an envelope for a letter.*

1. Open a letter (you can practice with BusinessLetterch03.doc, which you saved to your Practice folder back in Chapter 3).

2. Place your cursor next to the recipient's address.

3. Select Envelopes And Labels from the Tools menu.

4. When the Envelopes And Labels dialog box appears, click the Envelopes tab.

5. When the envelope options appear, as shown in Figure 8.3, the recipient's address appears in the Delivery Address box. If it doesn't appear, you can type in the address, or you can copy and paste it from the document.

6. Type your return address in the Return Address box. If a default return address displays and you do not want it to print, click the Omit checkbox.

7. Click the Print button.

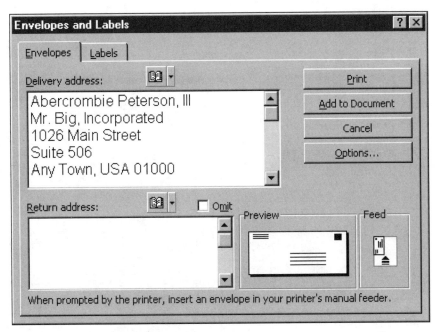

Figure 8.3 The Envelopes And Labels dialog box with the Envelopes option displayed.

To include the return address in a print out, make sure the Omit checkbox is not selected.

Task 11 *Printing a single mailing label.*

You can print a single mailing label with the current address.

1. Open a letter.

2. Place your cursor next to the recipient's address.

3. Select Envelopes And Labels from the Tools menu.

4. When the Envelopes And Labels dialog box appears, click the Labels tab.

5. When the label options appear, as shown in Figure 8.4, the recipient's address appears in the Address box. If it doesn't appear, you can type in the address, or you can copy and paste it from the document.

6. Select the Single Label option button from the Print area.

7. Click the Print button.

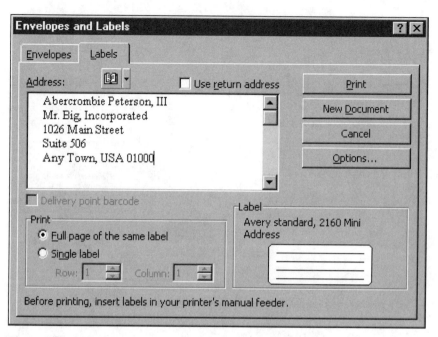

Figure 8.4 The Envelopes And Labels dialog box with the Labels option displayed.

Task 12 *Printing a sheet of mailing labels.*

You can plan ahead and print an entire sheet of mailing labels with the same address.

1. Open a letter (you can practice with BusinessLetterch03, which you saved to your Practice folder back in Chapter 3).

2. Place your cursor next to the recipient's address.

3. Select Envelopes And Labels from the Tools menu.

4. When the Envelopes And Labels dialog box appears, click the Labels tab.

5. When the label options appear, the recipient's address appears in the Address box. If it doesn't appear, you can type in the address, or you can copy and paste it from the document.

6. Select the Full Page Of The Same Label option button from the Print area.

7. Click the Print button.

Task 13   Adding an envelope to a document.

Once you create an envelope, you can add it to the current document so you can use it again.

1. Create an envelope, as explained in Task 11.

2. Click the Add To Document button.

Word returns you to the document and adds the envelope as the first page of the document.

Task 14   Creating a set of labels as a new document.

Once you create a set of labels, you can save them as a new document.

1. Create a set of labels, as explained in Task 12.

2. Click the New Document button.

When Word creates the new labels document, you can save it as you would a normal document.

 You cannot create a single label as a new document.

Practice Projects

Perform the following projects based on this chapter.

Project 1   Print a letter and a sheet of mailing labels.

1. Open BusinessLetterch03.doc.

2. Print two copies.

3. Print a sheet of mailing labels.

Answer to Project 1

Open BusinessLetterch03.doc from the Practice folder on your hard drive.

To print two copies of the letter, select Print from the File menu. When the Print dialog box appears, select the All option button from the Page Range list and then enter 2 in the Number Of Copies box. Click OK.

Place your cursor next to the recipient's address (Abercrombie Peterson, III). To print the mailing labels, select Envelopes And Labels from the Tools menu. When the Envelopes And Labels dialog box appears, click the Labels tab. When the label options appear, the recipient's address appears in the Address window. If it doesn't appear, you can type in the address, or you can copy and paste it from the document. Select the Full Page Of The Same Label option button from the Print area. Click the Print button.

Project 2   Add an envelope to a document.

1. Create an envelope for BusinessLetterch03.doc, and include the return address.

2. Add the envelope to the document.

3. Save the document as BusinessLetterch08.doc, and close it.

Answer to Project 2

From BusinessLetterch03.doc, place your cursor next to the address. To create the enve-lope, select Envelopes And Labels from the Tools menu. When the Envelopes And Labels dialog box appears, select the Envelopes tab. The address should appear in the Delivery Address box. Make sure the Omit checkbox is deselected, and type the return address into the Return Address box.

To add the envelope to the document, click the Add To Document button.

To save the document with a different name, select Save As from the File menu. When the Save As dialog box appears, enter "BusinessLetterch08.doc" in the File Name box and click the Save button. To close the document, select Close from the File menu.

If you are asked to include a return address with an envelope, you can copy and paste it, instead of typing the whole thing. First, select the return address and click the Copy button on the Standard toolbar to copy the return address to the Clipboard. Then, display the Envelopes And Labels dialog box. To paste the return address, place your cursor in the Return Address box, then use the Ctrl+V key combination.

Need To Know More?

Microsoft Word 97 Step by Step. Microsoft Press. Redmond, WA, 1997. ISBN 1-57231-313-7. Lesson 4 tells you everything you need to know about printing.

Text Tools

Terms you'll need to understand:

- √ Copy
- √ Cut
- √ Paste
- √ Format Painter
- √ Hyphenation
- √ Find and Replace
- √ Spelling
- √ Grammar
- √ Thesaurus

Skills you'll need to master:

- √ Selecting and typing over text
- √ Copying and pasting text
- √ Cutting and pasting text
- √ Applying text formatting to a paragraph with Format Painter
- √ Using hyphenation
- √ Searching and replacing text
- √ Searching and replacing a word
- √ Checking spelling and grammar
- √ Using the Thesaurus

Word has a variety of features for quickly editing and processing text that help you make your documents look more professional—and help you avoid making embarassing mistakes! When you take the test, it will ask you to prove your skills with basic Word functions such as cutting and pasting text, using hyphenation settings, searching and replacing text, and checking a document's spelling and grammar. In addition, the test may ask you to use the Thesaurus or it may present you with text formatting tasks that you can get through most efficiently with the Format Painter.

Editing And Processing Text

Editing and processing text means being able to select, delete, copy, and move text around. In addition, the Format Painter can help you quickly copy text formatting from one paragraph to another.

Task 1　Selecting and typing over text.

If the test asks you to select a word, line, or paragraph and type a new one, you can do this by selecting the text and typing over it. You can try this with any of the documents included on the practice disk.

1. Select a word, line, or paragraph either by placing your cursor at the beginning of the selection and then holding down the mouse key while dragging the cursor across the selection or by placing your cursor at the beginning of the selection and using one of the key combinations in Table 9.1.

2. Begin typing.

 The test expects you to know when it is appropriate to switch to Overtype mode—such as when replacing words at the end of a line or sentences at the end of a paragraph.

Task 2　Selecting and deleting text.

The easiest way to remove text is to select it and press the Delete key.

1. Select a word, line, or paragraph either by placing your cursor at the beginning of the selection and then holding down the mouse key while dragging the cursor across the selection or by placing your cursor at the beginning of the selection and using one of the key combinations in Table 9.1.

2. Press the Delete key.

Table 9.1 Key combinations for selecting text.	
Selection Functions	**Key Combinations**
Select text to the end of a word	Shift+Ctrl+left arrow
Select text to the end of a line	Shift+End
Select text to the beginning of a line	Shift+Home
Select text up one line	Shift+up arrow
Select text down one line	Shift+down arrow
Select text up one paragraph	Shift+Ctrl+up arrow
Select text down one paragraph	Shift+Ctrl+down arrow
Select text up one screen	Shift+PgUp
Select text down one screen	Shift+PgDn
Select text to the top of the next page	Shift+Ctrl+PgDn
Select text to the top of the previous page	Shift+Ctrl+PgUp
Select text to the end of a document	Shift+Ctrl+End
Select text to the beginning of a document	Ctrl+Shift+Home

Task 3   Copying and pasting text.

If the test asks you to copy text and place it in a new location, you can accomplish this with the Copy and Paste commands. When you copy or cut text, Word places the text on the system's Clipboard. The Clipboard is used for storing items so you can paste them into other parts of a document or into different files.

1. Select the text you want to copy.

2. Click the Copy button on the Standard toolbar, or use the Ctrl+C key combination. You can also click the selected text with your right mouse button, and select Copy from the shortcut menu.

3. Place your cursor where you want to insert the copied text.

4. Click the Paste button or use the Ctrl+V key combination.

 The Copy and Cut toolbar buttons are enabled only when you select text. The Paste toolbar button is enabled only when you have copied or cut something to the system's Clipboard.

Task 4 Cutting and pasting text.

To move text to a new location, use the Cut and Paste commands.

1. Select the text you want to move.

2. Click the Cut button on the Standard toolbar, or use the Ctrl+X key combination.

3. Place your cursor where you want to insert the cut text.

4. Click the Paste button, or use the Ctrl+V key combination.

What's the difference between cutting text and deleting text? When you cut text, Word copies it to the system's Clipboard so you can paste it into another file. When you delete text, it's gone.

HOLD That Skill!

If you make a mistake, don't forget our old friend Undo. To undo an action, click the Undo button on the Standard toolbar, select Undo from the Edit menu, or use the Ctrl+Z key combination.

Task 5 Applying text formatting to another paragraph with Format Painter.

Format Painter makes it easy to copy text formatting from one paragraph and apply it to another.

1. Click your cursor within the paragraph you want to copy the formatting from.

2. Click the Format Painter button on the Standard toolbar.

3. Click on the paragraph you want to copy the formatting to.

Word applies the copied text format.

If you select the Format Painter toolbar button by double-clicking it, you can apply formatting to lines and paragraphs throughout the document. The Format Painter stays active until you deselect the Format Painter toolbar button by clicking it.

Using Hyphenation

Hyphenation involves breaking a word in half with a hyphen when the word reaches the end of a line and doesn't fit, instead of moving the entire word down to the next line.

Task 6   Hyphenating text automatically.

1. Select Language from the Tools menu, and then select Hyphenation from the cascading menu.

2. When the Hyphenation dialog box appears, as shown in Figure 9.1, select the Automatically Hyphenate Document checkbox.

3. Click OK.

Task 7   Hyphenating text manually.

For more control over how words are hyphenated, you can hyphenate text manually.

1. Select the text to which you want to apply automatic hyphenation.

2. Select Language from the Tools menu, and then select Hyphenation from the cascading menu.

3. When the Hyphenation dialog box appears, select the Manual button.

4. When word identifies a word to hyphenate, the Manual Hyphenation dialog box appears, as shown in Figure 9.2.

5. Click Yes to hyphenate the word as Word suggests, or you can use the arrow keys to move the insertion point to a different part of the word and then click Yes.

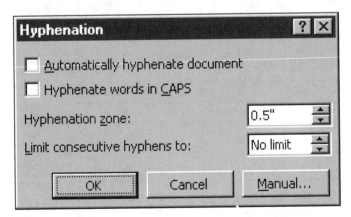

Figure 9.1   The Hyphenation dialog box.

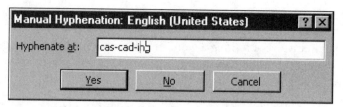

Figure 9.2 The Manual Hyphenation dialog box.

Searching And Replacing Text

You can search for a word, sentence, or character and automatically replace it with another word, sentence, or character with Word's Find And Replace feature.

Task 8   Searching and replacing text.

1. Select Replace from the Edit menu, or use the Ctrl+H key combination.

2. When the Find And Replace dialog box appears with the Replace tab selected, as shown in Figure 9.3, enter the term you want to search for in the Find What box and enter the term you want to replace it with in the Replace With box.

3. Click the Find Next button to locate the term in the Find What box without changing it. Word locates and highlights the term as it does when you use the Find command.

4. Click the Replace button to change a single occurrence of the term you're searching.

5. Click Replace All to automatically search for terms, and replace them throughout the entire document.

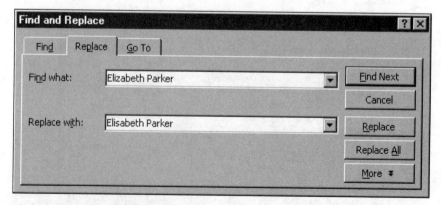

Figure 9.3 The Find And Replace dialog box with the Replace tab displayed.

When you're finished, click the Close button, or press the Esc key to close the Find And Replace dialog box and return to the document.

Spelling And Grammar

The test will ask you to use Word's spelling- and grammar-checking features to ensure accuracy in your documents. You can check for grammar errors, such as run-on sentences, and spelling errors together, or you can check for spelling errors only. In addition, Word highlights spelling and grammar errors with red and green lines, respectively, in the document so you can correct them while you're working.

Task 9   Checking spelling and grammar.

1. Select Spelling And Grammar from the Tools menu.

2. When the Spelling And Grammar dialog box appears, Word begins to search your document for possible errors.

3. When Word runs into a grammar problem, as shown in Figure 9.4, the sentence that contains the grammar problem appears in the top scroll box and Word's suggestions appear in the lower scroll box. Word displays misspelled words in red, and grammar problems in green.

➤ Retype the text shown in the top box, and click Change to correct the error.

➤ Click Ignore to leave the sentence unchanged.

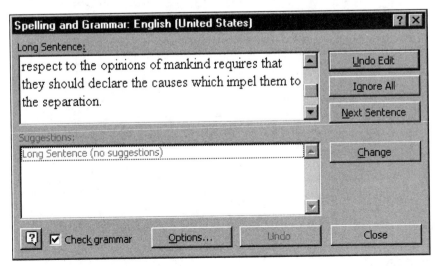

Figure 9.4   Checking grammar.

➤ Click Ignore All to leave all occurrences of the error unchanged throughout the document.

➤ Click Undo Edit to restore the original text.

➤ Click Next Sentence to move forward in the document.

4. When Word runs into a spelling problem, as shown in Figure 9.5, the sentence with the misspelled word appears in the top scroll box and a list of suggestions appears below. The spelling error displays in red.

➤ Select an item from the list of suggestions, and click Change to change this occurrence of the word. If the word you want to substitute does not appear on the list, you can select the misspelled word and replace it manually, and then click the Change button.

➤ Select an item from the list of suggestions, and click Change All to change all occurrences of the word throughout the document. If the word you want to substitute does not appear on the list, you can select the misspelled word and replace it manually, and then click the Change All button.

➤ Select an item from the list of suggestions, and click Ignore to leave the word unchanged and move forward in the document.

➤ Select an item from the list of suggestions, and click Ignore All to leave all occurrences of the word unchanged throughout the document.

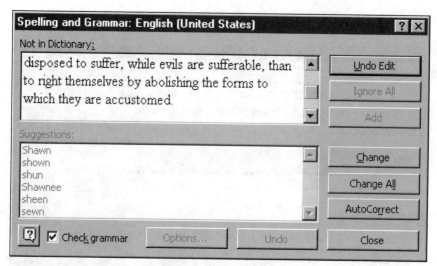

Figure 9.5 Checking spelling.

➤ Click Add to add the word to the custom dictionary so the application recognizes it from now on.

➤ Select an item from the list of suggestions, and click AutoCorrect to specify the error and the correction as an AutoCorrect entry so Word can automatically correct the word while you type from now on.

5. When Word finishes checking spelling and grammar, it notifies you with a message box. Click OK to return to the document. You can cancel spelling and grammar checking at any time by clicking the Cancel button, or you can close the dialog box by clicking the close box.

 You can also display the Spelling And Grammar dialog box by pressing the F7 key.

Task 10   *Checking spelling only.*

You can also run a quick spell check without checking grammar.

1. Select Spelling And Grammar from the Tools menu, or press the F7 key.

2. When the Spelling And Grammar dialog box appears, deselect the Check Grammar checkbox.

3. When Word runs into a spelling problem, as shown in Figure 9.5, the sentence with the misspelled word appears in the top scroll box and a list of suggestions appears below. The spelling error displays in red.

➤ Select a suggestion from the list, and click Change to change this occurrence of the word. If the word you want to substitute does not appear on the list, you can select the misspelled word and replace it manually, and then click the Change button.

➤ Select a suggestion from the list, and click Change All to change all occurrences of the word. If the word you want to substitute does not appear on the list, you can select the misspelled word and replace it manually, and then click the Change All button.

➤ Click Ignore to leave the word unchanged and move forward in the document.

➤ Click Ignore All to leave all occurrences of the word unchanged throughout the document.

➤ Click Add to add the word to the custom dictionary so the application recognizes it from now on.

➤ Click AutoCorrect to specify the error and the correction as an AutoCorrect entry so Word can automatically correct the word while you type.

4. When Word finishes checking spelling, it notifies you with a message box. Click OK to return to the document. You can cancel spell checking at any time by clicking the Cancel button, or you can close the dialog box by clicking the close box.

 The test may ask you to check spelling and to leave specific words unchanged.

Using The Thesaurus

Looking for just the right word? A thesaurus can help. And Word has one built in. You may be tested on whether you know how to use the Thesaurus.

Task 11   Using the Thesaurus.

1. Select a word.

2. Select Language from the Tools menu, and then select Thesaurus from the cascading list to display the Thesaurus dialog box, as shown in Figure 9.6.

3. The selected word appears in the Looked Up box, with a list of possible meanings in the Meanings box.

4. Select a word from the list to display a list of word choices in the Replace With Synonym scroll box.

5. Click the Replace button to replace the word and return to the document.

 You can also display the Thesaurus dialog box by using the Shift+F7 key combination.

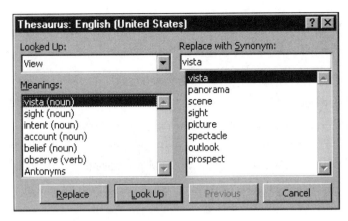

Figure 9.6   The Thesaurus dialog box.

Practice Projects

Perform the following projects based on this chapter.

Project 1   Process text.

1. Open Declarationch07.doc.

2. Reformat the paragraph above the third section break in the document with the text formatting from the paragraph before it.

3. Delete the first instance of the word "Massachusetts."

4. Move John Hancock's name to the top of the list with the rest of the representatives from Massachusetts.

Answer to Project 1

Open Declarationch07.doc.

Use the Go To command to locate the third section break. To copy formatting from the previous paragraph with the Format Painter, place your cursor within the previous paragraph and click the Format Painter button on the Standard toolbar. The cursor displays as a paintbrush while the Format Painter is active. To apply the formatting to the next paragraph, click Format Painter on the paragraph. Word reformats the paragraph.

To locate the first instance of Massachusetts that appears in the document, use the Find feature. When Word locates and selects the word Massachusetts, close the Find dialog box and press the Delete key to delete the word Massachusetts.

To begin moving John Hancock to a new location in the document, select the name John Hancock and click the Cut button on the Standard toolbar, or use the Ctrl+X key combination to cut the text. Use the Find command to locate the next place where the word "Massachusetts" appears. To paste the text into its new location, place the cursor to the left of the first person on the list of Massachusetts representatives. Click the Paste button on the Standard toolbar, or use the Ctrl+V key combination to paste the name John Hancock into the list. Press the Enter key to separate the two names.

Project 2   Search and replace text.

1. Replace the word "shewn" with "shown" throughout Declarationch07.doc.

Answer to Project 2

To display the Find And Replace dialog box, select Replace from the Edit menu. When the Find And Replace dialog box appears, enter the word "shewn" in the Find What box and the word "shown" in the Replace With box. To search and replace the text throughout the document, click the Replace All button. To return to the document, click the Close box or press the Esc key.

HOLD That Skill!

You can also include carriage returns when copying or cutting paragraphs. Before you select the text, display the document's paragraph markers by clicking the Show Paragraphs toolbar button on the Standard toolbar. When you select text, including the paragraph marker, Word automatically inserts the carriage return when you paste the text to a new location.

You can also move selected text to a new location by dragging the text. When you select text, the cursor changes into an arrow. Click on the text and hold the mouse button down, while dragging the text to its new location, then release the mouse button.

 You can also display the Find And Replace dialog box by using the Ctrl+H key combination.

Project 3   Check spelling and save the document.

1. Check the spelling in Declarationch07.doc.

2. Do not change states, personal names, or the words "usurpations" and "compleat".

3. Save the document as Declarationch09.doc and close it.

Answer to Project 3

To begin checking spelling without checking grammar, select Spelling And Grammar from the Tools menu.When the Grammar And Spelling dialog box appears, deselect the Check Grammar checkbox. To correct spelling errors, select Change All when Word flags a spelling error, so it doesn't check the same words twice.

To avoid changing the spelling for words that should remain as they are, click the Ignore All button when Word flags the words "usurpations" and "compleat." When Word finishes checking your spelling and displays the message box, click OK to return to the document.

To save the document with a different name, select Save As from the File menu. When the Save As dialog box appears, browse for the Practice folder, enter "Declarationch09.doc" in the File Name box, and click the Save button. To close the document, select Close from the File menu, or click the Close box for the document window.

Need To Know More?

 Microsoft Word 97 Step by Step. Microsoft Press. Redmond, WA, 1997. ISBN 1-57231-313-7. Lesson 2 covers copying and moving text, and Lesson 5 tells you how to search and replace text, to check spelling and grammar, and to use the Thesaurus.

Applying And Creating Styles, And Generating Outlines And Templates

Terms you'll need to understand:

- √ Styles
- √ Outlines
- √ Promote and demote
- √ Levels
- √ Document Map
- √ Templates

Skills you'll need to master:

- √ Applying styles
- √ Reformatting styles
- √ Creating new styles
- √ Generating outlines
- √ Displaying a Document Map
- √ Creating a template

Word's styles and outline features make it easy to quickly format and organize your documents. In addition, you can customize the templates that come with Word or create templates from scratch. The test won't ask you to create anything too complicated, such as a template for the testing center's brochures and newsletters (although the testing center could save money on graphic design consultants if it did). However, you may be asked to apply and edit styles, to create a new style, to work with an outline, or to save a document as a template.

Working With Styles

Word's styles give you an easy way to format headings, paragraphs, and other types of text by selecting text and choosing from options on the Formatting toolbar. The Normal template that comes with Word has basic styles built in, so you can start working with styles right away. In addition, you can create and edit your own styles.

Task 1   Applying a style.

Styles store text formatting attributes that you can apply by selecting them from the Style list, instead of having to format paragraphs and headings individually. When working on long documents, this helps you work a lot faster! When you apply a style, Word reformats the entire paragraph.

1. Click anywhere within a paragraph or line.

2. Select a style from the Style box on the Formatting toolbar.

Task 2   Applying a character style.

Word lets you format styles as paragraph styles and character styles, as explained in Task 4. Word automatically applies paragraph styles to the entire paragraph, regardless of what text you select. However, you can apply a character style only to the selected text while leaving the rest of the paragraph unchanged.

1. Select a word or words within a paragraph that has a style applied to it.

2. Select a style from the Style box on the Formatting toolbar.

Word applies the character style only to the text you selected.

If the test asks you to select a word or group of words within a paragraph and format it with a certain style, you can pretty much safely assume that the style indicated is a character style.

If you place your cursor on the line or paragraph and don't select any text, Word applies the style formatting to the entire paragraph, regardless of whether the style is a paragraph style or a character style.

Task 3   *Reformatting an existing style from within a document.*

The test may ask you to reformat an existing style. If the style has already been applied to text in the current document, you can easily reformat the paragraph without going to the Style dialog box.

1. Select a paragraph that is formatted in the style you want to change.

   ➤ To change text character formatting, use the Formatting toolbar to reformat the text, or you can select Font from the Format menu and reformat the text from the Font dialog box, as explained in Chapter 3.

   ➤ To change paragraph formatting and indents, select Paragraph from the Format menu and change the paragraph and indent settings from the Paragraphs dialog box, as explained in Chapter 4.

   ➤ To reformat tabs, select Tabs from the Format menu and change the tab settings from the Tabs dialog box, as explained in Chapter 4.

2. Select the style from the Style box on the Formatting toolbar.

3. When the Modify Style dialog box appears, as shown in Figure 10.1, select the option Update The Style to reflect recent changes.

4. Click OK.

Word applies the new style formatting to any lines or paragraphs within the document that have the same style assigned to them.

Task 4   *Creating a new style.*

You can create new styles by formatting text, selecting the text, and giving it a style name from the Style dialog box.

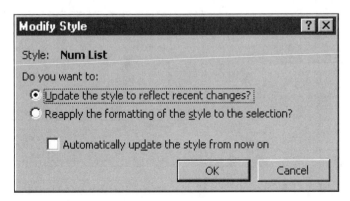

Figure 10.1   The Modify Style dialog box.

1. Format a line or paragraph as you want the style to appear.

2. Select the formatted text and then select Style from the Format menu.

3. When the Style dialog box appears, as shown in Figure 10.2, click the New button.

4. When the New Style dialog box appears, as shown in Figure 10.3, do the following:

   ➤ Enter a name for your new style in the Name box.

   ➤ To set up the style as a paragraph style, select Paragraph from the Style Type box. To set up the style as a character style, select Character from the Style Type box.

   ➤ Click OK.

5. When you return to the Style dialog box, Word adds the new style to the Styles list.

6. Click Apply to apply the new style, and return to the document.

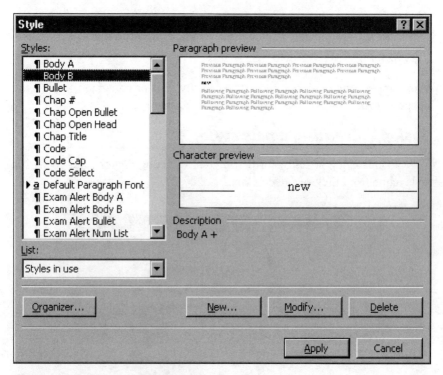

Figure 10.2 The Style dialog box.

Figure 10.3   The New Style dialog box.

The new style name will also appear when you click the Style box on the Formatting toolbar to apply a style.

 When you place your cursor on a line or paragraph, or select text, the style for the text displays in the Style box on the Formatting toolbar. The default style for text with no style applied is Normal. You can also display the Styles dialog box by using the Alt+O, and then S key combination.

Generating Outlines

Whether you have to write a term paper for school, or a proposal or report for work, chances are that you've had to write an outline at some point in your life. Word 97's outline feature makes it easy to create, organize, and rearrange outlines (which is a good thing, because the test may ask you to do just that).

First, you need to be familiar with the terms *levels*, *promote*, and *demote*. Outlines are by nature hierarchical: You organize headings and subheadings by level of importance, with level one headings (the Heading 1 style) as the most important. Other headings and topics are organized beneath these headings. When you promote a line, you format it as a higher-level heading. When you demote a line, you format it as a lower-level heading.

Task 5 Viewing a document as an outline.

In order to work with outlines, you have to switch to the Outline view. From the Outline view, you can easily arrange and prioritize items. When you view a document as an outline, it appears similar to the one shown in Figure 10.4.

1. Select Outline from the View menu.

2. The Outline view displays so you can begin working on your outline.

Word automatically displays text with the Heading 1 and Heading 2 styles as headings, and other text as items beneath the headings. You can use the Outlining toolbar buttons to arrange, organize, and prioritize your text, as explained in Table 10.1. You can collapse or expand headings to display or hide subheadings and text. When you assign headings to text, Word automatically applies its default heading styles.

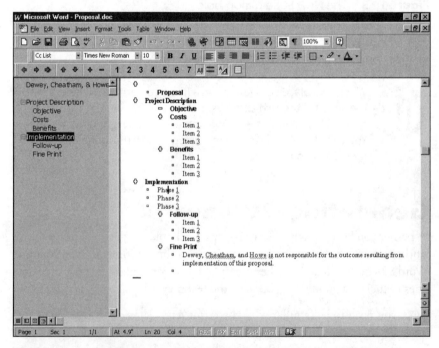

Figure 10.4 A document displayed in Outline view.

Table 10.1 The Outlining toolbar button functions.	
Outline Toolbar Button	**Function**
Promote	Moves a heading up one level
Demote	Moves a heading down one level
Demote to body text	Reformats a heading as body text
Move up	Moves the selected heading and text above the previous line
Move down	Moves the selected heading and text below the following line
Expand	Displays items organized beneath the selected heading
Collapse	Hides items organized beneath the selected heading
1-7	Indicates heading styles and levels, click to display or hide a heading level
All	Shows all heading levels
Show first line only	Displays only the first line of a paragraph
Show formatting	Displays text as formatted in the document

You can also display a document as an outline by using the Alt+V, and then O key combination.

Task 6   Promoting an item up a level.

1. Select the heading or line of text you want to promote.

2. Click the Promote button on the Outlining toolbar.

When you work with headings, Word moves the heading up one level and applies the next higher level heading style. For example, if you promote a level two heading (Heading 2), Word formats it in the Heading 1 style.

Task 7   Demoting an item down a level.

1. Select the heading or line of text you want to demote.

2. Click the Demote button on the Outlining toolbar.

When you work with headings, Word moves the heading down one level and applies the next lower level heading style. For example, if you demote a level 1 heading (Heading 1), Word formats it in the Heading 2 style and indents it in the Outline view.

 When promoting and demoting items for the test, look in the Style box to make sure you've promoted or demoted the item to the correct level!

Task 8   *Moving an item up or down in the outline.*

The Outline view also helps you move and rearrange text more quickly than you could do in the Normal or Page Layout views. You can select items and move them up or down in the document.

1. Select the text you want to move by clicking at the beginning of the text you want to move, holding down the Shift key, and clicking at the end of the text.

2. Click the Move Up button on the Outlining toolbar to move the text up in the outline, or click the Move Down button on the Outlining toolbar to move the text down in the outline.

3. Keep clicking until the text appears in the position where you want it to appear.

Displaying And Navigating A Document Map

A quick way to view a document's outline is to display it as a document map. The document map displays in a frame to the left of your document as a list of headings. You can quickly move around in your document by clicking the headings.

Task 9   *Displaying a document map.*

1. Select Document Map from the View menu.

The document map appears, as shown in Figure 10.5.

 Locating a document heading with the document map can be easier than using the Go To feature.

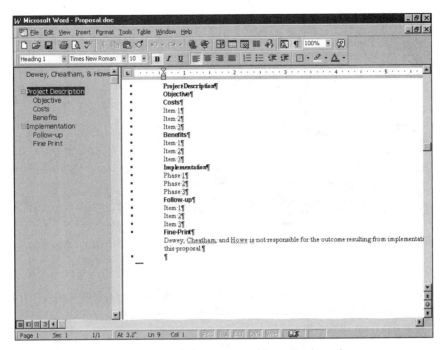

Figure 10.5   Document with Document Map displayed.

Task 10   *Navigating with a document map.*

1. Click an item on the document map list.

Word jumps you to the selected document heading.

Creating Templates

Outlines for standard company documents such as project proposals and sales reports make ideal templates. Templates store styles, text formatting, boilerplate text, graphics, headers, footers, and other document elements, so you don't have to create them all over again.

Task 11   *Saving a document as a template.*

1. Select Save As from the File menu.

2. When the Save As dialog box appears, as shown in Figure 10.6, enter a name for your template in the File Name box.

3. Select Document Template (*.dot) from the Save As Type list.

4. When Word places you in the Templates folder, click the Save button.

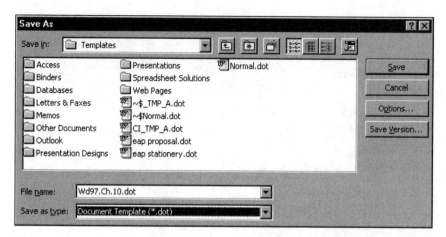

Figure 10.6 Saving a document as a template from the Save As dialog box.

You can now open a new document with this template, as explained in Chapter 2. By default, the templates you create appear when you click the General tab in the New dialog box.

Practice Projects

Perform the following projects based on this chapter.

Project 1   Apply and reformat a style.

1. Open the Proposal.doc practice document.

2. Change the Heading 1 style font to Arial.

3. Reformat the paragraph under the Fine Print heading as 8-point Arial.

4. Create a new style for fine print text and name it Fine Print.

5. Save the document as Proposalch10.doc.

Answer to Project 1

Open Proposal.doc from the practice disk.

To locate a heading formatted as Heading 1, display the document map by selecting Document Map from the View menu and select a level 1 heading.

 You can double-check whether the item you've selected is formatted in the Heading 1 style by checking the Style box on the Formatting toolbar.

To change the font for the Heading 1 style, select the text and then choose Arial from the Font box on the Formatting toolbar, then choose Heading 1 from the Style box. When the Modify dialog box appears, click the Update The Style To Reflect Recent Changes radio button. Click OK. Word applies the new formatting to all of the text formatted with the Heading 1 style. To jump to the Fine Print heading, select it from the document map. To reformat the paragraph, select it, then choose Arial from the Font box on the Formatting toolbar and select 8 from the Size box on the Formatting toolbar.

To create a new style from the selected paragraph, select Style from the Format menu. When the Style dialog box appears, click the New button. When the New Style dialog box appears, enter Fine Print for the new style in the Name box. Click OK. When you return to the Style dialog box, Word adds Fine Print to the Styles list. Click Apply to apply the new style and return to the document.

To save the document to the Practice folder on your hard drive as Proposalch10.doc, select Save As from the File menu. When the Save As dialog box appears, browse for the Practice folder on your hard drive, type "Proposalch10.doc" in the File Name box, and click the Save button.

Project 2   Work with an outline and save a template.

1. View Proposalch10 as an outline and display all headings.
2. Apply the Heading 1 style to the Objective heading.
3. Move the Objective heading above the Project Description heading.
4. Format the Implementation in the Heading 2 style.
5. Save the outline as a template and name it Company Proposal.

Answer to Project 2

To view Proposal.doc as an outline, select Outline from the View menu. To view all the headings, click the All button on the Outlining toolbar.

To format the Objective heading in the Heading 1 style, promote it to the highest level by selecting it and clicking the Promote button on the Outlining toolbar until Heading 1 appears in the Formatting toolbar's Style box.

To move the Objective heading above the Project Description heading, select the heading and click the Move Up button on the Outlining toolbar.

To format the Implementation heading as a Level 2 heading, select it and click the Demote button on the Outlining toolbar until Heading 2 appears in the Formatting toolbar's style box.

To save Proposalch10.doc as a template, select Save As from the File menu, enter "Company Proposal.dot" in the File Name box, select Template (*.dot) from the Save As type box, and then click the Save button.

The test may not specifically mention "promoting" or "demoting" headings. But if the test asks you to work with an outline and apply different heading styles, that's what it really wants you to do. Of course, you can also apply heading styles by selecting them from the Styles list. But in this context, you may lose points if you do it that way.

Remember that templates are saved with the .dot file name extension, not the usual .doc file name extension!

Need To Know More?

 Leonhard, Woody, Lee Hudspeth, and T.J. Lee: *Word 97 Annoyances*. O'Reilly and Associates, Inc. Sebastopol, CA, 1997. ISBN 1-56592-308-1. Chapter 6 talks about styles.

 Microsoft Word 97 Step by Step. Microsoft Press. Redmond, WA, 1997. ISBN 1-57231-313-7. Lesson 7 tells you how to work with styles and outlines. Chapter 8 provides information about using and creating templates.

 If you're connected to the Internet, select Microsoft on the Web from your Help menu and then select Microsoft Office Home Page from the cascading list. You can download useful templates and other goodies, learn how to use Word more effectively, and find other information.

Internet/
Intranet Documents

11

Terms you'll need to understand:

√   Intranet

√   Internet

√   Browsing

√   Word document/HTML document

√   Web page

√   Hyperlinks

√   Bookmarks

Skills you'll need to master:

√   Locating a document in a higher level folder

√   Locating a document on a network

√   Opening an HTML document

√   Saving a Word document as an HTML document

√   Creating hyperlinks

√   Linking to Bookmarks

Many of us are connected to the Internet as well as to an intranet. An *intranet* is an office network that works similarly to the Internet—except that only you and your co-workers can access it. Intranet services include File Transfer Protocol (FTP), which lets you save and get files from a server (in-house or on the Internet), and Hypertext Transfer Protocol (HTTP), which lets you distribute and view Web pages.

Although you should be familiar with these terms, don't worry about them too much. You don't need to take a course in server administration or Web page authoring to pass the test. Word 97 makes it easy for you to create, locate, open, and edit Web pages *locally* (on your computer or a server that you're directly connected to) and *remotely* (on an Internet server that you have to dial up in order to access).

If your computer isn't connected to a network or to the Internet, don't worry. You can still step through the exercises and prepare yourself for the test.

Browsing For Files

You may not have access to the Internet or to an intranet; however, proficient Word 97 users still need to know the basics of locating and working with files. Fortunately, all Office 97 applications are designed so you can work with files on local networks and remote servers the same way as you would work with files on your own computer. You'll first be tested on your ability to locate—or *browse*—for a file.

 Browsing the Web means using a Web browser to visit Web sites and view Web documents. Browsing for files means looking for files in the Open dialog box. In a way, both uses of the term "browsing" mean the same thing—looking for documents on somebody's computer.

Task 1 *Opening a document in a higher level folder.*

We've already talked about how to open documents in Chapter 2. However, to locate documents on a network, you need to be able to move up folder levels when browsing for files.

1. Select Open from the File menu, or use the Ctrl+O key combination.

2. When the Open dialog box appears, as shown in Figure 11.1, click the Up One Level button.

3. When the new list of folders appears, see if the folder you want displays in the list of folders. If it does not appear, click the Up One Level button again.

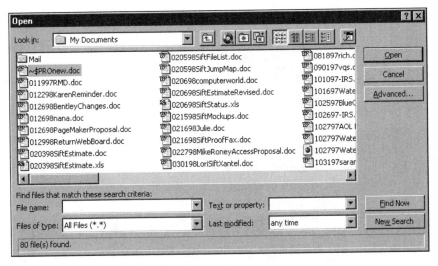

Figure 11.1   The Open dialog box.

4. When you see the folder you want in the list of folders, select it and click the Open button.

5. Select a document and click the Open button.

See? That isn't much different than opening a document in the same folder.

Task 2   *Opening a document on a network or on the Internet.*

You may be asked to open a document on a network or on the Internet. Don't worry if you aren't connected. Just familiarize yourself with these tasks, and you'll do fine.

1. Select Open from the File menu, or use the Ctrl+O key combination.

2. When the Open dialog box appears, display the list of available servers and computers from the Look In box by clicking it, as shown in Figure 11.2.

3. Select Network Neighborhood to display a list of local servers (computers that you're connected to through an Intranet or network).

4. Select Internet Locations to display a list of remote servers (computers that you can connect to via the Internet).

5. Select a server to display the files and folders located on the server.

6. Select a file and click Open.

You can also browse any local computers that appear on the list.

Figure 11.2 List of available servers and computers.

 If you work on a non-networked, standalone system, your Network Neighborhood and Internet Locations folders will be empty and you will not be able to perform the exercise in Task 2. But never fear. You can still ace the exam! Browsing for files on the Internet or on a Network works the same way as browsing for files on your own computer. Look over this chapter so you know what to look for, and you'll do fine.

 Follow the test instructions carefully. If the test asks you to open a document on a network or on the Internet, it will provide a server name and a file name. In addition, the instructions will probably tell you whether the file is local (in which case you'd look in Network Neighborhood) or remote (in which case you'd look in Internet Locations).

Task 3   Opening an HTML document.

Word also lets you view and edit HTML documents.

1. Select Open from the File menu, or use the Ctrl+O key combination.

2. When the Open dialog box appears, select HTML documents from the Files Of Type list.

3. Browse for the file, select the document, and then click the Open button.

When you're asked to open an HTML document or Web page, remember to select HTML documents from the Files Of Type list in the Open dialog box. Otherwise, Word won't display any HTML documents in the document list.

Don't let Web, Internet, and intranet terms throw you off. *HTML document* and *Web page* mean the exact same thing—a document you can view in a Web browser. In addition, the test may tell you to save a file to a *directory* on a server. Never fear. A directory is the same thing as a folder. A Web document can have either an .htm or an .html extension.

Saving HTML Documents

You can save Word 97 documents as Web pages to a server or to your computer. In an office setting, this enables your co-workers to view them in a Web browser or in Word 97. Because the Web does not support all of Word's features, documents may look different once you convert them.

Task 4   *Saving a file as an HTML document.*

1. From within a Word document, select Save As HTML from the File menu.

2. When the Save As HTML dialog box appears (as shown in Figure 11.3), the name of the current document with the .htm or .html file name extension appears in the File Name box, and HTML document is automatically selected from the Save As type box.

3. Browse for a folder or server to save your document to.

4. Click the Save button.

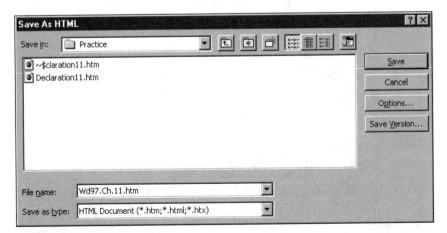

Figure 11.3   The Save As HTML dialog box.

Task 5 Saving a Web document to a network or the Internet.

The test may ask you to save a file to a server. If you're connected to a network, you can try this for yourself. Otherwise, you can walk through the steps below.

1. Select Save As HTML from the File menu.

2. When the Save As HTML dialog box appears, display the list of available servers and computers from the Save In box by clicking it, as shown in Figure 11.4.

3. Select Network Neighborhood to display a list of local servers.

4. Select Internet Locations to display a list of remote servers.

5. Select a server to display the files and folders located on the server.

6. If you're asked to save the file into a folder, select a folder and click the Open button.

7. When you finish looking for a server and a folder, click the Save button.

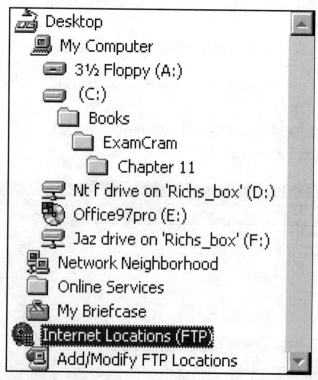

Figure 11.4 List of available local and Internet servers.

Making Links

Once you create a Web page by saving a Word document as an HTML document, you need to create links. Links enable users to click on them to jump to other Web pages. You can make links to a Web page on the same computer, on a network, within the current document, or on the Internet. In addition, Word helps you create three common types of links, as shown in Table 11.1.

If you're asked to save a Web document, be sure to follow the test instructions exactly.

Task 6   *Creating a link to an HTML document within a network or on the same computer.*

1. Select the text you want to link.

2. Click the Insert Hyperlink button on the Standard toolbar.

3. When the Insert Hyperlink dialog box appears, as shown in Figure 11.5, enter the name of the document in the Link To File or URL box.

4. When the Link To File dialog box appears, as shown in Figure 11.6, browse for and select a document as you would when opening a document; then click OK.

5. When you return to the Insert Hyperlink dialog box, the directory path appears in the Link To File or URL box.

6. Click OK to return to the document.

Word links the selected text.

You can make links to Word documents, Excel spreadsheets, Access databases, PowerPoint presentations, and other types of files—not just Web pages.

Table 11.1 Link types and results.	
Link Type	**Result**
http://	Links to a Web page on the Internet
ftp://	Links to a file on an FTP site
mailto:	Sends email

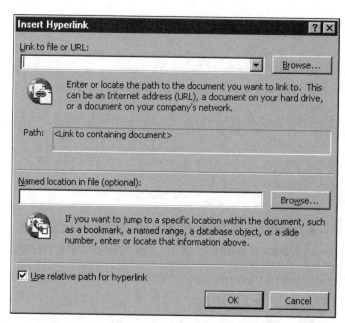

Figure 11.5 The Insert Hyperlink dialog box.

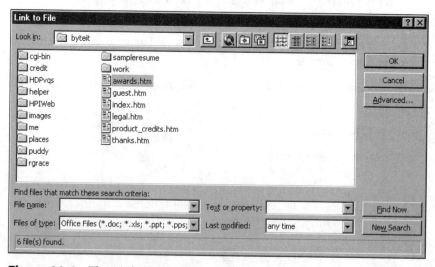

Figure 11.6 The Link To File dialog box.

Task 7 Creating a link to a Web page on the Internet.

You can also create a link to a Uniform Resource Locator (URL). A URL is a Web site's address on the Internet, as in http://www.microsoft.com/.

1. Select the text you want to link.

2. Click the Insert Hyperlink button on the Standard toolbar.

3. When the Insert Hyperlink dialog box appears, click the list arrow and select http:// from the Link To File or URL box; then enter a Web site address.

4. Click OK.

> If the text you want to link *is* a URL (as in, you can get more information from http://www.microsoft.com/), you can make a link by simply clicking anywhere on the URL and then clicking the Insert Hyperlink button. Word automatically inserts the link without you having to access the Insert Hyperlink dialog box.
>
> A URL can also point to a specific document on a Web site, as in http://www.microsoft.com/index.html.

Task 8   Creating a link to an FTP site.

The test may ask you to link to a file located on an FTP site, as in ftp://myserver.net.

1. Select the text you want to link.

2. Click the Insert Hyperlink button on the Standard toolbar.

3. When the Insert Hyperlink dialog box appears, select ftp:// from the Link To File or URL box; then enter the FTP site address.

4. Click OK.

Task 9   Creating an email link.

The test may ask you to set up an email link that people can click to send email to a specified address.

1. Select the text you want to link.

2. Click the Insert Hyperlink button on the Standard toolbar.

3. When the Insert Hyperlink dialog box appears, select MailTo from the Link To File or URL box; then enter an email address.

4. Click OK.

Working With Bookmarks

Before taking the test, you should also acquaint yourself with bookmarks. Bookmarks let you create a special kind of link that you can click on to jump to a place in the same document. Doing this is easy. First, you create a bookmark, then you make a link to it.

Task 10   Creating a bookmark.

You can create a bookmark in either a Word document or an HTML document.

1. Select the text that you want to create a bookmark for.

2. Choose Bookmark from the Insert menu.

3. When the Bookmark dialog box appears, as shown in Figure 11.7, enter a one-word title for your bookmark in the Bookmark Name box.

4. Click the Add button to add the bookmark to the list and return to the document.

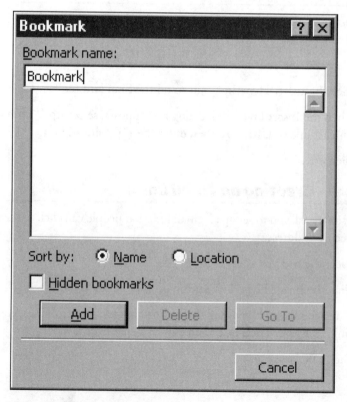

Figure 11.7   The Bookmark dialog box.

If bookmarks already exist in the document, they appear in the Bookmark dialog box's Bookmark Name list. You can remove a bookmark from the list by selecting it from the Bookmark Name list and clicking the Delete button.

HOLD That Skill!

You can also display the Bookmark dialog box by pressing ALT+I and then K. Bookmark names cannot have spaces in them.

Task 11   *Making a link to a bookmark.*

1. Select the text that you want to link to the bookmark.

2. Click the Insert Hyperlink button on the Standard toolbar.

3. When the Insert Hyperlink dialog box appears, click the bottom Browse button next to the Named Location In File box.

4. When the Bookmark dialog box appears, select a bookmark from the list and click OK to return to the Insert Hyperlink dialog box.

5. Click OK to return to the document.

Task 12   *Jumping to a bookmark.*

The test may ask you to locate a bookmark. This is easy.

1. Display the Bookmark dialog box by selecting Bookmark from the Insert menu.

2. Select an item from the Bookmark Name list.

3. Click the Go To button.

You can also search for bookmarks in a document with the Go To feature. When you select Bookmark from the Go To What list in the Go To dialog box, you can select a bookmark from the Bookmark Name list.

Practice Projects

Perform the following projects based on this chapter.

Project 1 Save a document as a Web page.

1. Open Declarationch09.doc.

2. Save it to the current folder as a Web page, and name it Declarationch11.htm.

3. Close the document.

Answer to Project 1

Open Declarationch11.doc by selecting Open from the File menu and browsing for the file.

Select Save As HTML from the File menu. When the Save As HTML dialog box appears, enter Declarationch11.htm in the File Name box. Click the Save button.

When you return to the document window, Declarationch11.htm appears. Select Close from the File menu.

 You may notice that when you save a document as an HTML file, some of the formatting changes. For example, the graphics and page numbers have disappeared. If you scroll down, you'll also notice that the column formatting is no longer applied. There *are* ways to create the graphics so they display in the Web page and to arrange elements so they look more like the original document; however, you won't be tested on them.

Project 2 Open an HTML document from the current folder and create a link.

1. Open Declarationch11.htm.

2. Find the text at the end of the document that reads "National Archives and Records Administration's Web site."

3. Link it to http://www.nara.gov/exhall/charters/declaration/declaration.html.

4. Link the text in which the URL appears.

Answer to Project 2

To open the HTML file, select Open from the File menu. When the Open dialog box appears, select HTML document from the Files Of Type box. Select Declarationch11.htm from the list of files and click the Open button.

Use the Find command to locate the text that reads "National Archives and Records Administration's Web site." Because the question mentions that this text is located at the end of the document, you can also use the scroll button to quickly scroll to the end of the document.

To create the link, select the text that reads "National Archives and Records Administration's Web site." Click the Insert Hyperlink button on the Standard toolbar. When the Insert Hyperlink button appears, select http:// from the Link To File or URL box, and then enter the address "www.nara.gov/exhall/charters/declaration/declaration.html". Click OK to return to the document. The linked text now appears with an underline to indicate a link.

 It is unlikely that the test would give you a long URL like the one shown in this example.

To turn an existing URL into a link, select the text in which the URL appears (http:// www.nara.gov/exhall/charters/declaration/declaration.html), and click the Insert Hyperlink button on the Standard toolbar. Word automatically links the URL without displaying the Insert Hyperlink dialog box, and the text appears with an underline to indicate a link.

Project 3   Locate a bookmark and link to a bookmark.

1. Locate the bookmark named States1.

2. Link the bookmarked text to the bookmark named States.

3. Save and close the document.

Answer to Project 3

To locate the bookmark, select Bookmark from the Insert menu, select an item from the Bookmark Name list (in this case, States1), and click the Go To button. Word jumps to the bookmarked text and selects the text.

To link the text (which reads "States") to the bookmark (in this case, States), select the text and click the Insert Hyperlink button on the standard toolbar. When the Insert Hyperlink dialog box appears, click the bottom Browse button (next to the Named Location In File box) to display the Bookmarks dialog box. Select a bookmark (in this case, States) and click OK. When you return to the Insert Hyperlink dialog box, click OK to finish making the bookmark link and return to the document.

To save and close the document, click the Save button on the Standard toolbar, then select Close from the File menu.

HOLD That Skill!

You can also display the Insert Hyperlink dialog box by using the Ctrl+K key combination.

Need To Know More?

 Leonhard, Woody, Lee Hudspeth, and T.J. Lee. *Word 97 Annoyances*. O'Reilly and Associates, Inc., Sebastopol, CA, 1997. ISBN 1-56592-308-1. Chapters 2 and 3 explain how to customize your Word 97 environment for efficiency and effectiveness.

 If you want to create Web pages, Word comes with a couple of Web page templates. Select New from the File menu; then click the Web Pages tab and select one to get started. You can also go to the Microsoft Office Web site for useful hints and resources. Select Microsoft on the Web from your Help menu, and then select Microsoft Office Home Page from the cascading list.

You can also get a quick rundown on which Word formatting features translate to the Web and which ones don't. Select Contents And Index from the Help menu. When the Contents And Index dialog box displays, select the Index tab, type "Web pages" in the text box, and then select Word 97 features from the list below.

Sample Proficiency Level Test

Congratulations. You've almost finished the Proficiency test chapters, and you're just about ready for the test. Now, wouldn't you like to walk into the testing center and ace the exam? Go for it—you can do it! This chapter tells you what to expect, what to memorize, how to prepare, and it even provides a sample test that you can run through. You can look up the answers for the sample test in the following chapter.

What To Expect

When you walk into the testing center, they will ask for your identification and payment for the test. Testing center personnel then set you up on the computer and explain how to begin (you cannot take this book nor anything else into the test room). First the computer will have you fill out a form with your name, company, and contact information. Then it launches the test program, provides instructions, and tells you how much time you have to complete the test.

When you begin taking your exam, the testing program launches Word for you. Lists of tasks appear in a dialog box. When you begin working, the dialog box disappears and the task appears on the status bar below the Word application window for you to refer to. When you complete an exercise, click a button to move on to the next one.

The test presents exercises in plain, straightforward language. If only your manager at work would do the same! Make sure you follow the instructions exactly. Forget all of the rules and procedures you follow at work, and do not save or close documents unless the test specifically tells you to do so. And rest assured: Although the wording of the questions will encourage you to use certain features, the test will *not* try to trick you.

What To Memorize

Practice makes perfect, and rote memorization can only go so far. The most important thing to remember is that the test is task-oriented. This means that the Word Proficiency Test has you perform exercises that mimic how people work in the real world. The best way to remember what you need to know for the test is to keep practicing. Because few of us use all of Word's features on a regular basis, you should also pay extra attention to unfamiliar tasks and Word functions. Although you don't have to memorize every little detail, you should at least be able to perform the tasks and practice projects in this book without having to look at the answers.

Important types of information to memorize include the following:

➤ **Features and commands located in drop-down menus** Remember which menu bar items contain which types of commands. For example, commands that involve working with files (such as Save, Print, and Page Set Up) are organized under the File menu. See Table 12.1 for a list of menu bar items and associated types of tasks.

➤ **Toolbars and toolbar buttons** Remember which toolbars help you with what. The Standard toolbar provides buttons for common functions (such as copying, pasting, and Undo) and displaying the Table and

Table 12.1	**Menu bar items and associated types of tasks.**	
File	**Edit**	**View**
Working with files	Working with text	Switching document views
Insert	**Format**	**Tools**
Inserting and creating	Formatting text	Helpful features

Drawing toolbars. The Format toolbar buttons and boxes help you format text. The Table toolbar lets you create and edit tables, and the Drawing toolbar contains all of your drawing tools.

➤ **Important key words and concepts**   Look carefully at the bulleted lists at the beginning of each chapter in the Proficiency test section of this book, so you don't get thrown for a loop during the test.

➤ **Helpful tools**   Word makes it easy for you to find and remember things—if you know how to use all the helpful tools that come with it. Find, Go To, Bookmarks, and the Document Map make it easy to locate words, headings, section breaks, bookmarks, tables, and graphics. Tooltips can also remind you of which toolbar buttons do what.

➤ **Think like Uncle Bill**   We mean Bill Gates, of course. Preparing for the Word Proficiency test is sort of like cramming for the SATs back in high school. Standard tests want you to think a certain way. The test questions provide clear clues about how it wants you to do things. For example, if the test asks you to type over a sentence, then switch to Overtype mode. If the test asks you to change heading styles while working on an outline, use the Promote and Demote buttons rather than apply styles from the Formatting toolbar's Style box.

➤ **Choices, choices, choices**   With the above in mind, you should also remember that Word often gives you more than one way to do things. But not always. For example, you can apply borders and shading to tables with the Tables And Borders toolbar or with the Borders And Shading dialog box. However, some table options are *only* available from the Tables And Borders toolbar. Depending on the task at hand, one method may work better than another one. We provide tips and notes throughout the book so you'll know when different methods are available. Familiarize yourself with them, and figure out which ones work best for you in different situations. As long as you can perform tasks quickly and accurately, and follow cues provided by the test exercises, you can work the way you normally do and easily pass the test.

If you master all the tasks and practice projects in the book, you should easily ace the exam. You can also use the Cram Sheet included at the front of this book to jog your memory.

Preparing For The Test

The best possible way to prepare for the test is to read this book while working with Word 97. Run through this book's tasks and practice projects, mark the ones you don't understand, and practice them until you get it right. You can also start applying what you've learned in this book to your daily work. You'll be more creative and productive, and, heck, you might even have a little fun. Try organizing your next project proposal in the Outline view, and creating AutoText entries and AutoCorrect entries to save yourself some typing. Set up character and paragraph styles for text formats that you frequently apply. Jazz up your documents with 3D graphics and slick-looking tables.

Test Exercises

We've provided you with some practice exercises in the following pages. You may remember some of these tasks from the previous chapters. Only this time, we've presented the exercises more closely to how you would perform them during the test. Copy the documents from the Proficiency folder on the Practice disk to a new folder on your computer, as you did when you first started reading this book. This way, you can work with a fresh set of documents. For answers to these practice projects, read Chapter 13.

 Yikes! Did you already save changes to the original documents on the practice disk? You can download a new set of practice documents from Elisabeth Parker's Web site at: http://www.byteit.com/WordExam/.

Exercise 1

1. Open Memorandum.doc.

2. Save Memorandum.doc as Memorandumch12.doc, and save it to a new folder named Practice.

3. In Memorandumch12.doc, format the lines of text that are colored red as a bulleted list, using the ❖ bullet style.

4. In Memorandum.doc, format the lines of text that are colored blue as a numbered list with the default number style.

5. Save and close the document.

Exercise 2

1. Open BusinessLetter.doc from the Proficiency folder on the practice disk.

2. Find the text that reads "To Whom It May Concern:".

3. Replace it with "Dear Mr. Abercrombie Peterson:".

4. In BusinessLetter.doc, insert today's date at the bookmark named "Date."

5. Use the Day, month, date, and year format.

6. Locate and select the text at the beginning of the letter that reads "Dewey, Cheatham, & Howe, Associates."

7. Change the text to 24-point Arial and make it bold.

8. Format the text in small caps and apply a wave underline.

9. Locate "Abercrombie Peterson, III."

10. Replace "III" with "the 3d".

11. Select the "d" in "3d" and format it as superscript text.

12. Create the line that reads "Dewey, Cheatham, & Howe Associates" as an AutoText entry, and name it Dewey, Cheatham.

13. Open a new document and insert the Dewey, Cheatham AutoText entry.

14. Close the new document without saving it and return to BusinessLetter.doc.

15. Create a new AutoCorrect Entry for "The Law Offices of Dewey, Cheatham, & Howe Associates" and name the AutoCorrect entry "DCH".

16. At the bottom of page 2, create a new line and enter the "DCH" AutoCorrect entry.

17. In BusinessLetter.doc, select "Dewey, Cheatham, & Howe, Associates" at the top of the page, and center the text.

18. In BusinessLetter.doc, select all the text starting with the salutation and ending with the closing ("Sincerely,").

19. Format the text as single-and-a-half-spaced text with 0-point line spacing before and 14-point line spacing after.

20. Go to the paragraph beginning "While we must give credit to...."

21. Select the paragraph and indent it 1" on the left and right.

22. Format the first line indent to 0.5".

23. Locate the tabbed list beneath the first heading in the document.

24. For the lines highlighted in red, set the first tab stop at 3" and align it to the center.

25. Position the second tab stop at 5" and make it a decimal tab.

26. For the line highlighted in blue, apply a dotted line leader to the tab and make it a decimal tab.

27. Print two copies of BusinessLetter.doc.

28. Print a mailing label for the recipient's address in BusinessLetter.doc.

29. Create an envelope for BusinessLetter.doc with a mailing and return address.

30. Add the envelope to the document.

31. Save and close BusinessLetter.doc, and rename the document BusinessLetterch12.doc.

Exercise 3

1. Open Declaration.doc.

2. Locate the list of signatures beginning with Georgia on page 4.

3. Format the entire list of states and names into three columns that are each 1.83" wide with 0.4" gutters between the columns.

4. Type the name "Samuel Adams" above the name John Adams.

5. Save the document.

6. In Declaration.doc, create a horizontal line underneath the words "A Transcription".

7. Make the line red and apply a 3-point line style.

8. Apply the round dot line style.

9. Make the line 6.5" long.

10. Select the two banners that appear alongside the words "Declaration of Independence."

11. Change them to five-point stars.

12. Change the fill to Light Blue.

13. Remove the border around the stars.

14. Apply 3D style 6 to the star on the left and 3D style 5 to the star on the right.

15. In Declaration.doc, change the top margin to 1.5" and the bottom margin to 1.5".

16. Create different headers for even and odd pages.

17. Insert page numbers in the even and odd page headers.

18. Align the right page number to the right and the left page number to the left.

19. In Declaration.doc, create a new section starting with the paragraph "He has refused..." and ending with the paragraph " He has excited...." Begin by finding the start of the section.

20. Begin the section on a new page and end the section with a page break.

21. Change the left and right margins for the new section to 1.5".

22. Save the document as Declarationch12.doc.

23. In Declaration.doc, reformat the paragraph above the third section break in the document with the text formatting from the previous paragraph.

24. Delete the first instance of the word "Massachusetts".

25. Move John Hancock's name to the top of the list with the rest of the representatives from Massachusetts.

26. Replace the word "shewn" with "shown" throughout Declaration.doc.

27. Check spelling for Declaration.doc. Do not check grammar or change the spellings for states, personal names, or the words "usurpations" and "compleat".

28. Save the document.

29. Save Declarationch12.doc to the current folder as a Web page and name it Declarationch12.htm.

30. Close the document.

31. Open Declarationch12.htm.

32. Find the text at the end of the document that reads "National Archives and Records Administration's Web site".

33. Link it to the URL: http://www.nara.gov/exhall/charters/declaration/declaration.html.

34. Link the text that writes out the URL, http://www.nara.gov/exhall/charters/declaration/declaration.html.

35. In Declarationch12.htm, locate the bookmark named States1.

36. Link the bookmarked text to the bookmark named States.

37. Save and close the document.

Exercise 4

1. Open a blank new document.

2. Create a table with three columns and three rows.

3. Close the document without saving it.

4. Open Table.doc. Make the text in the top row bold.

5. Change "Class 3" to "Class 2".

6. Add a row to the bottom of the table, type "4." in the first column, "Things" in the second column, and "Stuff" in the third column.

7. Add a row underneath the first table row, type "2." in the first column, "Gadgets" in the second column, and "Junk" in the third column.

8. Add a black, 1.5-point, solid line border to the entire table and all the cells.

9. Add 25% gray shading to the top row of the table.

10. Sort the list of items by number in ascending order.

11. Save the table as Tablech12.doc and close it.

12. Open Table2.doc.

13. Flip the text that says "Inventory" so it isn't backwards.

14. Align the text to the center of the table cell.

15. In Table2.doc, merge the table cells in the top row.

16. Type "MY TABLE" in capital letters in the top row.

17. Center the text and make it bold.

18. Save the file as Table2ch12.doc and close it.

Exercise 5

1. Open the Proposal.doc practice document.

2. Change the Heading 1 style to the Arial font.

3. Reformat the paragraph under the Fine Print heading as 8-point Arial.

4. Create a new style for fine print text and name it Fine Print.

5. Save the document.

6. Open Proposal.doc, and work on it as an outline.

7. Apply the Heading 1 style to the Objective heading.

8. Move the Objective heading above the Project Description heading.

9. Apply the Heading 2 style to the Implementation heading.

10. Save the document as a template, naming it Company Proposal.dot.

Answers To Sample Proficiency Level Test

This chapter contains the answers to the Chapter 12 test exercises.

Excercise 1

1. To open a document, select Open from the File menu. When the Open dialog box appears, select the drive or folder that contains the document from the Look In pull-down list. Double-click the appropriate folders in the list until you locate the one that contains the document (Memorandum.doc). Select the document and click the Open button.

2. To save a document with a different file name to a new folder, select Save As from the File menu. When the Save As dialog box appears, locate a drive and folder from the Save In pull-down list. Click the Create New Folder icon. When the New Folder dialog box appears, enter a name for the new folder (in this case, Practice). Select the new folder and click the Open button. From within the new folder, enter a new name (in this case Memorandumch12.doc) for your document in the File Name box. Click the Save button.

 If the test asks you to create a new folder, do not do it from the Windows Explorer. The test *only* asks you to perform tasks from within the Word application.

 You don't need to enter the .DOC file name extension. Microsoft Word adds it to your file name automatically.

3. In Memorandumch12.doc, select the lines of text that are colored red. Select Bullets And Numbering from the Format menu, and then click the Bulleted tab.Select the style shown from the Bulleted List options and click OK.

4. In Memorandumch12.doc, select the lines of text that are colored blue. Click the Numbering button on the Formatting toolbar.

5. To save a document (in this case, Memorandumch12.doc) with the same name and to close it, click the Save button on the Standard toolbar, then select Close from the File menu.

Exercise 2

1. To open a document, select Open from the File menu. When the Open dialog box appears, select the drive or folder that contains the document from the Look In pull-down list. Double-click the appropriate folders in the list until you locate the one that contains the document (BusinessLetter.doc). Select the document and click the Open button.

2. To locate text, display the Find dialog box from the Edit menu. When the Find dialog box appears, enter "To Whom It May Concern:" in the Find What box, and click the Find button. When Word locates and selects the words "To Whom It May Concern:", click the Close box to close the Find dialog box and return to the document.

3. Type "Dear Mr. Abercrombie Peterson:".

HOLD That Skill!

You can save yourself a little typing by simply entering "To Whom" in the Find dialog box's Find What box, double-clicking the OVR item on the status bar to switch to Overtype mode when you return to the document, and typing "Dear Mr. Abercrombie Peterson" over the entire salutation.

4. To locate a bookmark in a document, select Go To from the Edit menu. When the Go To dialog box appears, select Bookmark from the Go To What list and select or enter "Date" in the Enter Bookmark Name box; then click Go To. When the cursor moves to the bookmark, click the Close box or press the Esc key to return to the document.

5. Select Date and Time from the Insert menu, select a format from the list (in this case, the one that displays the day of the week, month, day, and year), and then click OK.

When the test asks you to locate an item by line number or page element (such as a section or table), it wants you to use the Go To command.

When locating a bookmark, you can use Go To, as explained above. Or, you can display the Bookmarks dialog box by selecting Bookmark from the Insert menu (or by pressing ALT+I, and then K), selecting the Bookmark from the list, and clicking the Go To button.

You can also display the Go To dialog box by using the CTRL+G key combination.

6. To begin reformatting the text in BusinessLetter.doc, scroll up to "Dewey, Cheatham, & Howe, Associates," and select the text.

7. To change the font size, select the number 24 from the Font Size box on the Formatting toolbar. To change the font, select Arial

from the Font box on the Formatting toolbar. To apply bold formatting to the text, click the Bold toolbar button on the Formatting toolbar.

8. To format the text in small caps and apply a wavy underline, display the Font dialog box by selecting Font from the Format menu, and click the Font tab. Select the Small Caps checkbox from the Effects list. Select Wave from the Underline box and click OK.

9. Scroll to Abercrombie Peterson, III.

In this exercise, it was easy to locate the text by scrolling. However, you can also use the Find command to help you locate text.

Determining the most efficient way to do things can help you get through the test faster. Applying small caps and a wave underline requires displaying the Font dialog box, so you could also apply all of the other font formatting from the same dialog box.

HOLD That Skill!

You can also display the Font dialog box by pressing ALT+O, and then F. You can select an entire line of text or paragraph by triple-clicking anywhere on the line or paragraph.

10. To locate "III" and replace it with "3d", select Replace from the Edit menu, enter "III" in the Find What box and "3d" in the With box, and click the Replace button. When Word replaces the text, press the Close box or the Esc key to return to the document

11. To apply superscript formatting to the "d" in "3d", select the "d", then choose Font from the Format menu. When the Font dialog box appears, click the Superscript checkbox from the Effects list, then click OK to return to the document.

12 To create an AutoText entry, select "Dewey, Cheatham, & Howe, Associates" in BusinessLetter.doc, then select AutoText from the Insert menu, and select New from the cascading list. When the Create AutoText dialog box appears, name the AutoText entry "Dewey, Cheatham".

13. Open a new document by selecting New from the File menu and choosing the Blank Document template. To insert the Dewey,

Cheatham AutoText entry, place your cursor in the document, select AutoText from the Insert menu and select Dewey, Cheatham from the cascading list (if you don't see it, select Company Name to display the Dewey, Cheatham option).

14. When Word inserts the AutoText entry, select Close from the File menu. When the dialog box appears and asks if you want to close without saving the document, click Yes.

15. To create an AutoCorrect Entry for "The Law Offices of Dewey, Cheatham, & Howe, Associates" named "DCH," select AutoCorrect from the Tools menu. When the AutoCorrect dialog box appears, select the AutoCorrect tab, enter "DCH" in the Replace box, and "The Law Offices of Dewey, Cheatham, & Howe, Associates" in the With box. Click the Add button and click OK.

16. Find page 2 by selecting Go To from the Edit menu or using the Ctrl+G key combination. When the Go To dialog box displays, select Page from the Go To What list and enter "2" in the Enter Page Number box. When you locate page 2, close the Go To window by clicking the Close button. To create a new line at the bottom of the page, scroll down to the bottom of the page, place your cursor at the end of the last line, and press the Enter key. To insert your AutoCorrect Entry, type "DCH". When Word inserts the AutoCorrect entry, select Close from the File menu. When the dialog box appears and asks if you want to close without saving the document, click OK.

Do not confuse AutoText and AutoCorrect. The test may ask you to work with one or both of these features.

17. To align the paragraph that reads "Dewey, Cheatham, and Howe, Associates" to the center, click anywhere on the line, and click the Center button on the Formatting toolbar.

18. In BusinessLetter.doc, select the line beginning with the Salutation ("Dear Mr. Abercrombie...") and press Ctrl+Shift, and then the down-arrow key to select paragraphs until you get to "Sincerely,".

19. To apply the spacing and line spacing options, select Paragraph from the Format menu, or use the Alt+O, and then P key combination. Select the Indents And Spacing tab. When the Indents And Spacing options appear, select 1.5 from the Line Spacing box and 14 points from the Spacing After box. Click OK to apply the line spacing options and return to the document.

HOLD That Skill!

You can also display the Paragraphs or Font dialog box by selecting it from the Shortcut menu. To display the shortcut menu, select a paragraph and click it with your right mouse button. When the shortcut menu appears, you can select an item.

20. Use the Find command to find the paragraph that begins with "While we must give credit to", and then select the paragraph.

21. To begin applying the indents to the paragraph, select Paragraph from the Format menu, or use the Alt+O, and then P key combination to display the Paragraph dialog box. Select the Indents And Spacing tab to display the Indents And Spacing options. To format the left and right indents, select the number 1 from the Indentation Left box and the number 1 from the Indentation Right box.

22. To create a first line indent, select First Line from the Special box; then enter .5 in the By box. Click OK to apply the indents and return to the document.

23. To locate the first heading in the document, select Go To from the Edit menu, choose Heading from the Go To What list when the Go To dialog box appears, enter 1 in the Heading Number box, click the Go To button, and then click the Close button when Word shows you the heading.

24. Select the lines highlighted in red, beginning with "Item" and ending with "Hospital bills". To begin formatting your tabs, display the Tabs dialog box by selecting Tabs from the Format menu. When the Tabs dialog box appears, click the Clear All button to remove the current tab settings. To create and format the first tab, enter 3" in the Tab Stop Position box and click the Set button. Now, select the item from the list of tab stop positions, click the Center radio button from the Alignment list, then click the Set button again.

25. To create and format the second tab, enter 5" in the Tab Stop Position box, and click the Set button. Now, select the second item from the list of tab stop positions (it should be 5"), click the Decimal radio button from the Alignment list, and then click the Set button. Click OK to apply your settings and return to the document.

26. To begin applying a dotted-line leader to a tab, select the line that is highlighted in blue, then select Tabs from the Format menu. When the Tabs dialog box appears, apply a dotted-line leader to

the tab stop by selecting the tab stop from the Tab Stop position list and clicking the second radio button (with the dotted line) from the Leaders list. Format the tab stop as a decimal tab by selecting the Decimal radio button from the Alignment list.

27. To print two copies of BusinessLetter.doc, select Print from the File menu. When the Print dialog box appears, select the All radio button from the Page Range list, and then enter 2 in the Number Of Copies box. Click OK to print and return to the document.

28. To print a mailing label, place your cursor next to the recipient's address (Abercrombie Peterson 3d). Select Envelopes And Labels from the Tools menu. When the Envelopes And Labels dialog box appears, click the Labels tab. When the Label options appear, the recipient's address appears in the Address window. If it doesn't appear, you can type in the address, or you can copy and paste it from the document. Select the Single Label radio button from the Print list. Click the Print button.

29. In BusinessLetter.doc, place your cursor next to the address. To create the envelope, select Envelopes And Labels from the Tools menu. When the Envelopes And Labels dialog box appears, select the Envelopes tab. The address should appear in the Delivery Address box. Make sure the Omit checkbox is deselected, and type the return address into the Return Address box.

30. To add the envelope to the document, click the Add To Document button.

31. To save BusinessLetter.doc with a different name, select Save As from the File menu. When the Save As dialog box appears, enter BusinessLetterch12.doc in the File Name box, and click the Save button. To close the document, select Close from the File menu.

Exercise 3

1. Open Declaration.doc by selecting Open from the File menu and finding the document in the pull-down list.

2. Use the Find command to find the word "Georgia.", then select the entire list of states and names.

3. To format the columns, select Columns from the Format menu. When the Columns dialog box appears, enter the number 3 in the Number Of Columns box. Because you were instructed to make the columns of equal width, select the Equal Column Widths checkbox. Enter 1.83" in the Width box to reset the column width. Enter .0.4" in the Spacing box to determine the column spacing. Choose Selected Text from the Apply To box and click OK.

4. Use the Find command to find the name "John Adams", then place the cursor before the name and press Return. Enter "Samuel Adams" in the blank line you have created above "John Adams."

5. Select Save from the File menu to save the document.

6. Use the Find command to locate the words "A Transcription." Display the Drawing toolbar by clicking the Drawing button on the Standard toolbar. If the Drawing toolbar appears as a floating toolbar, you can dock it by dragging it to the top, left, or bottom of the document window. Word switches to the Page Layout view. To create a line, click the Line button on the Drawing toolbar, click underneath the words "A Transcription", and drag the mouse horizontally across the page. Leave the line selected.

7. Color the line red by clicking the arrow to the right of the Line Color button and selecting Red from the Line Color options.

 Make sure you select the correct colors and styles. ToolTips tell you the name of each color or style when you pass your mouse button over them.

To apply the line style, click the Line Style toolbar button and select the 3-point line style.

8. To apply the line style, click the Dash Style toolbar button and select the Round Dot dash style.

9. To resize the line, select Borders And Shading from the Format menu. When the Format AutoShapes dialog box appears, select the Size tab. When the Size options appear, enter 6.5" in the Width box. Click OK to apply the line size and return to the document.

10. To begin editing the AutoShapes, switch to the Page Layout view, select the two banners, and click the Draw button on the Drawing toolbar.

11. To change the banners into five-point stars, select Change AutoShapes, select Banners and Stars, and then select the Change To Five-Point Star option and release the mouse key.

12. To change the fill to light blue, click the Fill Color button and select the Light Blue option.

13. To remove the border, click the Line Color button and select No Line.

When you need to apply the same changes to two shapes, you can select both of them and modify them simultaneously. Hold down the Shift key and click on both shapes.

14. To apply the first 3D style, select the left star, click the 3D button, and apply 3D style 6. To apply the second 3D style, select the right star, click the 3D button, and apply 3D style 6.

15. In Declaration.doc, select Page Setup from the File menu or use the Alt+F, and then U key combination to display the Page Setup dialog box. Click the Margins tab to display the Margins options. To change the top margin, enter 1.25" in the Top box. To change the bottom margin, enter 1.25" in the Bottom box. To apply the margins to the whole document, select Whole Document from the Apply To box. Click OK to return to the document.

16. To display the headers and footers view, go to page 1 in a document and select Header And Footer from the View menu. When Word places you in the header and displays the Header And Footer toolbar, click the Page Setup button. When the Page Setup dialog box appears, click the Layout tab. When the Layout options display, select the Different Odd And Even checkbox from the Headers And Footers list. Select Whole Document from the Apply To list; then click OK to return to the Header And Footer view. The header label indicates an odd page header.

17. To insert a page number, click the Insert Page Number button on the Header And Footer toolbar.

18. To align the odd page header page number to the right, click the Align Right button on the Standard toolbar. Click the Next button to add and align a page number for the even page. The header label now indicates an even page header. To insert a page number, click the Insert Page Number button on the Header And Footer toolbar. To align the even page header page number to the left, click the Align Left toolbar button on the Standard toolbar. Click the Close button to return to the document.

19. To locate the place where you need to start the new section, use the Find command to locate the words "He has refused".

Remember, when the test asks you to find groups of words, you can select the text and use the Ctrl+C key combination to copy it, and then use the Ctrl+V key combination to paste it into the Find What box, instead of entering it yourself.

20. Place your cursor at the end of the paragraph ending with the word "world", and then select Break from the Insert menu. When the Break dialog box appears, select Next Page from the Section Break list to start the section on a new page. Click OK. To locate the place where you need to end the section, use the Find command to locate the words "He has excited domestic insurrections amongst us." To end the section, place your cursor at the end of the paragraph and then select Break from the Insert menu. When the Break dialog box appears, select Next Page from the Section Break list to insert a section break that ends the section and starts a new page, and click OK.

21. To reset the margins, place your cursor anywhere within the new section; then select Page Setup from the File menu. Select the Margins tab to display the Margins options and enter 1.5" in the Left box and 1.5" in the Right box. Select the This Section option from the Apply To box and click OK.

22. To save the document as Declarationch12.doc, select Save As from the File menu, enter Declarationch12.doc in the File Name box and click the Save button.

23. Use the Go To command to locate the third section break. The paragraph above it reads "The 56 signatures on the Declaration appear in the positions indicated:". Place your cursor on the previous paragraph. Click the Format Painter button on the Standard toolbar. Click the Format Painter on the paragraph that reads "The 56 signatures on the Declaration appear in the positions indicated:". Word reformats the paragraph.

24. Use the Find command to locate the first instance of "Massachusetts". When Word locates and selects the word Massachusetts, close the Find dialog box and press the Delete key to delete the word Massachusetts.

25. To begin moving "John Hancock" to a new location in the document, select the name John Hancock and click the Cut button on the Standard toolbar, or use the Ctrl+X key combination to cut the text. Use the Find command to locate the next place where the word Massachusetts appears. Place the cursor to the left of the first person on the list of Massachusetts representatives. Click the Paste button on the Standard toolbar, or use the Ctrl+V key combination to paste the name "John Hancock" into the list. Press the Enter key to separate the two names.

26. Select Replace from the Edit menu, or use the CTRL+H key combination. When the Find And Replace dialog box appears, enter the word "shewn" in the Find What box and the word

"shown" in the Replace With What box. Click the Replace All button. Click the Close box to return to the document.

27. Select Spelling And Grammar from the Tools menu. When the Grammar And Spelling dialog box appears, deselect the Check Grammar checkbox, because the project does not ask you to check grammar. When Word flags a spelling error, select Change All so it doesn't check the same words twice. When Word flags the words "usurpations" and "compleat," click the Ignore All button. When Word finishes checking the spelling and notifies you by displaying a message box, click OK to return to the document.

28. To save a document with the same name, click the Save button on the Standard toolbar, or use the CTRL+S key combination.

29. Select Save As HTML from the File menu. When the Save As HTML dialog box appears, enter "Declarationch12.htm" in the File Name box. Click the Save button. When you return to the document window, Declarationch12.htm appears.

30. Select Close from the File menu.

 You may notice that when you save a document as an HTML file, some of the formatting changes. For example, the graphics and page numbers disappear. There are ways to create the graphics so they display in the Web page and to arrange elements so they look more like the original document; however, you won't be tested on them.

31. Select Open from the File menu. When the Open dialog box appears, select HTML document from the Files Of Type box. Select Declarationch12.htm from the list of files, and click the Open button.

32. Use the Find command to locate the text that reads "National Archives and Records Administration's Web site". Because the question mentions that this text is located at the end of the document, you can also scroll to the end of the document.

33. To create a link, select the text "National Archives and Records Administration's Web site", if it's not already selected. Click the Insert Hyperlink button on the Standard toolbar. When the Insert Hyperlink dialog box appears, select http:// from the Link To File or URL box and enter the address. Click OK to return to the document. The linked text now appears with an underline to indicate a link.

 The test will probably give you a short, uncomplicated URL that is easy to enter and remember.

34. To create a link from a URL, select the text that writes out the URL (http://www.nara.gov/exhall/charters/declaration/declaration.html) and click the Insert Hyperlink button on the Standard toolbar. Word automatically links the URL without displaying the Insert Hyperlink dialog box, and the linked text appears with an underline to indicate a link.

35. To locate the bookmark named States1, select Bookmark from the Insert menu to display the Bookmark dialog box, select an item from the Bookmark Name list, and click the Go To button. When Word jumps you to the bookmarked text and selects it (it should say "States"), close the Bookmark dialog box by clicking the Close button or pressing the Esc key. Leave the text selected.

36. To link the text to the bookmark named States, click the Insert Hyperlink button on the Standard toolbar. From the Insert Hyperlink dialog box, click the second Browse button next to the Named Location In File box. When the Bookmark dialog box appears, select an item (in this case "States") from the list and click OK. When you return to the Insert Hyperlink dialog box, click OK to apply the link and return to the document.

37. To save the document, select Save from the File menu or use the Ctrl+S key combination. To close the document, select Close from the File menu, or click the Close box in the document window.

Exercise 4

1. To open a new document from the Blank Document template, click the New Document toolbar button.

2. To create a table with three columns and three rows, click the Insert Table toolbar button. When the pop-up window appears, drag your cursor across three columns and down three squares until the status bar at the bottom of the pop-up window says 3×3 table. Release the mouse to insert the table.

3. To close a document without saving, select Close from the File menu. When a dialog box appears to ask if you want to close without saving, click Yes.

4. To open Table.doc, select Open from the File menu. When the Open dialog box appears, browse for the folder that contains the document and select Table.doc. To select the text in the entire table row, drag your cursor across the rows while holding down the mouse button, as you would normally select text. To bold the text, click the Bold button on the Formatting toolbar.

5. To change the text that says "Class 3" to "Class 2", select the text, and type over it.

You can move across cells in a table by pressing the tab key. This also automatically selects the text in the cell.

6. To add a row to the bottom of the table, place your cursor in the last table cell and press the Tab key.

7. To add a row underneath the first table row, place your cursor in the row below where you want the new row to appear (in this case, in the second row), and click the Add Row button on the Standard toolbar. To enter text in table cells, place your cursor in the first cell in the row, enter the text, and press the Tab key to move across the cells.

8. Display the Tables And Borders toolbar by clicking the Tables And Borders button on the Standard toolbar. To apply a border, select the cells that you want to apply the border to (in this case, the entire table). Select a solid line from the Line Style box. Select 1 1/2 points from the Line Weight box. Select Black from the Border Color box. Then click the Arrow next to the Borders button, select All Borders from the Borders pop-up box, then click the Borders button to apply the border.

9. To apply shading, select the cells you want to apply shading to (in this case, the top row). Click the arrow next to the Shading Color button, and select Gray-25% from the pop-up box. Click the Shading Color button to apply the shading.

You can also apply borders and shading by selecting Borders And Shading from the Format menu to display the Borders And Shading dialog box.

10. To sort table cell items in ascending numerical order, select the list of items (all of the table rows except for the first one), and click the Sort Ascending button on the Tables And Borders toolbar.

11. To save the table as Tablech12.doc, select Save As from the File menu, enter Tablech12.doc in the File Name box, and click the Save button. To close Tablech12.doc, select Close from the File menu.

You can also use this method to sort items in alphabetical order.

12. To open Table2.doc, select Open from the File menu and browse for the file.

13. To flip the text that says "Inventory" so it isn't backwards, place your cursor in the table cell and click the Change Text Direction on the Tables And Borders toolbar.

14. To align the flipped text in the center of the table cell, place your cursor in the table cell (it should still be there), and click the Center Horizontally button on the Tables And Borders toolbar.

HOLD That Skill!

When the text isn't flipped, the Center Horizontally button changes to a Center Vertically button.

The Change Text Direction and table cell alignment toolbars (Align Top, Align Center Vertically, and Align Bottom) are only available from the Tables And Borders toolbar.

15. To merge the table cells in the top row of Table2.doc, select the cells you want to merge, then click the Merge Cells button on the Tables And Borders toolbar.

16. To enter text in the newly merged table row, place your cursor in the table cell and type "MY TABLE".

17. To center the text and make it bold, select the text, then click the Bold button and the Center button. Both buttons are located on the Formatting toolbar.

18. To save the file with a different name, select Save As from the File menu, enter Table2ch12.doc in the File Name Box, and click the Save button. To close the file, select Close from the File menu.

Exercise 5

1. Open Proposal.doc by selecting Open from the File menu and finding the document in the pull-down list.

2. Use the Go To command to locate headings, until you find one formatted as Heading 1 (the style name displays in the Style box on the Formatting toolbar). Select the text; then choose Arial from the Font box on the Formatting toolbar. Select Heading 1 from the Style box. When the Modify dialog box appears, select the Update Style To Reflect Recent Changes radio button. Click OK.

3. Scroll to locate the Fine Print heading. Select the paragraph beneath it. Select Arial from the Font box on the Formatting toolbar and 8 from the Size box on the Formatting toolbar.

4. Select Style from the Format menu. When the Style dialog box appears, click the New button. When the New Style dialog box appears, enter Fine Print for the new style in the Name box. Click OK. Click Apply to apply the new style and return to the document. When you return to the Style dialog box, Word adds Fine Print to the Styles list.

5. Save the document by selecting Save from the File pull-down list.

6. To view Proposal.doc as an outline, select Outline from the View menu. To view all the headings, click the All button on the Outlining toolbar.

7. To promote the Objective heading to the highest level, click it and then click the Promote button on the Outlining toolbar until Objective stops moving to the left.

8. To move the Objective heading above the Project Description heading, click the Move Up button on the Outlining toolbar.

9. To demote Implementation one level lower, select it and click the Demote button on the Outlining toolbar once. To return to the Normal view, select Normal from the View menu.

10. To save Proposal.doc as a template, select Save As from the File menu, enter Company Proposal in the File Name box, select Document Template (*.dot) from the Save As Type box, and then click the Save button.

Expert Level

If you can do the following Word tasks, then you should take the Expert Word exam:

➤ Use advanced formatting and page layout options

➤ Create columns, headers, footers, endnotes, and footnotes

➤ Create and modify watermarks and graphics

➤ Create and modify charts

➤ Import worksheets and tables

➤ Create, modify, copy, and delete macros

➤ Create an index, table of contents, bookmark, and cross-reference

➤ Create and modify page, paragraph, and text borders and shading

➤ Create and work with a master document and subdocuments

➤ Track changes, create versions, and compare documents

➤ Perform mail merges

➤ Protect and unprotect a document or section of a document

Advanced Formatting And Page Layout

Terms you'll need to understand:

√ Widow

√ Orphan

√ Orientation

√ Header

√ Footer

√ Section break

√ Columns

Skills you'll need to master:

√ Controlling widow and orphan lines

√ Keeping lines in a paragraph together

√ Changing page orientation

√ Creating and customizing headers and footers

√ Inserting continuous, next page, odd, and even section breaks

√ Formatting columns

The secret to any well-written document is formatting; seriously—too much formatting distracts a reader and too little can bore a reader to tears. Here are some additional formatting features to whet your interest.

Text-Flow Options

Text flow refers to how your document moves from one word or one page to another. Controlling widows and orphans, keeping the lines of a paragraph together, and choosing the orientation of your document are all text-flow options.

You probably think that widows and orphans have to do with some old seaman's fund, but not in Word. A *widow* is the last line of a paragraph that is printed at the top of a new page, and an *orphan* is the first line of a paragraph that is printed at the bottom of the current page.

Task 1   Controlling widows and orphans.

1. Open the Ch14What document on the disk that's included with this book. Click at the end of the last sentence on page 1.

2. Click the Paragraph command on the Format menu, and then click the Line And Page Breaks tab.

3. Click the Widow/Orphan Control checkbox to select the option.

4. Close the dialog box and notice how the bullet's lines are kept together on the same page.

5. Save the document as Ch14.1What.

Task 2   Keeping lines together.

You can prevent the lines of a paragraph from being divided by a page break by using the Keep Lines Together option in the Paragraph dialog box.

1. Open the Ch14Say document on the disk.

2. Place the cursor in front of the last paragraph on page 1.

3. Click the Paragraph command on the Format menu, and then click the Line And Page Breaks tab, if necessary.

4. Click the Keep Lines Together option and then close the dialog box.

Note: Notice the Widow And Orphans option is selected. That option will not keep multiple lines of a paragraph together.

5. The paragraph is moved to the next page so that all the lines are together. Save the document as Ch14.1Say.

 You may have noticed that the Widow/Orphan control and Keep Lines Together options are in the same dialog box. You can set these options at the same time when applying them to the entire document.

Task 3   *Changing page orientation.*

Page orientation refers to how the document will be viewed and printed. There are two types of orientation: portrait and landscape. Portrait (Word's default orientation) specifies that the document will be viewed and printed with the short edge of the paper at the top. Landscape specifies that the document will be viewed and printed with the long edge of the paper at the top. Think of landscape orientation as turning a regular piece of 8 1/2"-by-11" paper on its side.

1. Open the Ch14What document on the disk, then click File|Page Setup.

2. Click the Paper Size tab and then click the Landscape option. Notice how the Height and Width boxes and the picture in the Preview section have changed.

3. Click the OK button, and then view your document in Print Preview.

4. Close the document *without* saving the changes.

Headers And Footers

Headers and footers are used to customize a document. *Headers* display at the top of each page, and *footers* display at the bottom of each page. You can customize your headers and footers in several ways. For example, you can display a header and/or footer on one page but not another. You can also display different headers and/or footers on different pages. You can even display the document name, the date, page numbers, customized text, and more in headers and footers.

 You must be in Page Layout view to see the headers and footers within your document.

Task 4   *Creating a header with different odd and even pages.*

1. Open the Ch14Office document from the disk, and move your cursor to the first page.

2. Click the Header And Footer command on the View menu.

3. Click the Insert Page Number button on the Header and Footer toolbar.

4. Press the Tab key twice and then type the name of the current section, as shown in Figure 14.1.

5. Click the Page Setup button and then click the Layout tab, if necessary.

6. Click the Different odd and even option and then close the dialog box.

7. Click the Show Next button, and insert the page number and the name of the document for the next section.

8. Click the Close button on the Header and Footer toolbar.

9. Save the document as Ch14.1Office.

Task 5   Creating a footer.

1. Open the Ch14.1Office document and move the cursor to the first page.

2. Double-click the header.

3. Click the Switch Between Header And Footer button.

4. Type "Revised on", press the spacebar, and then click the Insert Date button.

5. Press the Tab key and then type "Revision 1".

6. Press the Tab key and then type your name.

7. Click the Close button on the Header and Footer toolbar.

8. Save the document as Ch14.2Office.

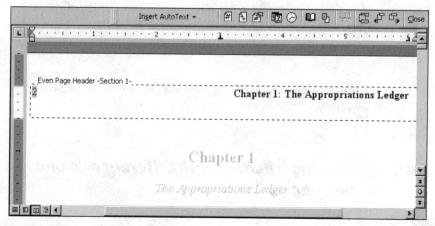

Figure 14.1   Creating a header.

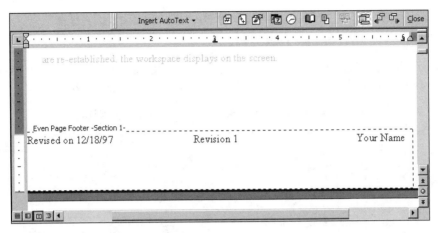

Figure 14.2   Creating a footer.

You now have professional-looking headers and footers, where the headers reflect the section and document names, and the footers are the same throughout the document (see Figure 14.2).

Section Breaks

You can use a *section break* to create a different header or footer for part of a document, or to change the formatting for a different section. A section break marks the end of a section and stores the section's formatting. Table 14.1 shows the four types of section breaks.

 Be careful when deleting a section break, because you'll also delete the formatting for the text above it. The text above the deleted section break will convert to the formatting of the following section.

Table 14.1 The four types of section breaks.	
Section Break	**Function**
Next Page	Creates a section break, starts a new page at the break, and then starts the new section on that page
Continuous	Creates a section break and starts the new section on the same page
Odd Page	Creates a section break and starts the new section on the odd-numbered page
Even Page	Creates a section break and starts the new section on the even-numbered page

Task 6   *Creating a section break and adding a different header.*

1. Move the cursor to the right of the last word in Chapter 1 in the Ch14.2Office document. This is where the section break is to occur.

2. Click Insert|Break and then click the Next Page Section Break option. Now Chapter 2 begins on its own page and is separated by a section break.

HOLD That Skill!

Other section break options:

- If your document is complete and has multiple pages, click the Continuous option.

- If you need to insert a page break to separate your document's sections (as in chapters), click the Next Page option.

- If you want to create a blank page between sections, use either the odd or even section break. The next section will start on the next even-numbered (or odd-numbered) page. For example, if the even section break falls on an even-numbered page, Word leaves the next odd-numbered page blank.

3. Click View|Header And Footer.

4. Click the Show Next button.

5. Click the Same As Previous button to deselect it.

6. Type the new header text, as shown in Figure 14.3.

7. Click the Close button on the Header And Footer toolbar, and then save the document as Ch14.3Office.

Because a section break allows each section to contain its own formatting, you can change the number format as well as the font style, size, and color in a header's section without affecting any other sections.

Columns

Another way to use section breaks is when adding columns. If your entire document is going to be formatted with the same column style, no section breaks are needed; however, if you're going to change column styles or add columns to one or more pages within a document, you need to insert section breaks.

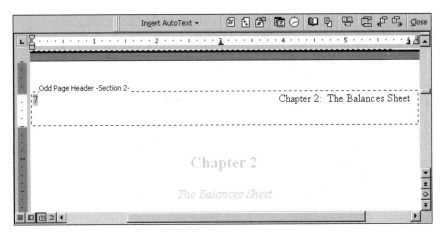

Figure 14.3   Creating a different header after a section break.

You can use a one-column format to create a banner heading that stretches across the columns. Select the heading and then click the 1 Column option from the Columns button on the Standard toolbar.

Task 7   *Creating columns.*

Creating columns is fast and easy with the Columns button on the Standard toolbar. You can format your entire document with columns from anywhere within the document.

1. Open the Ch14Say document from the disk.

2. Place the cursor to the left of the first word in the text, and then click the Columns button.

3. Use the mouse to select three columns.

4. Save the document as Ch14.2Say.

If you don't select any text, the entire document will be formatted with columns, including the title.

When you format existing text into columns, you can click the Normal View button to verify that continuous section breaks have been automatically added before and after the columns.

If you cannot see your columns, click the Page Layout View button (or click View|Page Layout).

Task 8   Using the Columns dialog box.

Sometimes you'll want to format your columns differently. You may want a larger space separating them, or you may want columns to be different widths.

1. Open the Ch14.2Say document.

2. Place the cursor to the left of the first word in column 1.

3. Click Format|Columns.

4. Click the Two Column option and deselect the Equal Column Width option. Next, make column one 3.5 inches, column two 2.5 inches, and the spacing 0.7 inches (see Figure 14.4).

5. Save the document as Ch14.3Say.

 If you don't need to create columns of differing widths, the most efficient way to format a document with up to four columns is to use the Columns button on the Standard toolbar.

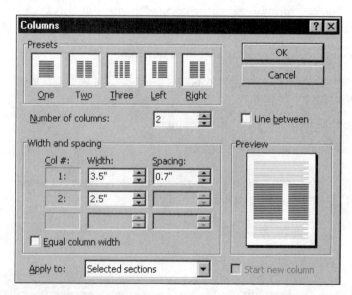

Figure 14.4   The Columns dialog box with the Two Column option selected.

Task 9   *Balancing column length.*

When a document is formatted with columns and some of the columns are longer than others, you can balance the text within the columns by inserting a section break.

1. Open the document Ch14Dog from the disk. Place the cursor at the end of the text in column 2.

2. Click Insert|Break and then click the Continuous Section Break option.

3. The columns are now balanced, as shown in Figure 14.5.

4. Save the document as Ch14.1Dog.

Task 10   *Keeping text in columns together.*

You can keep paragraph text together in columns just as you would in regular text. You can format your entire document or select a certain paragraph to keep together.

1. In any document, select a paragraph that you want to format, or perform the following step with a new document to format all paragraphs.

2. Click the Paragraph command on the Format menu, and then click the Line And Page Breaks tab.

3. Click the Keep Lines Together checkbox to select the option.

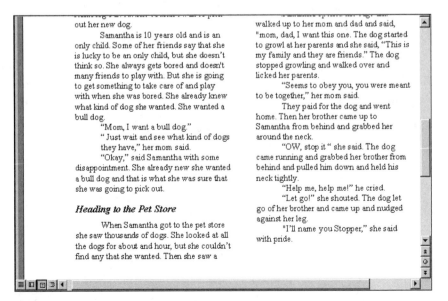

Figure 14.5   Balancing the text between the columns.

Column Breaks

You can insert a column break to force text to display in the next column.

Task 11   Inserting a column break.

1. Open the Ch14Dog document from the disk.

2. Place the cursor in front of the title Heading to the Pet Store.

3. Click Insert|Break and then click the Column Break option.

4. Save the document as Ch14.2Dog.

The heading and following text is now at the top of column 2, as shown in Figure 14.6.

Figure 14.6   Heading is in column 2 after inserting a column break.

Practice Projects

Perform the following projects based on this chapter.

Project 1   Control text.

Open the Ch14.3Office document.

1. Control orphans and widows for the entire document.

2. Keep all lines of the paragraph at the bottom of page 2 and top of page 3 together.

3. Save the document as Ch14.4Office.

Answer to Project 1

To control orphans and widows for the entire document, place the cursor at the beginning of the document, click FormatIParagraph, and then select the Widow/Orphan Control option. Do not select any text prior to checking this option; otherwise, it will only apply to the selected text.

Click the paragraph, click FormatIParagraph, and then select the Keep Lines Together option in the Paragraph dialog box, as shown in Figure 14.7.

Click FileISave As, change the name, click the disk drive from the Save In list box, and then click the Save button. Click the Close button on the document menu bar.

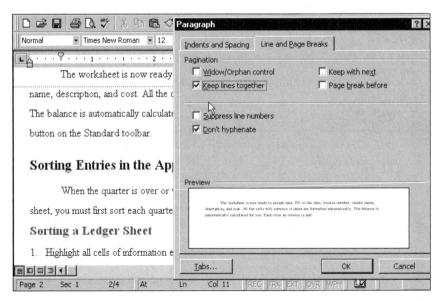

Figure 14.7   Keeping all lines of a paragraph on the same page.

Project 2 Create a header.

Open the Ch14Newsletter document from the disk.

1. Create a header that contains different header information for odd and even pages.

2. Perform the following instructions for the first (odd) document header: insert the date on the left side, type your name in the center, and then type "First Draft" on the right side.

3. Insert the document name on the right side of the second (even) document header.

4. Save the document as Ch14.1Newsletter.

Answer to Project 2

Move the cursor to the first page of the document. Click View|Header and Footer. Click the Page Setup button, and then select the Different Odd And Even option.

Click the Insert Time button, press the Tab key, type your name, press the Tab key, and then type "First Draft" (see Figure 14.8).

Click the Show Next button, press the Tab key twice, and then insert the name of the document (see Figure 14.9).

Click File|Save As, change the name, click the disk drive from the Save In list box, and then click the Save button.

Project 3 Create a footer.

Use the Ch14.1Newsletter document from Project 2 for this project.

1. Create a footer that repeats on every page.

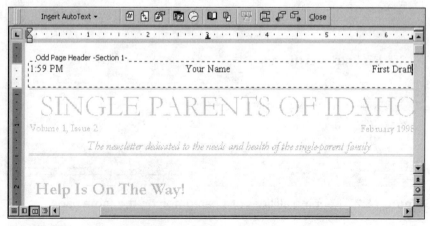

Figure 14.8   The odd-page header.

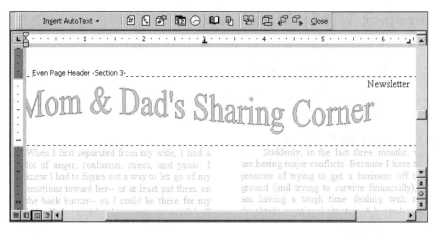

Figure 14.9   The even-page header.

2. Move to the middle of the footer, type the word "Page", and then insert the page number.

3. Save the document as Ch14.2Newsletter.

Answer to Project 3

Move the cursor to the first page of your document, double-click the header, and then click the Switch Between Header And Footer button.

Press the Tab key to move the cursor to the center of the footer, type the word "Page", press the spacebar, and then click the Insert Page Number button (see Figure 14.10). Click the Show Next button, and then click the Same As Previous button.

Click the Save button.

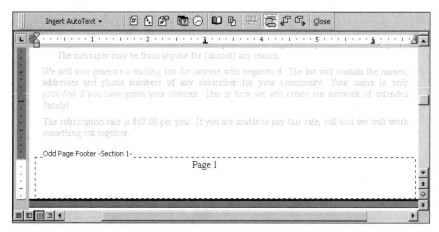

Figure 14.10   The footer contains the page number, which will appear on every page.

Project 4　Modify a header.

Use the Ch14.2Newsletter document from Project 3 for this project.

1. Modify the header on page 1 of your document.

2. Change your name to Cash Concepts and then close the header.

3. Save the document as Ch14.3Newsletter.

Answer to Project 4

Move to page 1 and double-click the header.

Delete your name, type "Cash Concepts", and then click the Close button (see Figure 14.11).

Click the Save button.

Project 5　Format columns.

Open the Ch14Poem document from the disk.

1. Format the title of the poem with one column, center the title, and then format the text with two columns.

2. Balance the column length so that the text is divided evenly between the columns.

3. Save the document as Ch14.1Poem.

Answer to Project 5

Select the title, click the Columns button, select the 1 Column option, and then click the Center button. Place the cursor to the left of the beginning text, click the Columns button, and then select the 2 Columns option (see Figure 14.12).

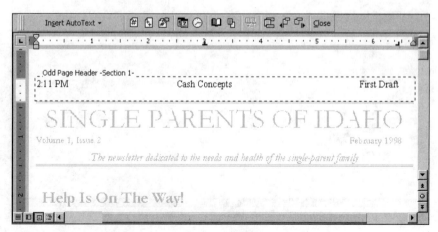

Figure 14.11　The header on page 1 has been modified.

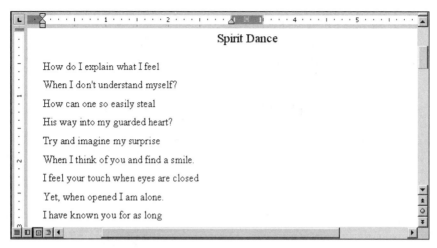

Figure 14.12 The Poem document with two columns.

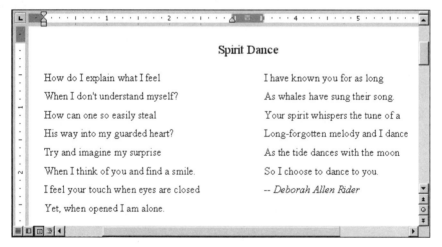

Figure 14.13 The Poem document with the text balanced between columns.

Insert a continuous section break at the end of the text (see Figure 14.13).

Click FilelSave As, change the name, click the disk drive from the Save In list box, and then click the Save button.

Project 6   Change page orientation.

Use the Ch14.1Poem document from Project 5 for this project.

1. Change the page orientation to landscape.

2. Save the document as Ch14.2Poem and close the document.

Answer to Project 6

Click File|Page Setup, click the Paper Size tab, if necessary. Click the Landscape Orientation option, and then verify the Whole Document option is selected in the Apply To list box. Close the dialog box.

Click the Save button, and then click the Close button on the document menu bar.

Need To Know More?

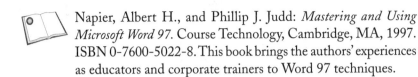 Napier, Albert H., and Phillip J. Judd: *Mastering and Using Microsoft Word 97.* Course Technology, Cambridge, MA, 1997. ISBN 0-7600-5022-8. This book brings the authors' experiences as educators and corporate trainers to Word 97 techniques.

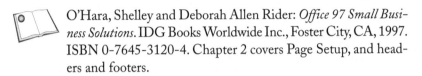 O'Hara, Shelley and Deborah Allen Rider: *Office 97 Small Business Solutions.* IDG Books Worldwide Inc., Foster City, CA, 1997. ISBN 0-7645-3120-4. Chapter 2 covers Page Setup, and headers and footers.

Shelly, Gary, Thomas Cashman, and Misty Vermaat: *Microsoft Word 97 Complete Concepts and Techniques.* Course Technology, Cambridge, MA, 1997. ISBN 0-7895-1338-2. A book in the Shelly-Cashman series. Offers a step-by-step approach to learning beginning and advanced skills in Word 97.

Swanson, Marie L.: *Microsoft Word 97—Illustrated Standard Edition: A Second Course.* Course Technology, Cambridge, MA, 1997. ISBN 0-7600-5141-0. An Illustrated Series book. Covers intermediate through advanced skills.

Zimmerman, Scott and Beverly Zimmerman: *New Perspectives on Microsoft Word 97—Comprehensive.* Course Technology, Cambridge, MA, 1997. ISBN 0-7600-5256-5. Part of the New Perspectives series. Offers case-based, problem-solving approaches to learning Word 97.

Graphics, Watermarks, And Special Characters

Terms you'll need to understand:

√ Graphic

√ Clip art

√ Watermark

√ Metafiles

√ Wrapping text

Skills you'll need to master:

√ Inserting clip art into your document

√ Positioning a graphic

√ Deleting a graphic

√ Wrapping text around a graphic

√ Inserting symbols and special characters

√ Inserting a watermark

√ Positioning a watermark

√ Modifying a watermark

Word 97 offers thousands of clip art images and more than one hundred photo images for your viewing pleasure. You can even add pictures from other sources and view them in the Clip Art Gallery dialog box. Word 97 also has a Web site you can visit where clip art images and photos are available to download to your computer.

Graphics

There are many types of graphics: clip art, pictures, WordArt, drawings, AutoShapes, charts, and more. You can also import graphic images from other programs. The most commonly used type of graphics in most word processing programs is clip art.

 Most clip art objects are *metafiles,* meaning they can be ungrouped and edited. You can ungroup and edit clip art images by selecting the image in your document and then clicking the Ungroup command from the Draw menu on the Drawing toolbar. You can then recolor shapes or sections of the picture independently of the other sections.

Task 1   Inserting and resizing a graphic.

Open the Ch14Dog document from the disk that's included with this book.

1. Place the cursor at the end of the sentence in the fourth paragraph in the first column (it starts with "Samantha is 10 years old"). Then click Insert|Picture|Clip Art.

2. Select any dog clip art or image from the Clip Art or Picture sheets by double-clicking the image.

3. Resize the image by dragging the sizing handles with the mouse, as shown in Figure 15.1.

 You can resize a graphic from its center, which maintains its height and width ratio, by holding down the Ctrl and Shift keys while dragging a corner sizing handle, as shown in Figure 15.1.

4. Save the document as Ch15.1Dog.

HOLD That Skill!

To quickly copy and paste your graphic, select the graphic while holding down the Ctrl key (a small plus sign will appear to the right of the mouse pointer); then drag the mouse and release. Voilà—two graphics with the ease of one.

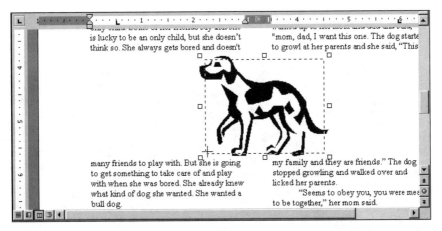

Figure 15.1   Resizing the inserted graphic.

Task 2   *Positioning and formatting a graphic and surrounding text.*

You can position a graphic anywhere on a document...even over text. You can choose to have your text flow around a graphic in several different ways.

1. In the document Ch15.1Dog, click the clip art to select it.

2. Right-click the graphic, and then click the Format Picture command on the shortcut menu.

3. Click the Wrapping tab, and then click the Tight wrapping style option.

4. Click the Both Sides Wrap To option.

5. Select 0.1" in the Left and Right Distance from text spin boxes.

6. Close the dialog box, save the document as Ch15.2Dog, and keep it open for the next task.

The text wraps around the graphic, as shown in Figure 15.2. You can resize or move the graphic, and the text will continue to flow around it.

You can adjust the amount of white space between the graphic and text by adjusting the spin boxes in the Distance From text group.

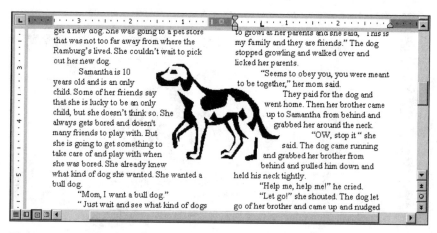

Figure 15.2   The text flows, or *wraps*, around the graphic.

Task 3   *Deleting a graphic.*

1. In the Ch15.2Dog document, click the graphic to select it.

2. Press the Delete key.

3. Close the document *without* saving.

The graphic is gone and the formatting is reversed, as shown in Figure 15.3.

Watermarks

A *watermark* is generally a graphic, WordArt, AutoShape, logo, or drawing that appears behind existing text in your document. A watermark appears lightly

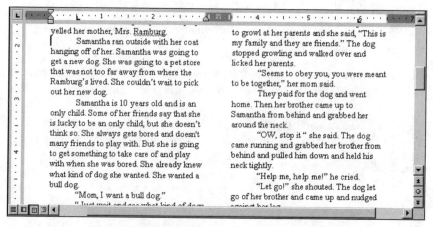

Figure 15.3   The graphic's formatting is reversed, and the document looks as it did before.

in the background of each printed page. You can also use a text box as a watermark to appear beneath your document text. A watermark must initially be placed in the header or footer of your document, but then it can be repositioned anywhere on the document you choose.

HOLD That Skill!

If you insert a watermark into a document with different odd and even headers, the watermark will show only on the pages in which it was placed (that is, either on the odd or even pages).

If you need to have different headers for the odd and even pages in your document, place the watermark on the first odd header *and* the first even header. You can copy and paste the watermark to make this task easier.

Task 4   Inserting a watermark.

Open the Ch14.4Office document that you created in Chapter 14.

1. Move to page 1 of your document, and then double-click the header.

2. Click Insert|Picture|Clip Art.

3. Select an image from the Clip Art or Picture sheet by double-clicking the image.

4. Position the image by dragging it into the body of the document. You can click the Show/Hide Document Text button to hide the text in your document if this is easier for you.

5. Resize the image by dragging the sizing handles with the mouse, as shown in Figure 15.4.

6. Close the header.

7. Save the document as Ch15.1Office, and keep it open for the next task.

You can view the effect of your watermark page by page, or you can click the Print Preview button on the Standard toolbar, as shown in Figure 15.5. If you repeat your watermark on odd and even header sections, you'll need to be certain that you use the Format Picture dialog box to maintain the same horizontal and vertical position as well as the height and width of the watermark (see Task 5).

 To edit your watermark, you must first view your header or footer. You can then select the watermark and modify it.

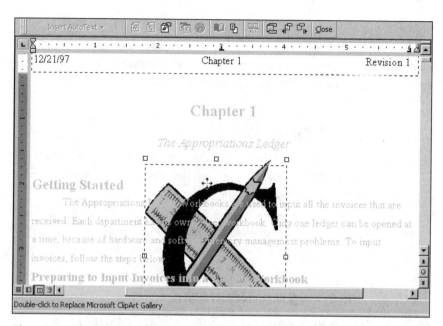

Figure 15.4 Moving and resizing a watermark with the document text visible.

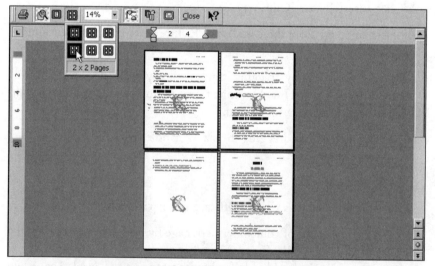

Figure 15.5 Previewing four pages of a document with a watermark on odd and even headers.

Task 5   Formatting a watermark.

In the Ch15.1Office document, use the tabs in the Format Picture dialog box to format the image (see Table 15.1 for each sheet in detail).

1. Double-click the header, right-click the watermark image, and then click the Format Picture command on the shortcut menu.

2. Click the Picture tab (if necessary), click the Color list arrow in the Image Control group, and then click the Watermark option from the list.

3. Click the Wrapping tab, and then click the None option in the Wrapping Style group.

4. Click the Position tab, and then click the Move Object With Text option to deselect it.

Note: If you're inserting a watermark into two headers, note the horizontal and vertical positions on the first header and repeat them on the second.

5. Click the Lock Anchor option, and then verify that the Float Over Text option is selected.

6. Click the Size tab, and then verify that the Lock Aspect Ratio and Relative To Original Picture Size options are checked.

7. Click the OK button and save the document as Ch15.2Office.

Note: If you're inserting a watermark into two headers, note the height and width settings on the first header and repeat them on the second.

Table 15.1   The Format Picture dialog box options.

Sheet	Option	Result
Colors And Lines	Color list box	Creates a background color for the watermark.
	Line list box	Creates a lined border around the watermark.
Size	Height spin box	Adjusts the height of the watermark.
	Width spin box	Adjusts the width of the watermark.
	Height Scale	Adjusts the scale height of the watermark based on the original image.
	Width Scale	Adjusts the scale width of the watermark based on the original image.

(continued)

Table 15.1   The Format Picture dialog box options *(continued)*.

Sheet	Option	Result
	Lock Ratio Aspect	Forces the height and width of the selected object to maintain their proportion to one another.
	Relative To Original Picture Size	Calculates the height and width percentages under Scale, based on the original size of the picture.
Position	Horizontal Position	Determines the amount of space between the left edge of the watermark and the left edge of the page, margin, or column.
	Vertical Position	Determines the amount of space between the top edge of the watermark and the top of the page, margin, or column.
	Move Object With Text	The watermark will move with the paragraph to which it is anchored. Word changes the Horizontal From list box to Column and changes the Vertical From list box to Paragraph.
	Lock Anchor	Anchors the watermark to the page and position to which it has been placed.
	Float Over Text	Takes the watermark out of the text layer and places it in the drawing layer, where it can be moved above or beneath the text.
Wrapping	Wrapping Style	Allows you to select the way text wraps around a picture. Use the None option for a watermark.
	Wrap To	Allows you to further select how the text wraps around the graphic. These options are not available with the None option selected as the wrapping style.
	Distance From Text	Allows you to select the distance between the text and the graphic. These options are not available with the None option selected as the wrapping style.
Picture	Crop From	Determines the amount to crop from the left, right, top, and bottom sides of the watermark. If you enter negative numbers, white space is added to the selected sides.

(continued)

Sheet	Option	Result
	Image Control Color	Determines the color for the image. Automatic keeps the original picture color. Use the Watermark option to select preset brightness and contrast settings that work well for watermarks.
	Image Control Brightness	Allows you to manually change the brightness levels for your watermark. Use either the slide switch or the spin box to adjust the brightness percentages.
	Image Control Contrast	Allows you to manually change the contrast levels for your watermark. Use either the slide switch or the spin box to adjust the contrast percentages.
Text Box	Internal Margin	Allows you to adjust the amount of space you want between the left, right, top, and bottom edges of the selected text box and the text within it.
	Convert To Frame	Converts the selected text box to a Word frame. A frame cannot be used as a watermark.

Table 15.1   **The Format Picture dialog box options *(continued)*.**

Watermarks As Text

Sometimes you will want to add a watermark that is text-based, such as a message that appears beneath the body of a document.

Task 6   *Creating a text watermark.*

Open a new, blank document.

1. Click View|Header and Footer.

2. Click the Drawing button on the Standard toolbar, and then click the Text Box button on the Drawing toolbar.

3. Create a text box on the document, as shown in Figure 15.6.

4. Select the Baskerville Old Style font (or equivalent), select 24 point, 25% Gray text color, and then bold and italics.

5. Enter the following text: "Thanks To Your Business We Are A Success!"

6. Adjust the size of the text box so all the text is visible (see Figure 15.6).

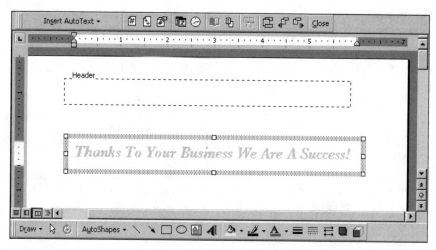

Figure 15.6 Creating a text-based watermark.

7. Right-click the text box border, and then click the Format Text Box option.

   Note: If the Format Text Box option is ghosted, then try clicking the text box border again. When the text box is selected, there is no I-beam blinking inside the text box.

8. Click the Wrapping tab, select the Through option, click the Positions tab, select the Lock anchor checkbox, and then make sure the Move object with text checkbox is not selected.

9. Click the Colors and Lines tab, click the Color list arrow in the Fill group, and then select the None option. Click the Color list arrow in the Line group, select the None option, and then click the OK button.

10. Click the Zoom list arrow on the Standard toolbar, and select the Whole Page option, as shown in Figure 15.7.

11. Center the text box on the page, and then close the Headers and Footers toolbar.

12. Save the document as Ch15TextWatermark, and then close the document.

Special Characters

Special characters can be symbols, such as the ones you use as bullets. They can also be international characters, typographic characters, and symbols such as an arrow or happy face.

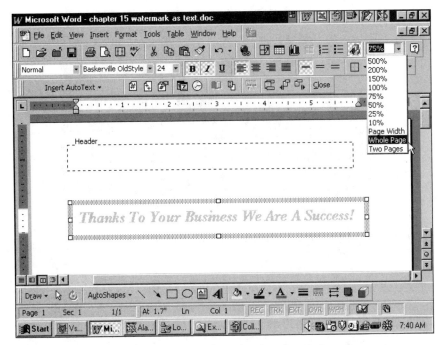

Figure 15.7 Using the Zoom box to display the entire page.

You can insert a character or symbol by typing the character code on the keyboard. Word will automatically add certain symbols, such as when you type two hyphens after a word (--), an *em dash* replaces the hyphens.

Task 7   *Inserting symbols.*

Open the Ch15Designs document from the disk.

1. Place the cursor in front of the first item on the list (Elephant), and then click Insert|Symbol.

2. Click the Symbols tab, if necessary.

3. Click the Font list arrow and select the Animals symbol set. If your computer doesn't have Animals, select another set to use for this task.

4. Select the Elephant symbol, and then click the Insert button (see Figure 15.8).

5. Drag the Symbol dialog box to the right (but don't cover the vertical scroll bar) so you can see the list.

6. Click in front of the next animal in the list, find an appropriate symbol, and then insert it.

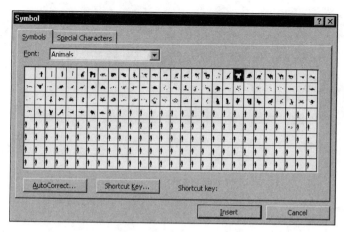

Figure 15.8 The Symbol dialog box with the Animals symbol set selected.

7. Continue inserting animals, and then find another symbol set that best fits the rest of the items in the list, such as Holidays for the Angel and Cupid, and Zapf Dingbats for the Fairy (see Figure 15.9).

8. Close the dialog box when you're finished, resize the symbols to 36 point for the animals and 20 point for the others, and then add color to each one.

9. Insert a line where necessary to create a consistent distance between each item.

10. Select the list and format it into two columns using the Columns button.

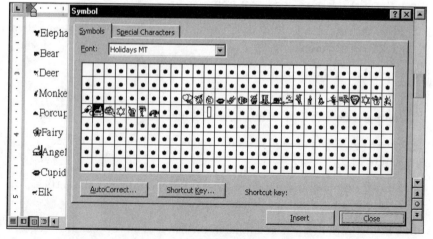

Figure 15.9 Inserting symbols with the dialog box remaining open.

11. Save the document as Ch15.1Designs and close it.

Your document should resemble Figure 15.10.

Task 8   *Inserting typographic symbols.*

Open the Ch15Trademark document from the disk.

1. Click between the words "the" and "symbol" in the first paragraph, click Insert|Symbol, and then click the Special Characters tab.

2. Find the Registered character and insert it, as shown in Figure 15.11. Notice that you can also use the keyboard shortcut Alt+Ctrl, and then R to insert it.

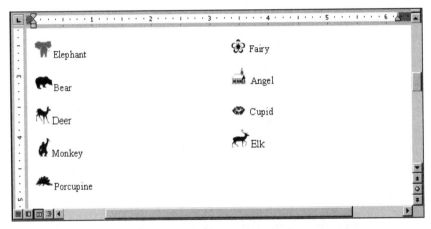

Figure 15.10   The document's list now has formatted symbols.

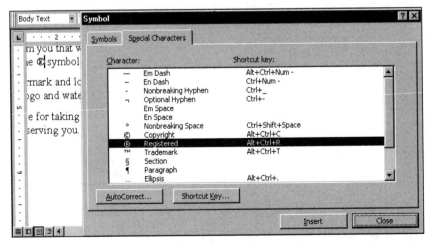

Figure 15.11   Inserting a typographic character into a document.

HOLD That Skill!

You can type (r) to create the Registered symbol and (tm) to create the Trademark symbol. Experiment with different symbols, such as two hyphens and a greater than symbol (-->) to create an arrow (→).

3. Close the dialog box, select the symbol, click the Bold button, and then change the font size to 14 point.

4. Click between the words "the" and "symbol" in the second paragraph, and then press the Alt+Ctrl, and then T key combination.

5. Select the symbol, click the Bold button, and then change the font size to 14 point.

6. Place the cursor in front of the third paragraph, click Insert|Symbol, change to the Symbol font, click the heart, and then click the Shortcut Key button.

7. Press the Alt+H key combination, and then click the Assign button if the shortcut is unassigned (see Figure 15.12).

8. Close both dialog boxes, and then Press the Alt+H keys to insert the heart in front of the third paragraph. Format it as 14 point, bold, and red.

9. Save the document as Ch15.1Trademark and close it.

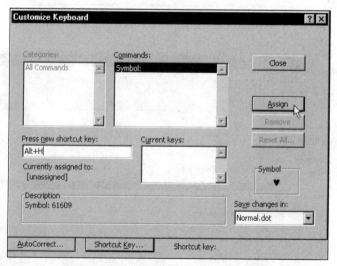

Figure 15.12   Assigning a symbol to your own keyboard shortcut.

You can also create international characters using the keyboard, as shown in Table 15.2.

You can use the nonbreaking space special character to keep two words together. For example, I want the words David Jolly to appear on the same line and not be separated by a soft page break, so I selected the space between the words and pressed Ctrl+Shift+Spacebar.

Now when the words near the end of the line, they will both wrap to the next line.

You can use keyboard shortcuts to enter symbols or special characters. You can also assign your own shortcut to symbols.

Table 15.2	The keyboard shortcuts for creating international characters.
Character	**Keyboard Shortcut**
à, è, ì, ò, ù, À, È, Ì, Ò, Ù	Ctrl+' (accent grave), the letter
á, é, í, ó, ú, ý, Á, É, Í, Ó, Ú, Ý	Ctrl+' (apostrophe), the letter
â, ê, î, ô, û, Â, Ê, Î, Ô, Û	Ctrl+Shift+^ (caret), the letter
ã, ñ, õ, Ã, Ñ, Õ	Ctrl+Shift+~ (tilde), the letter
ä, ë, ï, ö, ü, ÿ, Ä, Ë, Ï, Ö, Ü, Ÿ	Ctrl+Shift+: (colon), the letter
å, Å	Ctrl+Shift+@, the letter
æ, Æ	Ctrl+Shift+&, a or A
œ, Œ	Ctrl+Shift+&, o or O
ç, Ç	Ctrl+, (comma), c or C
ø, Ø	Ctrl+/, o or O
¿ ¡	Alt+Ctrl+Shift+?, Alt+Ctrl+Shift+!
ß	Ctrl+Shift+&, s

Practice Projects

Perform the following projects based on this chapter.

Project 1   Insert and resize a graphic.

Open the Ch14Newsletter document from the disk.

1. Delete the text box that contains the letter W, type a "W" in front of the first word to make it Welcome, and then click in front of the word Welcome.

2. Select and insert a graphic from the Microsoft Clip Gallery, and then resize it to the approximate size of the text box you deleted.

3. Save the document as Ch15.1Newsletter.

Answer to Project 1

Select the text box, press the Delete key, add the W to make the first word Welcome, and then place the cursor in front of the first paragraph.

Display the Microsoft Clip Gallery from the Insert menu, hold down the Ctrl and Shift keys while dragging the lower-right corner sizing handle on the graphic to resize it.

Click File|Save As, change the name, click the disk drive from the Save In list box, and then click the Save button.

Project 2   Format a graphic and surrounding text.

Use the Ch15.1Newsletter document from Project 1 for this project.

1. Wrap the text around your graphic on three sides.

2. Adjust the distance between your graphic and the surrounding text to 0.1" on the top and bottom and 0.2" on the right.

3. Add a semitransparent violet fill and a line border that's 0.75" thick and colored 80% gray.

4. Save the document as Ch15.2Newsletter, and then close the file.

Answer to Project 2

Display the Format Picture dialog box from the shortcut menu, and click the Wrapping tab. Click the Square option in the Wrapping Style group, and then click the Right option in the Wrap To group.

Change the numbers in the Distance From Text group spin boxes to 0.1" for the Top and Bottom options, and 0.2" for the Right option.

Click the Colors and Lines tab, click the Fill Color list box, and select Violet from the color palette. Click the Semitransparent option. Click the Line Color list box, and select the 80% gray color from the color palette. Verify that the line weight is .75 point (change it if necessary). See Figure 15.13.

Click File|Save As, change the name, click the disk drive from the Save In list box, and then click the Save button. Click the Close button on the document menu bar.

Project 3   Insert a watermark.

Open the Ch14.2Poem document that you created in Chapter 14.

1. Create a watermark from a clip art image, and then resize the image from its center, if necessary.

2. Hide the document text and then center the watermark on the page.

3. Save the document as Ch15.1Poem.

Answer to Project 3

View the header on the first page of your document. Insert a clip art image from the Microsoft Clip Gallery on the Insert menu. Resize the image by holding down the Ctrl and Shift keys while dragging a sizing handle with the mouse.

Click the Show/Hide Document Text button, and then drag the watermark to the center of the page.

Click the Save button.

Figure 15.13   The newsletter with a graphic and formatting.

Project 4   Format a watermark.

Use the Ch15.1Poem document you saved in Project 3.

1. Format the watermark as Watermark and adjust the brightness to 90%.

2. Anchor the watermark to the page and make sure it's on the drawing layer.

3. Verify that there is no text wrapping.

4. Close the dialog box by clicking the OK button, and then save the document as Ch15.2Poem.

Answer to Project 4

Display the Format Picture dialog box from the shortcut menu, and click the Watermark option from the Color list box on the Picture sheet. Use either the slide box or spin box to adjust the watermark's brightness.

Deselect the Move Object With Text option, and select the Lock Anchor option on the Position sheet. Verify that the Float Over Text option is selected.

Verify that the None option is selected in the Wrapping Style group on the Wrapping sheet.

The document should resemble Figure 15.14.

Project 5   Create a text watermark.

1. Open a new, blank document, and then create a text watermark that says, "Celebrating our 50th year". Make sure all the text is visible.

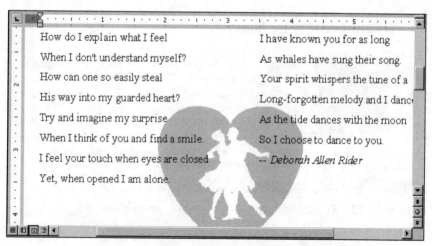

Figure 15.14   The document with a formatted watermark.

2. Center the watermark on the page and then close the document, saving it as Ch15.1WatermarkProject.

Answer to Project 5

Click the New button on the Standard toolbar, click View|Header And Footer, click the Drawing button on the Standard toolbar, click the Text Box button on the Drawing toolbar, and then create a text box on the document. Type, "Celebrating our 50th year!", and adjust the size of the text box so all the text is visible.

Click the Zoom list arrow on the Standard toolbar and select the Whole Page option, center the text box on the page, and then close the Headers And Footers toolbar. Click the Save button on the Standard toolbar, and then save the document as Ch15.2Water-markProject. Close the document.

Project 6   Insert special characters.

1. Open a blank document, and find three different ways to create the registered and trademark symbols.

2. Create a sad face, a thin right arrow, and then place a nonbreaking space between two words.

3. Close the file.

Answer to Project 6

Click the New button on the Standard toolbar. Type "(r)", press Ctrl+Alt+R, and click Insert|Symbol, click the Special Characters tab, and then click the Registered option. Type "(tm)", press Ctrl+Alt+T, and click Insert|Symbol, click the Special Characters tab, and then click the Trademark option.

Type ":(" for the sad face, "<—" for the arrow, and select the space between two words and press Ctrl+Shift+Spacebar.

Click the Close button.

Need To Know More?

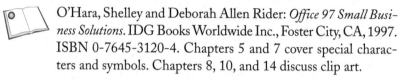 Napier, Albert H. and Phillip J. Judd: *Mastering and Using Microsoft Word 97.* Course Technology, Cambridge, MA, 1997. ISBN 0-7600-5022-8. This book brings the authors' experiences as educators and corporate trainers to Word 97 techniques.

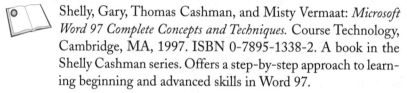 O'Hara, Shelley and Deborah Allen Rider: *Office 97 Small Business Solutions.* IDG Books Worldwide Inc., Foster City, CA, 1997. ISBN 0-7645-3120-4. Chapters 5 and 7 cover special characters and symbols. Chapters 8, 10, and 14 discuss clip art.

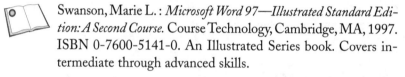 Shelly, Gary, Thomas Cashman, and Misty Vermaat: *Microsoft Word 97 Complete Concepts and Techniques.* Course Technology, Cambridge, MA, 1997. ISBN 0-7895-1338-2. A book in the Shelly Cashman series. Offers a step-by-step approach to learning beginning and advanced skills in Word 97.

Swanson, Marie L.: *Microsoft Word 97—Illustrated Standard Edition: A Second Course.* Course Technology, Cambridge, MA, 1997. ISBN 0-7600-5141-0. An Illustrated Series book. Covers intermediate through advanced skills.

Zimmerman, Scott and Beverly Zimmerman: *New Perspectives on Microsoft Word 97—Comprehensive.* Course Technology, Cambridge, MA, 1997. ISBN 0-7600-5256-5. Part of the New Perspectives series. Offers case-based, problem-solving approaches to learning Word 97.

Worksheets And Charts

16

Terms you'll need to understand:

√ Embed

√ Link

√ Drag and drop

√ Import

√ Datasheet

√ Chart

Skills you'll need to master:

√ Importing a worksheet into a table

√ Embedding a worksheet

√ Modifying a worksheet in Word

√ Performing calculations in a table

√ Updating fields in a worksheet

√ Creating a chart

√ Modifying a chart

Microsoft Word 97 has the ability to import worksheets from Excel as well as to create them right in your document. You can calculate the data you enter, modify the data, and even create a chart from the data. And you thought Word was just another word processor!

One of the most obvious advantages to having the ability to display worksheet data and charts in your document is that you can format and print this data along with your text document. This is especially handy when creating financial forecasts and other business and presentation documents.

Import And Modify A Worksheet

There are four ways to import a worksheet into Word:

➤ Cut and paste allows you to import a static copy of the worksheet data, and it can't be modified. If you change the data once you have imported it into Word, the totals aren't automatically recalculated. Import a worksheet by selecting all the data you want to import from an Excel worksheet, click either the Copy or Cut button, display the Word document, move the cursor to the place where you want to paste the data, and then click the Paste button.

➤ Drag and drop allows you to import a worksheet by dragging selected Excel data to the Microsoft Word button on the taskbar. When the Word document displays, release the mouse button and the data is placed in the document. Drag-and-drop responds like an embedded worksheet when the data is modified. The drag-and-drop method can be used in two ways:

  ➤ Drag the data to the Word button with the left or right mouse button to move or copy the data to Word.

  ➤ Display Excel and Word either tiled or side by side, select the Excel data to import, drag the data to the Word document, and then release the mouse button to drop the data into the document.

➤ Embedding allows you to edit the data by double-clicking the embedded worksheet. The Excel toolbars and menu bar are displayed, and totals will automatically recalculate when the figures are changed. The modified data is not updated in the original Excel worksheet, however. Select the data in the Excel worksheet, click the Copy button, display the Word document, and then click Edit|Paste Special. Click the Paste option, and then click Microsoft Excel Worksheet Object in the As box.

➤ Linking allows you to edit the data by double-clicking the linked worksheet, which displays the original Excel worksheet. When you change the data in a linked worksheet, it's updated in the document as well. Select the data in the Excel worksheet, click the Copy button, display the Word document, and then click Edit|Paste Special. Click the Paste Link option, and then click Microsoft Excel Worksheet Object in the As box.

 If hard disk space is at a premium, use the Link option. A linked file is not an actual copy of the worksheet—it's a pointer to the original worksheet. The Excel worksheet is called the *source* document, and the Word document is called the *destination* document.

Task 1   *Embedding a worksheet in a Word document.*

Open the Excel file Ch16Books from the disk that was included with your book.

1. Open a blank Word document.

2. Click the Excel button on the taskbar to display the Excel worksheet.

3. Select the data, including all the headers and titles.

4. Using the right mouse button, drag the data to the Word button on the taskbar.

   Make sure the mouse pointer is an arrow and not a hollow plus sign; otherwise, you'll get the shortcut menu (see Figure 16.1).

 Sometimes it seems like the Word document won't display, but if you keep the pointer paused over the Word button on the taskbar, the Word document will eventually appear.

5. When the Word document appears, release the mouse button and then select Copy from the shortcut menu to copy the data to the document.

6. Save the file as Ch16.1Books and close the file.

You now have an embedded worksheet in your document that you can modify using Excel's toolbars and menus.

Task 2   *Modifying an embedded worksheet.*

Modifying an embedded worksheet in Word is as simple as modifying it in Excel. You'll be able to recalculate totals, change headers, format numbers, and more.

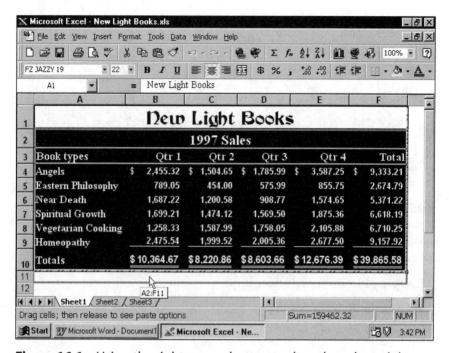

Figure 16.1 Using the right mouse button to drag the selected data to the Word button.

Note: Remember that any changes you make to an embedded worksheet will not be reflected in the original Excel workbook. Only a linked worksheet updates any modifications made to the imported data.

1. Double-click on the Ch16.1Books worksheet. The Word toolbars and menu bar are replaced by Excel's toolbars, formula bar, and menus, as shown in Figure 16.2.

2. Change Eastern Religion to Eastern Philosophy.

3. Change the first quarter total for the Angels book type to $2,895.55.

4. Click anywhere outside the worksheet to deselect it.

5. Save the document as Ch16.2Books and close it.

Notice the Quarter 1 total has changed to include the new figure (see Figure 16.3). Compare the embedded worksheet with the original. The original Excel worksheet has not changed to reflect the changes made to the embedded worksheet.

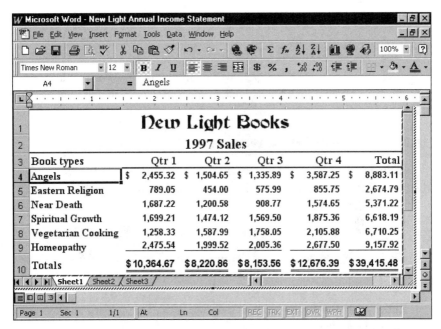

Figure 16.2   Modifying an embedded worksheet displays the Excel menu bar and toolbars.

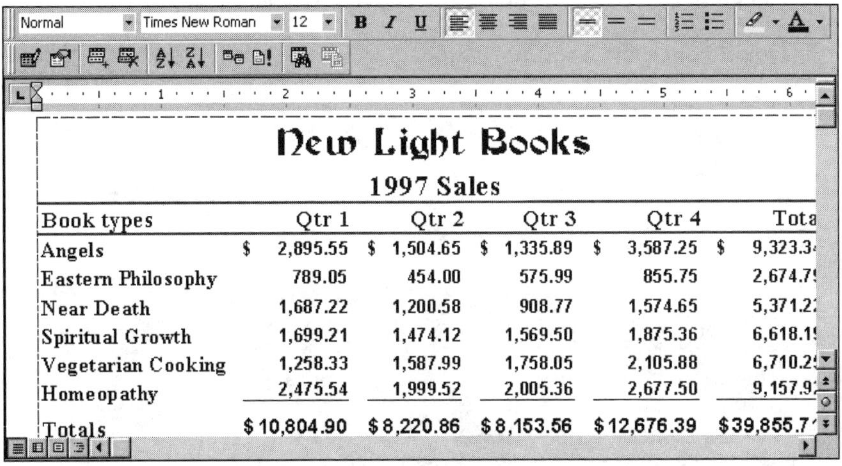

Figure 16.3   Once the embedded worksheet is deselected, the Word menu bar and toolbars are displayed.

Import And Modify A Worksheet In A Word Table

Importing a worksheet into a table will maintain all the Word table formatting. You can update the table data when the source data changes by selecting the Insert Data As Field checkbox in the Database dialog box.

Task 3   Importing a worksheet into a table.

Open a new blank Word document, and use the Ch16Books worksheet from the disk for this next task. With the new Word document active, perform the following steps to import the worksheet data:

1. Display the Excel worksheet, and then select cells A3 through F10.

2. Click the Name box and type "import_range" (see Figure 16.4).

3. Display the new Word document.

4. Right-click any visible toolbar, and then select Database to display the Database toolbar.

5. Click the Insert Database button on the Database toolbar.

6. Click the Get Data button on the Database dialog box.

7. Double-click the workbook name.

Book types	Qtr 1	Qtr 2	Qtr 3	Qtr 4	Total
Angels	$ 2,455.32	$ 1,504.65	$ 1,335.89	$ 3,587.25	$ 8,883.11
Eastern Religion	789.05	454.00	575.99	855.75	2,674.79
Near Death	1,687.22	1,200.58	908.77	1,574.65	5,371.22
Spiritual Growth	1,699.21	1,474.12	1,569.50	1,875.36	6,618.19
Vegetarian Cooking	1,258.33	1,587.99	1,758.05	2,105.88	6,710.25
Homeopathy	2,475.54	1,999.52	2,005.36	2,677.50	9,157.92
Totals	$ 10,364.67	$ 8,220.86	$ 8,153.56	$ 12,676.39	$ 39,415.48

Figure 16.4   Naming the selected worksheet range.

If you cannot see the workbook name in the Open Data Source dialog box, click the Files Of Type list arrow and select either the MS Excel Worksheets or the All Files option.

8. Click the import_range option in the Named Cells Or Range text box of the Microsoft Excel dialog box.

   Note: If you want to merge only certain records, you can use the Query Options button. You'll need to specify your selection criteria. You can filter and sort records as well as select criterion fields.

9. Click the Table AutoFormat button to format the table with fonts, colors, and borders.

   Note: You have a plethora of formatting choices, and you can customize the style further with the formatting options checkboxes. Select the style you prefer and then select or deselect formatting options. Figure 16.5 shows the table of worksheet data with the Columns 3 option. All the formatting checkboxes are selected, in addition to the Last Column and Last Row options in the Apply Special Formats group, which will offset the totals.

10. Click the Insert Data button on the Database dialog box.

11. Verify that the All option is selected, and then check the Insert Data As Field option.

Book types	Qtr 1	Qtr 2	Qtr 3	Qtr 4	Total
Angels	$2,455.32	$1,504.65	$1,335.89	$3,587.25	$8,883.11
Eastern Religion	789.05	454.00	575.99	855.75	2,674.79
Near Death	1,687.22	1,200.58	908.77	1,574.65	5,371.22
Spiritual Growth	1,699.21	1,474.12	1,569.50	1,875.36	6,618.19
Vegetarian Cooking	1,258.33	1,587.99	1,758.05	2,105.88	6,710.25
Homeopathy	2,475.54	1,999.52	2,005.36	2,677.50	9,157.92
Totals	$10,364.67	$8,220.86	$8,153.56	$12,676.39	$39,415.48

Figure 16.5   The Excel data is inserted into a formatted Word table.

If you don't click the Insert Data As Field option, you won't be able to update your table fields when the Excel worksheet changes.

12. Save this document as Ch16.3Books.

You now have a formatted table in your Word document that can be updated if the original worksheet values change.

You can modify a worksheet in many ways. You can change the text and numeric formatting, adjust the height and width of cells, sort, insert formulas, as well as add or delete cells, rows, and columns.

Task 4 Updating fields in a table.

When changes to fields are made in your Excel worksheet, you can update your table fields with the Update Field button on the Database toolbar. Use the Ch16.3Books document you created in Task 3.

1. Open the Ch16Books worksheet from the disk, and change the Angels Qtr 3 total to $1,785.99 and the Eastern Religion book type to Eastern Philosophy.

2. Save and close the worksheet, and then return to your Word document.

3. Click the table anywhere to select it, and then click the Update Field button (see Figure 16.6).

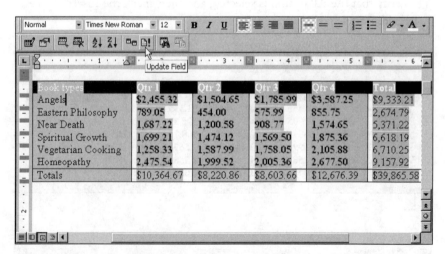

Book types	Qtr 1	Qtr 2	Qtr 3	Qtr 4	Total
Angels	$2,455.32	$1,504.65	$1,785.99	$3,587.25	$9,333.21
Eastern Philosophy	789.05	454.00	575.99	855.75	2,674.79
Near Death	1,687.22	1,200.58	908.77	1,574.65	5,371.22
Spiritual Growth	1,699.21	1,474.12	1,569.50	1,875.36	6,618.19
Vegetarian Cooking	1,258.33	1,587.99	1,758.05	2,105.88	6,710.25
Homeopathy	2,475.54	1,999.52	2,005.36	2,677.50	9,157.92
Totals	$10,364.67	$8,220.86	$8,603.66	$12,676.39	$39,865.58

Figure 16.6 The table fields have been updated.

4. Save the Word document as Ch16.4Books and keep it open for the next task.

 You can also update the fields by pressing the F9 key.

As you can see, the worksheet does not need to be open when you're updating fields.

 Any changes you make to the table, such as adding cells or inserting rows, will be removed when you use the Update Field button if the changes are not on the original worksheet as well.

Task 5   Modifying a worksheet in a table.

The cells of the table are referred to the same way as an Excel worksheet. The first column is column A and the first row is row 1. Therefore, the first cell is cell A1. The table's range is A1:F8, which reads as A1 to F8.

1. Click the Draw Table command on the Table menu. The Tables And Borders toolbar displays, and the mouse pointer resembles a pencil.

 If the toolbar is floating, you can dock it on any side of the screen by dragging it to a side with the mouse. Figure 16.7 shows the toolbar docked at the bottom of the screen.

2. Draw a cell beneath the totals that begins in the Qtr 3 column and ends in the Total column (see Figure 16.7); then draw a vertical line to extend the line separating Qtr 4 from Total (columns E and F), thus splitting the cell in two. Click anywhere on the document to stop the drawing feature.

3. Click in the cell that spans columns D and E and type "Annual Average Sales".

4. Highlight (or select) the entire table.

5. Click the Border Color button on the Tables And Borders toolbar and select a color.

6. Click the Border button list arrow and select the Outside Border option.

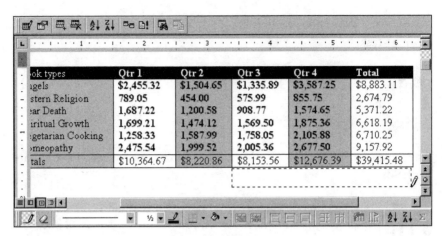

Figure 16.7   Drawing a cell on the table.

7. Move to the ruler on the left side of the screen and widen the Totals row, as shown in Figure 16.8.

> If there is no ruler, switch to Page Layout view.

8. Select all currency fields, and then click the Align Right button on the Formatting toolbar.

9. Select all headings in row 1 and then click the Center button.

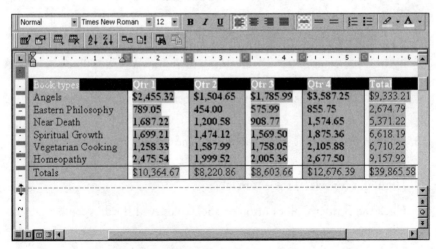

Figure 16.8   Widening a table row.

10. Save the document as Ch16.5Books and keep it open for the next task.

 If your cursor is to the right of the last cell of any row in the table, you can easily insert a new row by pressing the Enter key.

Performing Calculations In A Table

Although you should use Excel for complex table calculations, you can use Word to update field calculations, and to find averages, percentages, totals, and many other types of functions.

Task 6   *Calculating an average.*

You can use the Formula dialog box to create and format a formula for any cell or group of cells in your table. Using the AVERAGE formula can be a simple way to find out how your company's profits are averaging over an entire period, such as a year.

1. Click in the new, empty cell you added beneath the Totals column.

2. Click the Formula command on the Table menu.

3. Delete the SUM(ABOVE) formula but leave the equals sign (=).

   Note: The equals sign tells Word that the next set of commands is a formula.

4. Click the Paste Function list arrow, and then click the AVERAGE function.

5. Type "F2:F7" for the argument (inside the parentheses). This will average all the annual book totals.

6. Click the Number format list arrow and then click the $#,##0.00; ($#,##0.00) format option. This will display your result with the dollar sign, two decimal places, and negative values in parentheses. Close the dialog box.

7. Return to the Word worksheet, and use the Align Right button to align the AVERAGE result.

8. Save the document as Ch16.6Books.

The SUM(ABOVE) function seems to be the only function that gives the desired results on the test, so use cell references for any other function.

Charts

When presenting data, you can use a chart to provide a unique visual interpretation. You can use a chart in Word in three ways:

➤ Create a chart from imported worksheet data

➤ Import an Excel chart

➤ Use Word's datasheet option to create a chart

Importing an Excel chart is the same as importing a worksheet. To add a chart using Word, Microsoft Graph must be installed.

Creating Charts

When a chart is created with Microsoft Graph, Word provides a datasheet with sample data entered. A *datasheet* is a worksheet that Word provides for your chart's data input.

Task 7   Creating a chart from imported data.

You can use Excel data to create a chart by copying the data range in Excel and pasting it to the datasheet in Word. You can also use an embedded Excel worksheet to copy the data, as shown in the following steps:

1. Open the Ch16.1Books document you created in Task 1, double-click the embedded worksheet, and then select the data range to include column and row headings and all data, excluding all totals (range A3:E9).

2. Click the Copy button and deselect the embedded worksheet.

3. Click Insert|Picture|Chart.

4. Click the Select All button on the datasheet (it's the header button in the upper-left corner of the datasheet to the left of the column headers and above the row headers). Press the Delete key. Click in cell A1 of the datasheet, and then click the Paste command on the Edit menu of the Chart Standard toolbar.

5. Close the datasheet and deselect the chart.

6. Save the file as Ch16.7Books and close it.

HOLD That Skill!

Another way to import data is to display the sample chart and datasheet, and then click the Import File button on the Chart toolbar. In order to import only the data fields and header rows, you must type in the range (for example, A3:E9). The named range (for example, import_range) is not recognized in this Import File dialog box.

If you select the Entire Sheet option, you'll need to delete the rows and columns that do not contain chart data from the datasheet, such as titles and totals.

Task 8   *Creating a chart using a Word table.*

Open the Ch16.3Books document you created in Task 3 for this task.

1. Click anywhere in the table to activate it.

2. Click the Select Table command on the Table menu.

3. Click Insert|Picture|Chart. The chart and datasheet appear and include the table data, as shown in Figure 16.9.

4. If there are rows and columns with totals, you'll want to delete them by right-clicking the column or row heading and then clicking the Delete

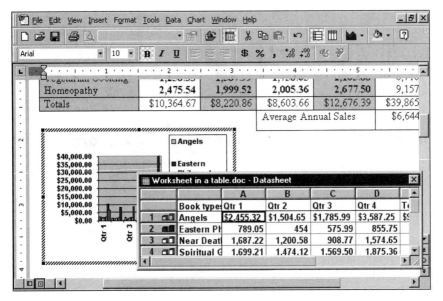

Figure 16.9   The table data is inserted into the datasheet and chart.

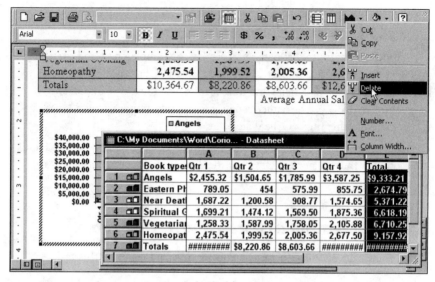

Figure 16.10 Using the shortcut menu to delete a column.

command on the shortcut menu (see Figure 16.10). Delete the Average row, if one exists.

5. Click the View Datasheet button on the Chart toolbar to hide the datasheet, and then click anywhere on the document to deselect the chart.

6. Save the document as Ch16.8Books.

Modifying Chart Elements

Modifying a chart can be accomplished in different ways. You can use menus and the Chart toolbar to modify the chart elements, or you can right-click the chart elements to modify them.

Task 9   Repositioning and enlarging a chart.

Use the Ch16.8Books document you created in Task 8 for this task.

1. Single-click the chart to select it.

2. Drag the chart to the 3" mark on the *vertical* ruler.

3. Double-click the chart to place it in edit mode.

4. Click the View Datasheet button on the Chart toolbar to hide the datasheet.

5. Widen the perimeter of the chart horizontally to the 5-1/2-inch mark and vertically by 3 1/2 inches.

6. Widen the plot area on all four sides, as shown in Figure 16.11.

7. Save the document as Ch16.9Books.

Task 10   Changing the chart type and adding a title.

Use the Ch16.9Books document you created in Task 9 for this task.

1. Click Chart|Options and then click the Titles tab.

2. Type "Annual Sales" in the Chart Title text box.

3. Click the Legend tab, and then click the Show Legend option to deselect the legend.

 You can also right-click the legend to format or remove it.

4. Click the By Column button on the Chart toolbar to view the series by the datasheet columns.

5. Click the Chart Type button list arrow, and change the chart type to a 3-D column chart.

6. Deselect the chart and save the document as Ch16.10Books.

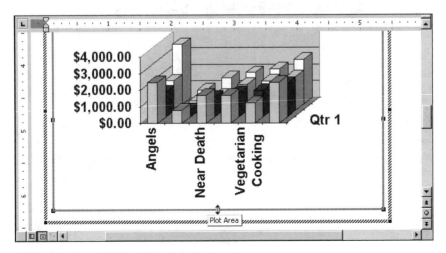

Figure 16.11   Widening the plot area.

Task 11 Modifying the font on the axes and changing the 3-D view.

Use the Ch16.10Books document you created in Task 10 for this task.

1. Select the chart, click the Category axis to select it, and then use the Chart Formatting toolbar to change the font size to 11 point and to angle the text downward.

 To align text, use the Format Axis button and the Alignment tab to angle the text. You can change the angle of the text by using the Degrees spin box, by dragging the red diamond in the Orientation box, or by clicking the Vertical Text box.

2. Click the Value axis and change the font size to 11 point.

3. Click the Series axis and change the font to Times New Roman, point size 11, and bold.

4. Click the 3-D View command on the Chart menu and adjust the chart's angle and rotation for maximum visibility, as shown in Figure 16.12.

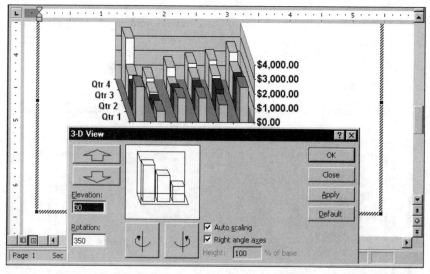

Figure 16.12 Using 3-D View to adjust the chart's angle and rotation.

Practice Projects

Perform the following projects based on this chapter.

Project 1   Import a worksheet in a table.

In Excel, open Ch16Supplies from the disk.

1. Name the range in the worksheet that is to be imported into Word.

2. Import the worksheet into a Word table with font and color formatting. Link it to the worksheet so that it will reflect changes.

3. Change the original worksheet and save it. Update the Word table to reflect the changes.

4. Save the file as Ch16Project1.

Answer to Project 1

Select the header row and columns to be imported (A3:G12). Click the Name box and type a range name.

Open a new Word document, display the Database toolbar, and then click the Insert Database button to begin the import. Select the workbook that contains the worksheet, and then select the range. Select a format style in the Table AutoFormat dialog box. Click the Insert Data As Field option.

Open the original worksheet and make changes. Save the worksheet. Return to the Word table document, click the table to activate it (if necessary), and then click the Update Field button.

Click File|Save As, change the name, choose the folder where you want to save the file, and then click the Save button.

Project 2   Perform tabular calculations.

Open the file Ch16.6Books that you created in Task 6.

1. Insert a row in the middle of the table. Name the row header "Fantasy", enter zero for the first three quarters, and then enter 455.01 in Quarter 4.

2. Find the total for the row Fantasy, maintaining the same format as the rest of the column data. Find the new total for the Qtr 4 and Total columns. Format their results with two decimal places to the right, a comma, a dollar sign, and negative values in parentheses.

3. Delete the Average Sales total, and then find the average with the new row. Format the result as you did in step 2.

4. Save the document as Ch16Project2.

Answer to Project 2

Place the cursor to the right of the last cell directly above the new row placement (see Figure 16.13). Press the Enter key and then add the name and figures to each column.

Place the cursor in the Total cell for the new row, and then click the Formula command on the Table menu. Type "=SUM(A5:B5)" in the Formula text box, and then click the #,##0.00 option in the Number Format list box. Delete the Qtr 4 cell in E9, and use the Formula dialog box to find the sum of cells E2:E8, formatting it with the $#,##0.00; ($#,##0.00) option. Delete the Totals cell in F9, and use the Formula dialog box to find the sum of cells F2:F8, formatting it with the $#,##0.00;($#,##0.00) option.

 You can use the =SUM(LEFT) or the =SUM(ABOVE) formula in place of the cell references. Be aware, however, that these functions do not always provide the desired results within the test. Cell references are more accurate.

Delete the Average Sales cell in F10, and then use the Formula dialog box to find the average of cells F2:F8, formatting it with the $#,##0.00;($#,##0.00) option.

Click FilelSave As, change the name, choose the folder where you want to save the file, and then click the Save button.

Project 3   Create a chart from imported data.

Use the Excel file Ch16Supplies from the disk.

1. Create a chart in a new document using the Import File button, charting only the columns Qtr 1 through Qtr 3. Widen the chart to the 6" mark and lengthen it to the 4" mark.

2. Format the legend to appear on the right, in a regular 9-point Times New Roman font.

3. Format the Value axis to currency with a bold 10-point Arial font.

4. Format the Category axis with a bold 12-point Times New Roman font.

5. Type "Quarterly Sales" for the chart title and "1997" for the Category axis. Resize the Category axis title to 14 points, and

	Qtr 1	Qtr 2	Qtr 3	Qtr 4	Total
	$2,455.32	$1,504.65	$1,785.99	$3,587.25	$9,333.21
phy	789.05	454.00	575.99	855.75	2,674.79
	1,687.22	1,200.58	908.77	1,574.65	5,371.22

Figure 16.13 The cursor placed to the right of the last cell for adding a row.

move the title down toward the bottom of the chart. Resize the Title axis title to 18 points, and move the title up toward the top of the chart.

6. Save the file as Ch16Project2 and then close it.

Answer to Project 3

Open the Excel file Ch16Supplies, note the import range, and then close Excel. Click Insert|Picture|Chart to display the sample chart and datasheet, click the Select All button on the datasheet, press the Delete key, click in the cell above row 1 and to the left of column A, and then click the Import File button on the Chart toolbar. Double-click the Excel file Ch16Supplies on the disk that was included with your book. Type the import range (B3:E12). When the data is displayed in the datasheet (see Figure 16.14), verify that the By Row button is selected, and then click the View Datasheet button to hide the datasheet. Drag the right side of the chart to the 6" mark, and then drag the bottom of the chart to the 4" mark.

Right-click the legend and then click the Format Legend command. Click the Font tab, and select Times New Roman in the Font list box, Regular in the Style box, and 9 in the Font Size box. Close the dialog box.

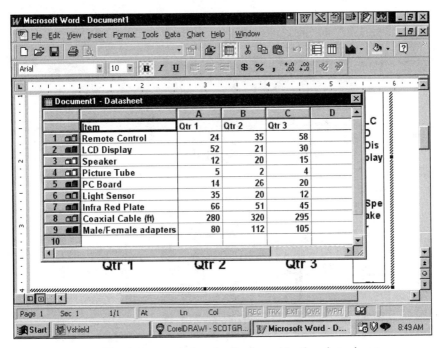

Figure 16.14   The imported data is displayed in the datasheet.

Right-click the Value axis, click the Format Axis command, click the Number tab, and then select Currency from the Category list. Click the Font tab, verify that Arial is selected in the Font list box, select Bold in the Style box, and then select 10 in the Font Size box.

Right-click the Category axis, click the Format Axis command, click the Font tab, and select Times New Roman in the Font list box, Bold in the Style box, and then 12 in the Font Size box.

Click Chart|Chart Options and then click the Titles tab, if necessary. Type "Quarterly Sales" in the Chart Title text box, and then type "1997" in the Category (x) axis text box. Close the dialog box. With the 1997 title still selected, click the Font Size list box and then click 14. Drag the title down with the mouse. Click the Quarterly Sales title to select it, click the Font Size list box, and then click 18. Drag the title up with the mouse.

Click File|Save As, change the name, choose the folder where you want to save the file, and then click the Save button.

Your chart should resemble Figure 16.15.

Project 4   Create a chart from embedded data.

Use the document Ch16.1Books for this project.

1. Create a chart at the 2" mark on the vertical ruler using only the Item and Total Sales columns.

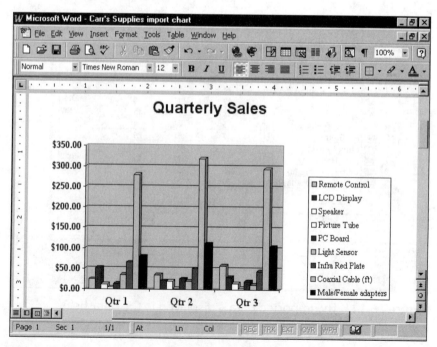

Figure 16.15   A chart that has been created from imported data.

2. Widen the chart to the 5" mark on the horizontal ruler and lengthen it to the 5" mark on the vertical ruler.

3. Delete the legend, view the chart by columns, and enlarge the plot area.

4. Format the Category axis with the headings on a -45 degree angle. Format the font as a regular 10-point Times New Roman font.

5. Scale the Value axis with a 750 major unit scale. Format the font as a regular 10-point Times New Roman font.

6. Format each data series with a different color and with a gradient vertical shading fill effect.

7. Deselect the chart and then save the file as Ch16Project4. Close the file.

Answer to Project 4

Double-click the embedded worksheet. Select the data range to include column and row headings and all data, excluding the row of totals (range A1:F7). Click the Copy button, click outside the worksheet to deselect it, and then place the cursor at the 2" mark on the vertical ruler. Click Insert|Picture|Chart, click the Select All button, press the Delete key, and then click in the cell up and to the left of cell A1 of the datasheet. Click the Paste button, select columns A through D, right-click, and then click the Delete command.

Click the View Datasheet button to hide the datasheet. Drag the right side of the chart to the 5" mark, and then drag the bottom of the chart to the 5" mark.

Double-click the legend and then click the Clear command. Click the By Columns button. Click the plot area of the chart, and drag the boundaries to widen and lengthen the plot area.

Right-click the Category axis, click the Format Axis command, click the Font tab, and select Times New Roman in the Font list box, Regular in the Style box, and then 10 in the Font Size box. Click the Alignment tab, and then select a –45 degree angle in the Orientation group.

Right-click the Value axis, click the Format Axis command, click the Number tab, and then select Currency from the Category list. Click the Font tab, select Times New Roman in the Font list box, select Regular in the Style box, and then select 10 in the Font Size box. Click the Scale tab and type "750" in the Major Unit box.

Click one of the data series bars twice (don't double-click), right-click the bar, and then click the Format Data Point command. Click the Patterns tab and then click the Fill Effects button. On the Gradient tab, click the Color list arrow, select a color, and then click the Vertical shading style.

Click anywhere outside of the chart to deselect it and then click File|Save As, change the file name, and then click the Save button.

Your completed chart should resemble Figure 16.16.

Project 5 Create a chart from a table.

Use the Ch16.3Books document from Task 3.

1. Chart the data in columns A through E, excluding the Totals row.
2. Save the file as Ch16Project5.

Answer to Project 5

Open Ch16.3Books, and then drag the mouse across columns A through E, as shown in Figure 16.17. Click Insert|Picture|Chart. Right-click row 7 on the datasheet, and then click the Delete command.

Click File|Save As, change the name, choose the folder where you want to save the file, and then click the Save button.

Project 6 Modify a chart.

Use the Ch16Project5 file you created for Project 5 in the following steps:

1. Move the chart down the page one inch, remove the legend, and increase the length and width of the chart by 2" each.

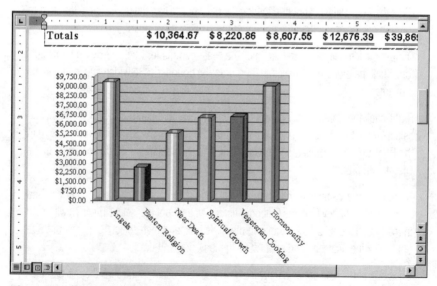

Figure 16.16 The chart's data series have gradient fill effects, and the headers display below each bar.

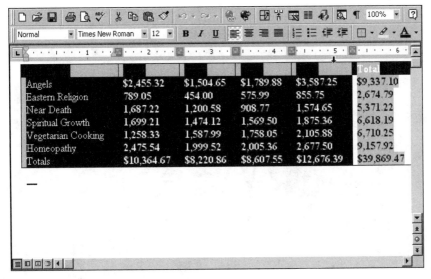

					Total
Angels	$2,455.32	$1,504.65	$1,789.88	$3,587.25	$9,337.10
Eastern Religion	789.05	454.00	575.99	855.75	2,674.79
Near Death	1,687.22	1,200.58	908.77	1,574.65	5,371.22
Spiritual Growth	1,699.21	1,474.12	1,569.50	1,875.36	6,618.19
Vegetarian Cooking	1,258.33	1,587.99	1,758.05	2,105.88	6,710.25
Homeopathy	2,475.54	1,999.52	2,005.36	2,677.50	9,157.92
Totals	$10,364.67	$8,220.86	$8,607.55	$12,676.39	$39,869.47

Figure 16.17   Selecting columns in a table.

2. Add the title "Sales Analysis" to the chart, change the font to Century Schoolbook (or a similar font), and then change the point size to 19.

3. Change the chart type to a 3-D Pyramid chart, and then change the angle and rotation of the chart until all chart elements are visible.

4. Change the Value axis font to a bold, 10-point Arial font, the Category axis to a 10-point Times New Roman font with a -45 degree angle, and the Series axis to a 10-point Times New Roman font with a -30 degree angle.

5. Save the file as Ch16Project6 and close the file.

Answer to Project 6

Single-click the chart to select it. Drag the chart down 1" on the vertical ruler. Double-click the chart. Right-click the legend and then click the Clear command. Widen the perimeter of the chart horizontally and vertically by 2".

Click ChartIChart Options and then click the Titles tab. Type "Sales Analysis" in the Chart Title text box. Close the dialog box and with the title still selected, click the Format Chart Title button on the Chart toolbar. Click the Font tab, select Century Schoolbook or a similar font in the Font list box, and then select 19 in the Font Size box.

Click the Chart Type button list arrow, and then select the 3-D Pyramid Chart option.

Click ChartI3-D View and adjust the chart's elevation to 27 and the rotation to 284. (See Figure 16.18 for the completed chart.)

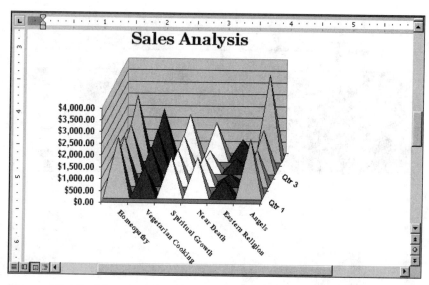

Figure 16.18 The completed pyramid chart with three axes.

Click File|Save As, change the name, choose the folder where you want to save the file, and then click the Save button.

Need To Know More?

Napier, Albert H. and Phillip J. Judd: *Mastering and Using Microsoft Word 97*. Course Technology, Cambridge, MA, 1997. ISBN 0-7600-5022-8. This book brings the authors' experiences as educators and corporate trainers to Word 97 techniques.

O'Hara, Shelley and Deborah Allen Rider: *Office 97 Small Business Solutions*. IDG Books Worldwide Inc., Foster City, CA, 1997. ISBN 0-7645-3120-4. Chapters 5 through 7 offer basic to intermediate techniques for creating a letterhead, mail merge, fax cover sheet, and more.

Shelly, Gary, Thomas Cashman, and Misty Vermaat: *Microsoft Word 97 Complete Concepts and Techniques*. Course Technology, Cambridge, MA, 1997. ISBN 0-7895-1338-2. A book in the Shelly Cashman series. Offers a step-by-step approach to learning beginning and advanced skills in Word 97.

Swanson, Marie L: *Microsoft Word 97—Illustrated Standard Edition: A Second Course*. Course Technology, Cambridge, MA, 1997. ISBN 0-7600-5141-0. An Illustrated Series book. Covers intermediate through advanced skills.

Zimmerman, Scott and Beverly Zimmerman: *New Perspectives on Microsoft Word 97—Comprehensive*. Course Technology, Cambridge, MA, 1997. ISBN 0-7600-5256-5. Part of the New Perspectives series. Offers case-based, problem-solving approaches to learning Word 97.

Reference Material

Terms you'll need to understand:

√ Footnotes and endnotes

√ Note reference mark

√ Heading styles

√ Table of contents

√ Styles

√ Index

√ Cross-reference

√ Bookmarks

Skills you'll need to master:

√ Working with footnotes and endnotes

√ Applying styles to headings

√ Creating a table of contents

√ Creating an index

√ Using a cross-reference

√ Inserting a bookmark

Reference material is any text or documentation that clarifies, explains, directs, or gives credit to specific text in your document. For example, footnotes and endnotes usually credit (name) the originating author or work. A table of contents, index, and cross-reference direct the reader to specific areas of the document. It may seem complicated to create reference material for your document, but with Word it's as easy as putting on your shoes.

Footnotes And Endnotes

Footnotes and endnotes provide a reference for text in your document. They can be considered a comment or explanation of the referenced text. You can use both footnotes and endnotes within the same document. Footnotes typically appear at the bottom of the page that contains the text reference, whereas endnotes generally appear at the end of the document.

A footnote or an endnote contains a note reference mark that appears as a superscript character next to the referenced text as well as the note text, which appears separately at the bottom of a page or at the end of the document.

You'll be using the file Ch17Handbook from the disk that was included with your book for all the tasks in this chapter.

Task 1   Inserting a footnote.

1. Click to the right of the text "equal opportunity employer" in the first sentence on page 1, as shown in Figure 17.1.

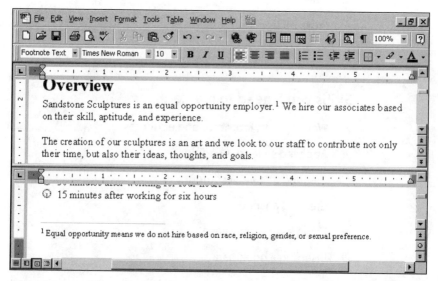

Figure 17.1   The split pane shows the noted sentence and its footnote.

2. Click Insert|Footnote and then select the Footnote option in the Footnote And Endnote dialog box. Verify that the AutoNumber option is selected, and then click the OK button.

3. Type "Equal opportunity means we do not hire based on race, religion, gender, or sexual preference" in the Footnote pane at the bottom of the document. Next, right-click the footnote and then click the Go To Footnote command to return to your sentence in the document.

HOLD That Skill!

The AutoNumber option will automatically renumber your footnotes if you move, add, or delete a footnote from the document.

The note reference mark and the note text are linked. You can place the cursor in front of the reference mark in the document text or the Note pane, and then double-click to move between them. In order to move between a footnote and the note text by double-clicking, you must be in Page Layout view.

4. Rest your mouse pointer on the reference mark in the document, and the footnote will display like a ScreenTip.

5. Double-click the reference mark, and you are taken to the footnote for viewing or editing.

6. Type the footnote "As defined in the 1996 OSHA Guidelines for Employee/Employer Relations, page 251, § 2 ¶ 15." for the "Harassment" heading on page 4.

Remember, you can leave the Symbol dialog box open and continue working in the document if you need to insert more than one special character.

7. Type the footnote "www.SandstoneSculptures.net was established 12/28/97." for the sentence "We are making incredible leaps into the future with our ability to sell our products on the Internet." on page 5.

If Word uses AutoFormat to format your text (such as a Web site as a hyperlink), you can reverse the formatting by clicking the Undo button once.

Task 2   Inserting an endnote.

Inserting an endnote is like inserting a footnote:

1. Click to the right of the heading "Breaks" on page 2.

2. Click Insert|Footnote and then click the Endnote option in the Foot-note And Endnote dialog box.

3. Verify that the AutoNumber option is selected.

   Note: Notice that the AutoNumber sequence has changed from 1, 2, 3, to I, II, III, for endnotes.

 As with footnotes, the AutoNumber option will automatically re-number your endnotes if you move, add, or delete an endnote from the document.

4. Click the Options button to display the Note Options dialog box, as shown in Figure 17.2.

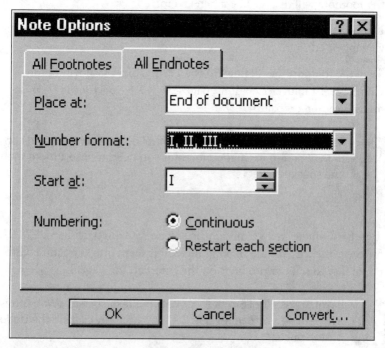

Figure 17.2   The numbering option is changed to I, II, III.

5. Click the Number Format list arrow and select the I, II, III numbering option.

6. Type "Exceeds OSHA standards" in the Endnote pane at the end of your document.

7. Place your cursor one line above the note pane, and press Ctrl+Enter to insert a page break and place the endnotes on their own page.

 Remember, the note reference mark and the note text are linked. You can place the cursor in front of the reference mark in the document text or the Note pane, and then double-click to move between them. To move between a footnote and the note text by double-clicking, you must be in Page Layout view.

8. Rest your mouse pointer on the reference mark in the document, and the endnote will display like a ScreenTip.

9. Double-click the reference mark, and you are taken to the endnote for viewing or editing.

Revising Footnotes And Endnotes

You can move, insert, delete, and copy footnotes and endnotes. You can also convert a footnote into an endnote, and vice versa.

Task 3   *Converting a footnote to an endnote.*

To view all your footnotes, you must be in Normal view.

1. Click View|Footnotes, right-click the second footnote, and then click the Convert To Endnote command on the shortcut menu, as shown in Figure 17.3.

   Note: Notice how the footnotes have renumbered themselves to accommodate for the change.

2. Click the Footnotes list arrow and select the All Endnotes option. The converted endnote is placed in the correct order according to its location in the document.

 You can click the Convert button on the Note Options dialog box to convert all footnotes to endnotes, and vice versa.

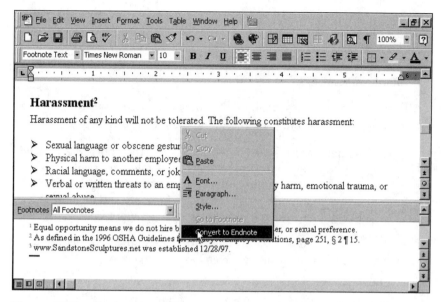

Figure 17.3 Converting a footnote to an endnote.

3. Click the Close button on the Note pane to return to normal editing mode.

Task 4 Copying a footnote or endnote.

1. Select the note reference mark in your document that you want to copy and then click the Copy button.

   Note: Do not select the footnote or endnote text in the Note pane.

2. Place the cursor to the right of the text that you want noted and then click the Paste button.

3. Display the Note pane. Notice that the new note is placed within the existing notes.

 You can copy a note reference mark by selecting the mark and holding down the Ctrl key while dragging it to the new location. This method isn't efficient if you're copying to a different page.

Task 5 Moving a footnote or endnote.

1. Select the note reference mark in your document for the "Harassment" heading on page 4 and then click the Cut button.

   Note: Do not select the footnote or endnote text in the Note pane.

2. Place the cursor to the right of the "Types of Harassment" heading and then click the Paste button.

3. Display the Note pane and notice the moved note's location.

You can move a note reference mark by selecting the mark and dragging it to the new location. This method isn't efficient if you're moving it to a different page.

Task 6   Deleting a footnote or endnote.

Deleting a footnote or endnote is as easy as 1, 2, 3. Actually, it's as easy as 1, as shown in the following step:

1. Select the note reference mark you want to delete and then press the Delete key.

   Note: Do not select the footnote or endnote text in the Note pane.

Save the document as Ch17.1Handbook and close it.

Table Of Contents

A table of contents appears at the beginning of a document; it lists the headings of each chapter and any sections within each chapter and their corresponding page numbers. Before you can create a table of contents, you must apply heading styles to the headings.

Another way to apply heading styles is by applying outline level heads, which consist of paragraph formats you can use to assign levels 1 through 9 to paragraphs in your document. You can also create a table of contents using your own custom headings.

Task 7   Applying built-in heading styles.

Word has nine different built-in heading styles, labeled Heading 1 through Heading 9. Heading 1 can be used for the chapter title or the first major heading in your document.

1. Open the file Ch17Draft from the disk that was included with your book.

2. Select the first major heading, labeled "Section 1." Click the Style list arrow and select the Heading 1 style, as shown in Figure 17.4.

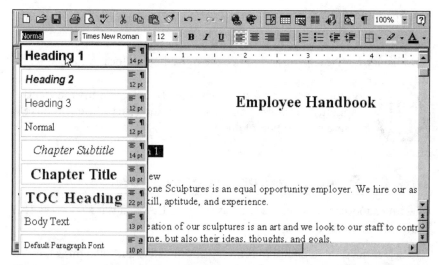

Figure 17.4 Applying the Heading 1 style to the first major heading.

3. Move to the first subheading under Section 1, labeled "Overview," and apply the Heading 2 style from the Style list box.

4. Scroll the document and format the following headings with the Heading 2 style: "Dress Regulations," "Breaks," "Hours/Overtime/Flex Time," "Sick Leave/Vacation," and "Harassment."

5. Scroll to the heading "Sick Leave/Vacation," and apply the Heading 3 style to the "Accrual" and "Usage" subheadings.

6. Scroll to the heading "Harassment," and apply the Heading 3 style to the "Types of Harassment" subheading.

Task 8   Adding a style to the Style list box.

When you click the Style list box, only three built-in headings appear. In order to apply the built-in Heading 4 style, you must add it to the list.

1. Select the "Verbal" subheading under "Types of Harassment" and then click Format|Style.

2. Click the List box list arrow in the Style dialog box, and then click the All Styles option, as shown in Figure 17.5.

3. Scroll to the Heading 4 option in the Style list box and then click the Apply button.

4. Apply the Heading 4 style to the subheadings "Sexual" and "Physical."

5. Save the file as Ch17.1Draft.

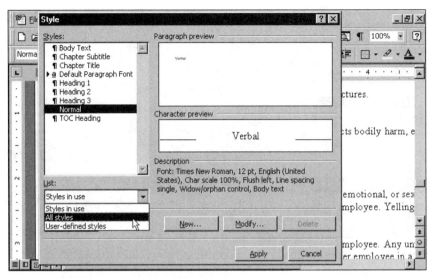

Figure 17.5   Selecting the All Styles option in the List box.

Task 9   Creating a table of contents using built-in heading styles.

Use the document Ch17.1Draft from Task 8 for this task.

1. Place the cursor in front of the "Section 1" heading on page 1, and press Ctrl+Enter to insert a page break.

2. Click to the right of "Employee Handbook" on page 1 and add two blank lines. Don't worry about the style.

3. Click Insert|Index And Tables, and then click the Table of Contents tab.

4. Click the Distinctive design in the Formats list box.

5. Select .... (dotted lines) in the Tab Leader option, show four heading levels, and verify that the Show Page Numbers and Right Align Page Numbers boxes are checked (see Figure 17.6). Click the OK button.

You now have a table of contents that was relatively painless to create. Save the document as Ch17.2Draft and close it.

Task 10   Creating a table of contents using custom heading styles.

You can use heading styles that you have already created in your document to design your table of contents. Use the document Ch17.1Handbook for this task.

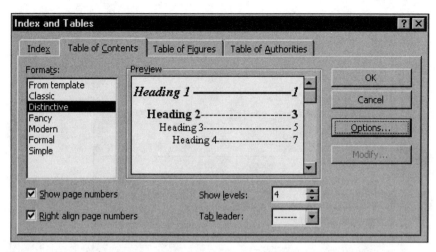

Figure 17.6 Creating a table of contents using built-in headings.

1. Place the cursor in front of the "Section 1" heading on page 1, and press Ctrl+Enter to insert a page break.

2. Click to the right of "Employee Handbook" on page 1 and add two blank lines. Don't worry about the style.

3. Click Insert|Index And Tables, and then click the Table of Contents tab.

4. Click the Options button.

5. Scroll down the Available Styles window, and make sure the Section Title heading has a 1 in the TOC level box.

6. Type a "2" in the TOC level box for Heading 1, a "3" for Heading 2, and a "4" for Heading 3. You can delete the numbers for headings 4 through 9, but it's not essential (see Figure 17.7).

7. Close the Table Of Contents Options dialog box, and then click the Classic design in the Formats list box.

8. Select the .... (dotted lines) in the Tab Leader option, and verify that the Show Page Numbers and Right Align Page Numbers boxes are checked.

Note: When you select custom styles from the Table of Contents Options dialog box, the number of levels is already determined, so the Show Levels box disappears.

9. Save the document as Ch17.2Handbook.

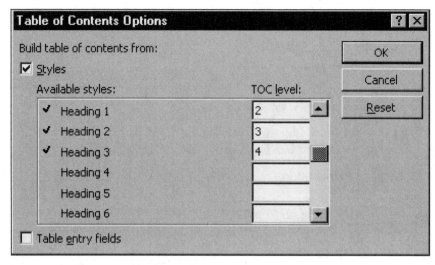

Figure 17.7   The Table Of Contents Options dialog box.

HOLD That Skill!

An easy way to add a new style to the Style list box is to add formatting to selected text and then name it in the Style list box.

Here's an example: Select the words "Employee Handbook on page 1". Apply the following formatting from the Font dialog box: Century Schoolbook BT font (or a similar font), 30 points, Bold, Engraved, Dark Red, and expand the characters by 1 point. Click the Center button. Then click the Style list box and type "Handbook Title". Press the Enter key.

Index

An index generally appears at the end of a document; it lists words and/or phrases in a document, including the page numbers where they appear.

Before you can create the index, you'll need to mark the entries—that is, words and phrases—you want to include. When compiling the index, Word will sort the index entries alphabetically, remove any duplicate entries, and include the page numbers of the entries.

Task 11   Marking entries for an index.

Use the document Ch17.2Handbook for this task.

1. Click Insert|Index And Tables, and then click the Index tab.

2. Click the Mark Entry button.

   Note: The Mark Index Entry dialog box displays and will remain open until you mark all your entries and close the dialog box.

3. Select the heading "Overview" on page 2.

4. Click in the Mark Index Entry dialog box to activate it. The selected text appears in the Main Entry dialog box, as shown in Figure 17.8.

5. Click the Mark button.

   Note: If you want all occurrences of a word or phrase marked, you can click the Mark All button once the text is inserted into the Main Entry box.

6. Select the text "equal opportunity employer" in the first sentence, click the Mark Index Entry dialog box, and then click the Mark button.

7. Scroll the document and mark the "Dress Regulations" heading.

8. Mark the "Breaks" heading, click in the Subentry text box, type "Eight hour day", and then click the Mark button. Type "Six hour day" in the Subentry text box, click Mark, type "Four hour day" in the Subentry text box, and then click Mark.

9. Mark the "Hours/Overtime/Flex Time" heading, select the word "Overtime" in the same heading, click Mark, and then select "Flex Time" and click Mark.

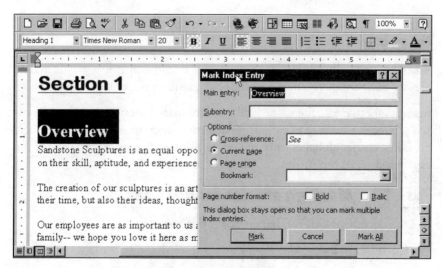

Figure 17.8   Selecting entries for the index.

Be sure to select the heading text and not the marked text when selecting multiple entries in the same heading. Marked text is surrounded in brackets (see Figure 17.9).

10. Mark the "Sick Leave/Vacation" heading.

11. Mark "Sick Leave" and then add "Accrual" and "Usage" as subentries. Repeat this for "Vacation."

12. Mark the "Harassment" heading and then mark "Types of Harassment" as a subentry.

13. Mark "Company Financial Overview" and then close the dialog box. Keep the document open for the next task.

Task 12   Creating the index.

1. Move to the last page of the document below the chart (remember you won't see charts or headers in Normal view), and press Ctrl+Enter to insert a page break.

2. Click the new blank last page.

3. Click Insert|Index And Tables, and then click the Index tab.

4. Click the Fancy design in the Formats list box.

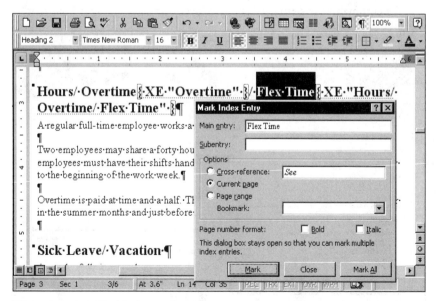

Figure 17.9   Marking text for separate index entries.

5. Click the Right Align Page Numbers box to select it, and then select the ...... (dotted lines) Tab Leader option.

6. Click the OK button to create the index and save the document as Ch17.3Handbook.

You can insert a heading for the index by clicking the index to select it, adding lines, and then typing a heading (see Figure 17.10).

You can also use a concordance file to automark all your entries. A *concordance file* is an index file that contains a column that lists the document text you want to index and a second column that lists the index entries that will be used to create the index from the text in the first column.

Cross-Reference

You can add a cross-reference to your index in two ways. One way is to add it while you're marking your text entries for your index, and the other is to use the Cross-reference dialog box to add all your cross-references at once. The latter option will also allow you to place a cross-reference anywhere in your document.

Task 13   *Inserting a cross-reference.*

Use the document Ch17.3Handbook for this task.

1. Scroll to the "Breaks" heading, and place the cursor between the "y" and the comma in the sentence "For employees working an eight hour day,".

2. Press the spacebar, type "(see also", and then click Insert|Cross-reference.

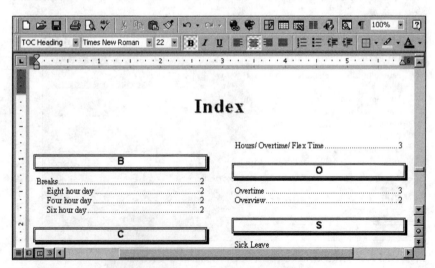

Figure 17.10   The completed index and a heading.

3. Click the Reference Type list arrow and select the Heading option.

4. Verify that the Heading text option is displayed in the Insert Reference To list box.

5. Click the "Hours/Overtime/Flex Time" heading in the For Which box, click the Insert button, click the "Sick Leave/Vacation" heading, click the Insert button, verify that the Insert Text As A Hyperlink option is selected, and then close the dialog box.

 If you insert text as a hyperlink, you can click the cross-reference and it will jump you to the actual text that was referenced.

6. Select the text "see also" and then click the Italics button.

7. If the cross-referenced headings aren't formatted as hyperlinks, use the keyboard to place the cursor in front of the "Hours/Overtime/Flex Time" heading, select the heading, and then click the Hyperlink style in the Style list box. Repeat this for the "Sick Leave/Vacation" heading.

Note: If the Hyperlink style isn't showing, select it in the Style dialog box.

8. Type a comma and a space between the headings, and then type the ending parenthesis (see Figure 17.11).

9. Save the document as Ch17.4Handbook.

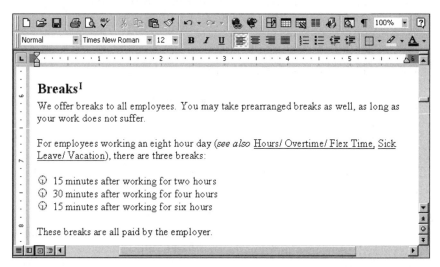

Figure 17.11   The cross-references are formatted and inserted into the document.

Bookmarks

Bookmarks in Word work much like the ones you stick in a book—except these bookmarks won't fall out. Bookmarks are used for marking an entry for an index or cross-reference. They allow you to jump to a particular location in your document. You can select text, tables, graphics, and more with bookmarks.

Task 14   Inserting a bookmark.

Use the document Ch17.4Handbook for this task.

1. Select the text "Name of Employee" on page 1.

2. Click Insert|Bookmark, type "Employee_Name" in the Bookmark Name text box, click the Add button, and then close the dialog box. Keep the document open for the next task

 You can enter multiple words for your bookmark name, but there can be no spaces. Use an underscore to keep words from running together, such as Use_Bookmark.

Task 15   Going to a bookmark.

Use the document Ch17.4Handbook from the previous task for this task.

1. Click the Next Page button once or twice.

2. Click Insert|Bookmark, click the bookmark Employee_Name in the Bookmark Name list box, and then click the Go To button.

3. Close the dialog box and replace the bookmark text with the name Allyson Hummel.

4. Save the document as Ch17.5Handbook.

 Remember, to go to a bookmark, you still use the Bookmark command on the Insert menu.

You can leave the Bookmark dialog box open and go to as many bookmarks as you like. Close the Bookmark dialog box when you're finished.

You can use the Bookmark and Hyperlink features on the Insert menu to mark all the entries in a table of contents or index as hyperlinks. When a page number is clicked, the reader jumps to the page and heading.

Practice Projects

Perform the following projects based on this chapter. Use the file Ch17Handbook from the disk that was included with your book for these projects (unless otherwise instructed).

Project 1   Create footnotes and endnotes.

1. Insert an endnote and change its options so that it appears at the end of each section and is numbered with the letters a, b, c.

2. Insert two footnotes so that they appear beneath the noted text.

3. Convert all footnotes to endnotes.

4. Delete an endnote.

5. Convert one endnote back to a footnote.

Answer to Project 1

Click to the right of the text you want to reference with an endnote. Click InsertIFootnote. Click the Endnote option. Click the Options button and then click the All Endnotes tab. Click the Number Format list arrow and select the a, b, c numbering option. Click the Place At list arrow and select the End of Section option. Type the note in the Endnote pane at the end of the section.

Click to the right of the text you want to reference with a footnote. Click InsertIFootnote. Click the Footnote option. Click the Options button and then click the All Footnotes tab. Click the Place At list arrow and select the Beneath The Text option. Type the note in the Footnote pane beneath the text. Click the Footnote command again and insert a second footnote.

Click InsertIFootnote and then click the Options button. Click the Convert button, and then click the Convert All Footnotes To Endnotes option.

Go to the endnote you want to delete in the text and select the note reference mark. Press the Delete key.

In Normal view, click the ViewIFootnotes. Click the Footnotes list arrow and select the All Endnotes option. Right-click the endnote you want to convert, and then click the Convert To Footnote command on the shortcut menu.

Project 2   Design a table of contents with built-in heading styles.

1. Apply built-in heading styles for the first three heading levels.

2. Design the table of contents with tab leaders, right-justified page numbers, and three heading levels.

Answer to Project 2

Move through the document, select headings, and apply Heading 1 through Heading 3 from the Style box, as needed.

Insert a page break with Ctrl+Enter. Click the new blank page to activate it. Click Insert|Index and Tables. Click a design in the Formats list box, select a Tab Leader option, select three heading levels, and make sure the Show Page Numbers and Right Align Page Numbers boxes are checked.

Project 3 Design and insert an index.

1. Select the text you want to include in your index.
2. Design the index with tab leaders, right-justified page numbers, and two columns.

Answer to Project 3

Click Insert|Index and Tables. Mark the entries to include in the index by selecting the text and then clicking the Main Entry text box and clicking the Mark button.

Move to the end of your document and insert a page break to create a blank page. Click the new blank last page. Click Insert|Index and Tables. Click a design in the Formats list box. Click the Right Align Page Numbers box to select it and then select a Tab Leader option.

Project 4 Create a cross-reference in the index.

1. Use the Cross-reference dialog box to place a Heading cross-reference in the index with the text *"See also"*.

Answer to Project 4

Insert a blank line where you want the cross-reference to appear. Type the introductory text. Click Insert|Cross-reference. Click the Reference Type list arrow and select Heading. Click the Insert Reference To list arrow and Heading text. Click the text you want the cross-reference to use in the For Which box.

Project 5 Insert a bookmark.

1. Insert a bookmark in your document.
2. Go to your bookmark.

Answer to Project 5

Place your cursor where you want a bookmark. Click Insert|Bookmark. Type a name for the bookmark.

Click Insert|Bookmark. Click the bookmark in the Bookmark Name list box. Click the Go To button.

Need To Know More?

 Napier, Albert H. and Phillip J. Judd: *Mastering and Using Microsoft Word 97.* Course Technology. Cambridge, MA, 1997. ISBN 0-7600-5022-8. This book brings the authors' experiences as educators and corporate trainers to Word 97 techniques.

 Shelly, Gary, Thomas Cashman, and Misty Vermaat: *Microsoft Word 97: Complete Concepts and Techniques.* Course Technology, Cambridge, MA, 1997. ISBN 0-7895-1338-2. A book in the Shelly Cashman series. Offers a step-by-step approach to learning beginning and advanced skills in Word 97.

 Swanson, Marie L.: *Microsoft Word 97—Illustrated Standard Edition: A Second Course.* Course Technology, Cambridge, MA, 1997. ISBN 0-7600-5141-0. An Illustrated Series book. Covers intermediate through advanced skills.

 Zimmerman, Scott and Beverly Zimmerman: *New Perspectives on Microsoft Word 97—Comprehensive.* Course Technology, Cambridge, MA, 1997. ISBN 0-7600-5256-5. Part of the New Perspectives series. Offers case-based, problem-solving approaches to learning Word 97.

Borders
And Shading

Terms you'll need to understand:

√ Borders

√ Point size

√ Shading

Skills you'll need to master:

√ Creating a border around a graphic or chart

√ Using art borders

√ Shading a paragraph

Word 97 makes adding borders and shading to your document simple and fun. You can shade just a single paragraph or the entire document. You can add a border to a single character or an entire page. You can apply shading and borders to text, graphics, text boxes, charts, and more.

Open the file Ch18Income from the disk that was included with this book, and use it for all of the tasks in this chapter.

Borders

Adding borders to your document can enhance its readability and keep your readers' interest.

Task 1 Adding a border to a graphic or chart.

1. Right-click the "Sales Analysis" chart on page 2, and then click the Format Object command on the shortcut menu.

2. Click the Colors And Lines tab.

3. Select the Teal line color, the 4 1/2 point thick top line and thin bottom line style, and change the weight to 4 points. Close the dialog box.

4. Click the Print Preview button, zoom out to 90%, click the Magnifier button to deselect it, and then center the chart across the page, as shown in Figure 18.1.

5. Close the Print Preview screen, deselect the chart, and then save the document as Ch18.1Income. Keep it open for the next task.

Task 2 Adding a page border to an
entire document.

You can add a page border to one page or to all the pages of your document. You need to be in Page Layout view to see page borders on the screen.

1. Click Format|Borders And Shading, and then click the Page Border tab.

You can click the Show Toolbar button to close the Borders And Shading dialog box and display the Tables And Borders toolbar, instead. You cannot set options or select an art border from the toolbar.

2. Select the third line style from the bottom in the Style list box, as shown in Figure 18.2.

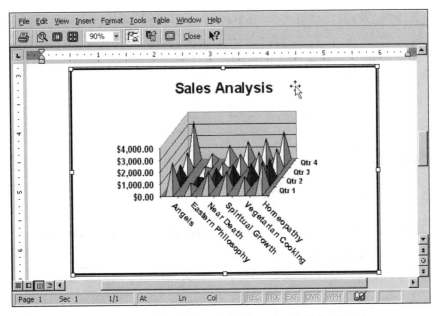

Figure 18.1　Centering the chart with a border in Print Preview edit mode.

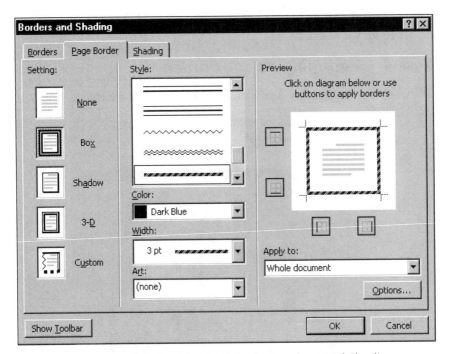

Figure 18.2　Page border selections in the Borders And Shading dialog box.

3. Select the Dark Blue color, adjust the width to 3 points, and then apply the settings to the whole document.

4. Save the document as Ch18.2Income and keep the document open for the next task.

Note: Some of the line styles do not have adjustable widths.

Modifying Borders

You can easily modify a border by changing its attributes in the appropriate dialog box.

Task 3   Modifying a border around a graphic or a chart.

1. Right-click the chart, click the Format Object command on the shortcut menu, and then click the Colors And Lines tab.

2. Place a thick top line and thin bottom line border around the graphic, and change the weight to 1.5 points (see Figure 18.3).

3. Deselect the chart. Save the document as Ch18.3Income and keep it open for the next task.

Task 4   Modifying a page border.

1. Click Format|Borders And Shading, and then click the Page Border tab.

2. Change the line style to the second to the last option in the Style list box, as shown in Figure 18.4.

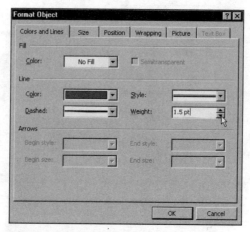

Figure 18.3   Changing the attributes of a chart border.

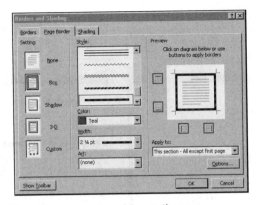

Figure 18.4   Changing page border attributes.

3. Change the color to Teal and adjust the width to 2 1/4 points.

4. Under Apply To, select This Section - All Except First Page option, as shown in Figure 18.4.

5. Click the Options button, and then click the Measure From list arrow and select Text.

6. Click the Align Paragraph Borders And Table Edges With Page Border checkbox to select it.

7. Change the distance on all four sides of the text to 5 points.

   Note: The Align Paragraph Borders And Table Edges With Page Border option will align any paragraph borders and tables with the page border all through the selected section. It eliminates spaces between adjoining borders. If the edge of a table is only 10 1/2 points (or the width of one character) away from the page border, Word will align the edge of the table to the border.

8. Deselect the Surround Header and Surround Footer checkboxes, if necessary.

9. Close the dialog boxes and click the Print Preview button.

10. Click the Multiple Pages button and view the first two pages of your document. Notice that the title page has no border, and the table is aligned with (or snapped to) the border on the left side, as shown in Figure 18.5.

11. Click the Borders And Shading command from the Format menu on the Print Preview toolbar.

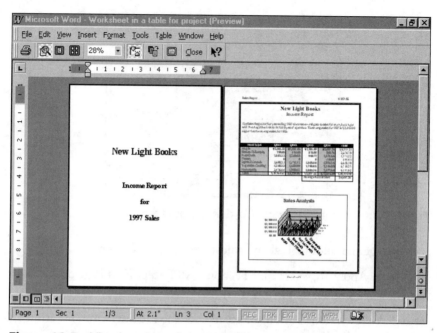

Figure 18.5 Viewing your changes in Print Preview mode.

12. Deselect the Align Paragraph Borders And Table Edges With Page Border option and increase the left and right text margins to 8 points.

13. Close the dialog box, and you will return to Print Preview mode where you can view the results of your changes and make further modifications to your document. Save the document as Ch18.4 and keep it open for the next task.

You can deselect the Magnifier button and edit your document right in Print Preview mode. This is a good place to adjust the table borders to center the table on your page and reposition your chart or text.

Art Border

If you have ever worked with Microsoft Publisher, you know about those neat decorative page borders. Now, you can use most of those same borders in Word.

Task 5   Adding an art border to one page of a document.

You can choose to have a different border on every page, if you want, but it won't look professional—only busy. You may want to exclude or change the border on a specific page, however, to set the page apart from the rest of the document.

1. Insert a continuous section break at the bottom of page 1.

   Note: You can also insert a Next Page section break and then delete the page break. Switch to Normal view to see the breaks.

2. With the cursor on page 1, click Format|Borders And Shading and then click the Page Border tab.

3. Click the Art list box and select the art border shown in Figure 18.6.

4. Change the color to Teal and then change the size to 25 points.

5. Click the Apply To list box and select the This Section option.

6. Click the Options button, and select the Text option from the Measure From list box.

7. Set the distance from the text to 2 points on all four sides.

8. View the first two pages in Print Preview mode to see if the borders are complementary to each other, as shown in Figure 18.7.

9. Save the document as Ch18.5Income and keep it open for the next task.

Shading

Shading is used to enhance a document. You can use shading to add or change the color of a table's background, to color the background of a text box, and to shade a paragraph or specific text.

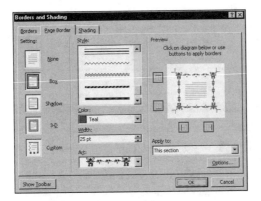

Figure 18.6   Art border selection with preferences.

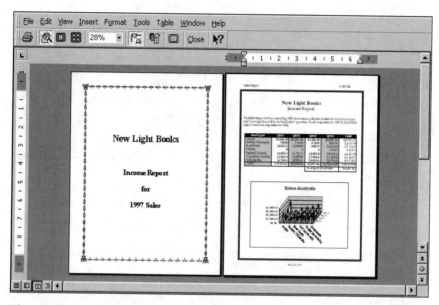

Figure 18.7 Print preview of document showing the first two pages.

Task 6 *Shading a paragraph.*

You can shade a paragraph to make it stand out. You don't have to highlight an entire paragraph to shade it, as long as the cursor is anywhere within it.

1. Click the paragraph on page 3 that begins with the sentence, "New Light Books intends to open another store in Scottsboro, Idaho", as shown in Figure 18.8.

2. Right-click a toolbar and select the Tables And Borders toolbar. You can also use the Borders And Shading command on the Format menu, but

Figure 18.8 A shaded paragraph with colored and bolded text.

it's easier to test several colors from the toolbar than by displaying the Borders And Shading dialog box each time.

3. Click the Shading Color button arrow and click the 20% Gray color option.

4. Bold the text and change the text color to Teal.

5. Save the document as Ch18.6Income and keep it open for the next task.

Task 7   *Shading a table.*

Shading a table is relatively painless with the Tables And Borders toolbar.

1. Move to the table on page 2, and select only the heading row.

2. Display the Tables And Borders toolbar, click the Shading Color button, and then click the Teal color.

3. Click the Font Color button on the Formatting toolbar, and then click the White color. Repeat for the row with the totals.

4. Select the row with the average sales and total. Click the Teal font color.

5. Select the Qtr 1 column of data, excluding the header and totals rows (see Figure 18.9), click the Shading Color button, and then click the Gray-15% color. Repeat for the data in the Qtr 3 and Total columns.

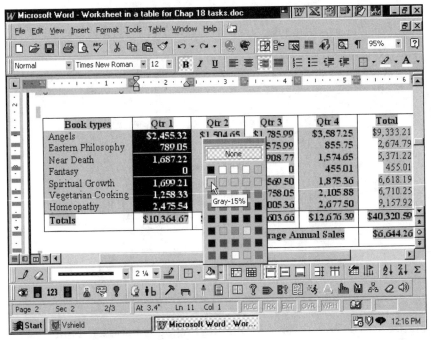

Figure 18.9   Shading the columns in a table.

6. Deselect the table, save the document as Ch18.7, and keep it open for the next task.

Task 8 Shading a page.

To shade a page, you have to select all the paragraphs on the page.

1. Move to page 1 and select all the text.

2. Click Format|Borders And Shading, and then click the Shading tab.

3. Click the Style list arrow in the Patterns group, scroll to the bottom of the list, and then select the Light Trellis style.

4. Click the Color list arrow and then select Teal.

5. Click the Page Border tab, and select the This Section option in the Apply To list box.

 Whenever you change any attributes in the Borders And Shading dialog box, you must reapply all the formatting in the Apply To list box prior to closing the dialog box. The Apply To list box always defaults back to the Whole Document option whenever the dialog box is displayed.

6. Close the dialog box and move to the end of the text.

7. The text on page 1 doesn't go to the end of the page, so move to the end of the text and then press the Enter key until the shading is at the bottom of the page.

8. View pages 1 and 2 in Print Preview mode (see Figure 18.10), close Print Preview mode, save the document as Ch18.8Income, and close it.

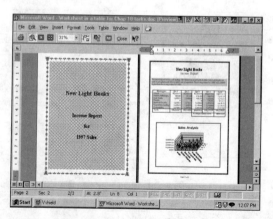

Figure 18.10 Viewing the formatting on pages 1 and 2 in Print Preview mode.

Practice Projects

Perform the following projects based on what you've learned in this chapter. Open the file Ch18Project.doc from the disk that was included with your book and use it for all the following projects.

Project 1   Create a border around a graphic.

1. Place a thick top line and thin bottom line border around the graphic on page 2.

2. Select the dark blue color and adjust the width to 4 points.

3. Save the document as Ch18.1Project.

Answer to Project 1

Right-click the graphic and then click the Format Picture command. Click the Colors And Lines tab. Select Dark Blue in the Color list box.

Select the 4 1/2 point thick top line and thin bottom line option (second to last option in the Style list box), and then change the weight to 4 points in the Weight spin box. Close the dialog box. Your border should resemble the one shown in Figure 18.11.

Click File|Save As, click the Save In list box, locate the folder where you want to save the document, rename it Ch18.1Project, and then click the Save button. Keep the document open for the next project.

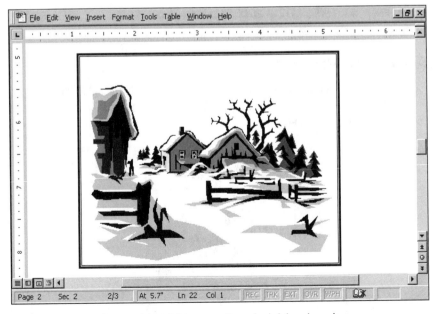

Figure 18.11   A graphic with a two-line dark blue border.

Project 2 Add a page border.

1. Add the page border, shown in Figure 18.12, to your document.

2. Change the color of the art border to dark blue and resize the border to 20 points.

3. Apply the border to only the first page (do not use a section break).

4. Set the margins to 4 points on all sides, measuring from the text. Do not surround headers or footers; also, do not snap tables and paragraph edges to the border.

Answer to Project 2

Click Format|Borders And Shading and then click the Page Border tab. Select the black-and-white art border, shown in Figure 18.12, from the Art list box.

Click the Color list arrow and select the Dark Blue option. Set the art border to 20 points in the Width spin box.

Click the This Section - First Page Only option from the Apply To list box.

Click the Options button and select the Text option from the Measure From list box. Set the left, right, top, and bottom margins to 4 points. Deselect the Surround Headers and Surround Footers checkboxes, if necessary. Verify that the Align Paragraph Borders And Table Edges With Page Border checkbox is deselected. Your page border should resemble Figure 18.13.

Project 3 Modify a graphic border.

Change the graphic border to three lines and resize the border to 10 points.

Answer to Project 3

Right-click the graphic and click the Format Picture command. Click the Colors And Lines tab. Click the 6 point three-line option in the Style list box, and adjust the weight to 10 points, as shown in Figure 18.14.

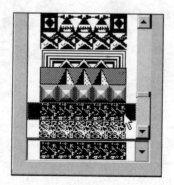

Figure 18.12 The black-and-white art page border.

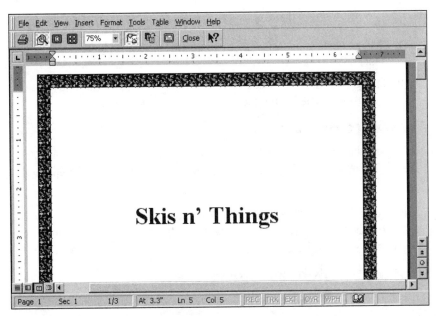

Figure 18.13   A page border added to the first page of a document.

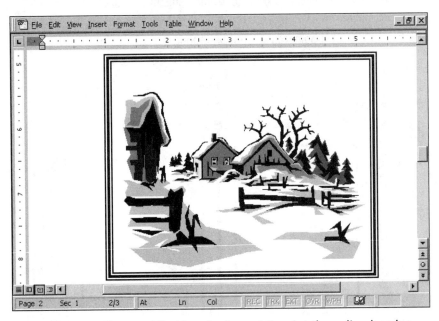

Figure 18.14   The modified border has a 10-point three-line border.

Project 4   Modify a page border.

1. Change the page border width to 10 points and apply it to the whole document.

2. Change the margins to 1 point for the top and bottom margins and 4 points for the left and right margins, measuring from the text.

Answer to Project 4

Click Format|Borders And Shading and then click the Page Border tab. Change the border to 10 points in the Width spin box. Click the Whole Document option in the Apply To list box.

Click the Options button and verify that the Text option is displayed in the Measure From list box. Change the top and bottom margins to 1 point and the left and right margins to 4 points, as shown in Figure 18.15.

Project 5   Shade a paragraph.

Use the Tables And Borders toolbar for this project.

1. Shade the paragraph on page 3 that begins "Skis n' Things intends to begin carrying the following items in the Fall of 1998" dark blue, and change the font color to white.

2. Create a 2 1/4 point red line border around the paragraph.

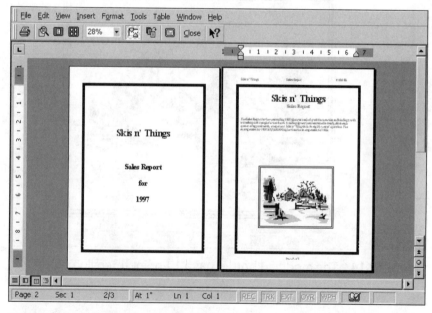

Figure 18.15   The first two pages with the new settings in Print Preview mode.

Answer to Project 5

Click anywhere in the paragraph to select it. Right-click a toolbar and select the Tables And Borders toolbar. Click the Shading Color button arrow and select the Dark Blue option. The font color should automatically be white, but if it's not, highlight the text, and then click the Font Color button on the Formatting toolbar and select the White option.

Verify that a thin line border is showing in the Line Style box in the Tables And Borders toolbar. Select the 2 1/4 point line size from the Line Weight list box. Click the Border Color button and select the Red option. Select the Outside Border option from the Border button. Your paragraph should resemble Figure 18.16.

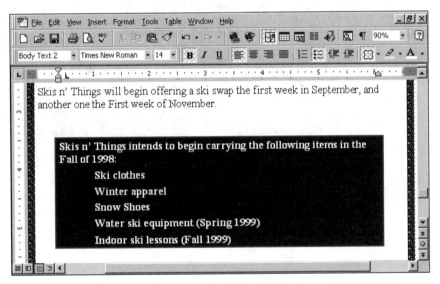

Figure 18.16   A shaded paragraph with white text and a red border.

Need To Know More?

Napier, Albert H., and Phillip J. Judd: *Mastering and Using Microsoft Word 97*. Course Technology, Cambridge, MA, 1997. ISBN 0-7600-5022-8. This book brings the authors' experiences as educators and corporate trainers to Word 97 techniques.

O'Hara, Shelley and Deborah Allen Rider: *Office 97 Small Business Solutions*. IDG Books Worldwide Inc., Foster City, CA, 1997. ISBN 0-7645-3120-4. Borders are discussed in Chapter 9.

Shelly, Gary, Thomas Cashman, and Misty Vermaat: *Microsoft Word 97 Complete Concepts and Techniques*. Course Technology, Cambridge, MA, 1997. ISBN 0-7895-1338-2. A book in the Shelly-Cashman series that offers a step-by-step approach to learning beginning and advanced skills in Word 97.

Swanson, Marie L.: *Microsoft Word 97—Illustrated Standard Edition: A Second Course*. Course Technology, Cambridge, MA, 1997. ISBN 0-7600-5141-0. A book in the Illustrated series that covers intermediate through advanced skills.

Zimmerman, Scott and Beverly Zimmerman: *New Perspectives on Microsoft Word 97—Comprehensive*. Course Technology, Cambridge, MA, 1997. ISBN 0-7600-5256-5. Part of the New Perspectives series. Offers a case-based, problem-solving approach to learning Word 97.

Macros

Terms you'll need to understand:

√ Macro

√ Assign

√ Keyboard shortcut

√ Template

√ Visual Basic editor

Skills you'll need to master:

√ Recording a macro

√ Assigning a macro to a keyboard shortcut

√ Assigning a macro to a toolbar button

√ Creating a new toolbar

√ Creating a template with macros

√ Deleting a macro

√ Editing a macro using the Visual Basic editor

√ Copying a macro

√ Renaming a macro

A macro can perform redundant tasks for you, which can save you hours of extra work every month—and we can all use more time. A macro records and saves keystrokes and mouse clicks, and then repeats them when you run it.

Making Macros

Recording a macro is extremely easy. Once you have recorded your macro, you can choose to run it from the Macros dialog box, by using a keyboard shortcut, or by clicking a button you've created.

Task 1   Recording a macro.

1. Open a blank document and click Tools|Macro|Record New Macro.

2. Type the macro name, "Our_Letterhead", in the Record Macro dialog box, as shown in Figure 19.1, and then click the Store Macro In: list arrow and select the current document.

 A macro name can contain up to 80 letters and numbers, but the name must begin with a letter. You cannot use spaces or symbols in a macro name. However, you can use the underscore character to separate words.

3. Click the OK button. The Stop Recording toolbar displays with two buttons: the Stop button and the Pause button. The Pause button enables you to pause recording temporarily and then resume recording.

4. On the Formatting toolbar, click the Center button, click the Bold button, and then select the Arrus Black BT font (or similar) and a font size of 20.

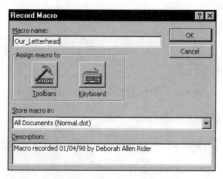

Figure 19.1   The Record Macro dialog box.

5. Type "Sandstone Sculptures Ltd.", press the Enter key, click the Bold button to deselect it, select a 16-point font size, type "2120 Falls Brook Way", press the Enter key, and then type "Scottsboro, WA 98000".

6. Press the Enter key, select a 14-point font size, and then type "509-244-8552".

7. Click the Stop button on the Stop Recording toolbar.

8. Save the document as Letterhead Document.

Your letterhead should resemble Figure 19.2.

Task 2   Assigning a macro to a toolbar button.

Now that you've created the macro, you can run it from the Macros dialog box or you can assign it to a toolbar button. A button is much easier to use because you don't have to display a dialog box to run the macro. Use the Letterhead document throughout these tasks.

1. Click the Customize command on the Tools menu.

2. Click the Commands tab.

3. Scroll down the Categories list and click the Macros item.

4. Drag the name of the macro you just created to the Formatting toolbar.

Figure 19.2 Creating a letterhead macro.

The easiest place to put a button that runs a macro during the test is on the menu bar, to the right of the Help menu. Don't bother taking the time to give the button a picture (unless you're directed to)—just place it, record the macro, and then use it.

5. While still in the Customize dialog box, right-click the new button and then click the Text Only (In Menus) command from the shortcut menu. This will remove the text so that the button resembles the other buttons.

6. Right-click the button again and point to the Change Button Image command. A list of all available button images displays. You can select one of these or create your own image.

7. Click the Edit Button Image command.

8. Click the Clear button in the Button Editor dialog box to delete the Macro icon, and then draw a picture of a sheet of paper with a letterhead, as shown in Figure 19.3.

9. Close the dialog boxes and return to your document. Point to the new button, and a ScreenTip will display your macro name.

10. Save the document.

 If you do not have ScreenTips enabled, you can do so by clicking the Options tab in the Customize dialog box from the Tools menu.

Use the New button on the Standard toolbar to open a blank document and try out the new macro button you have created. Your screen should resemble Figure 19.4.

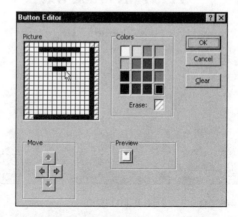

Figure 19.3   Drawing a button image in the Button Editor dialog box.

Figure 19.4   Using the macro button.

Task 3   *Recording a macro and assigning it to a keyboard shortcut.*

Some people are more comfortable using the mouse to perform operations and some prefer using the keyboard. Here's a way to assign a macro to a keyboard shortcut:

1. Double-click the REC button on the status bar.

2. Name the macro "LetterFooter" in the Record Macro dialog box, and then click the Store Macro In: list arrow and select the current document.

3. Click the Keyboard button.

4. Press and hold the Alt key, and then type the letter "L" in the Customize Keyboard dialog box, as shown in Figure 19.5.

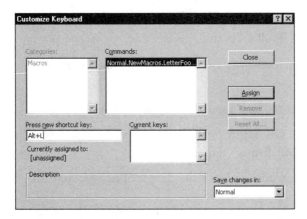

Figure 19.5   Assigning a macro to a keyboard shortcut.

5. Click the Assign button.

Note: If the keys you choose are assigned to another command, then select a different key combination. You can use either the Alt or Ctrl key when assigning a shortcut; however, the Ctrl key combination is usually reserved for default shortcuts created by Word. For example, to toggle the bold character formatting on and off you can press Ctrl+B.

6. Click the Close button. Your macro is now recording.

7. Click View|Header And Footer and then click the Switch Between Header And Footer button.

8. Tab to the center of the footer and type "Page" followed by a space.

9. Click the Page Number button.

10. Close the footer.

11. Click the Stop button on the Stop Recording toolbar.

12. Save the document.

Test the macro in a new document to make sure it works properly.

Task 4   Assigning a new macro to a button and making a new toolbar.

This is similar to Task 2, only you'll assign the macro to the button before you start recording.

1. Double-click the REC button.

2. Name the macro "FormLetter" in the Record Macro dialog box, and then click the Store Macro In: list arrow and select the current document.

3. Click the Toolbars button.

4. Click the Toolbars tab in the Customize dialog box, and then click the New button.

5. Name the toolbar "Sandstone" , as shown in Figure 19.6.

6. Click the OK button to close the New Toolbar dialog box, and an empty toolbar will display on the screen.

7. Click the Commands tab and drag your new macro name to the new toolbar.

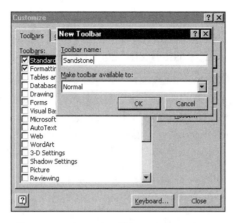

Figure 19.6   Creating a custom toolbar.

8. Right-click the macro button, and then click the Text Only (In Menus) command.

9. Right-click the button you created for the letterhead, and then click the Copy command.

10. Right-click the new button, and then click the Paste command.

11. Use the button editor to change the new button image so that it resembles a letter (see Figure 19.7).

12. Drag the Our_Letterhead button to the new toolbar, as shown in Figure 19.7, and then close the dialog box.

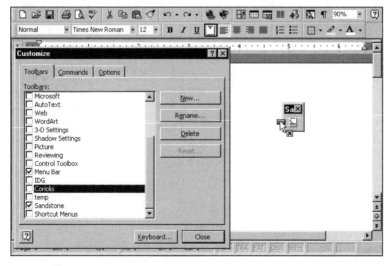

Figure 19.7   Dragging a button to a new toolbar.

13. You're now recording the form letter macro. Increase the font size for all the text in the document to 12 points, and then insert the date by using the Insert menu. The date is left-aligned with the Body Text style applied and two lines below the letterhead.

14. Leave enough lines to insert name, company, and two address fields below the date. Include a line before the name and after the second address (six lines total). Type "Dear" and then press the spacebar. Next, type a colon (:).

15. Type the body of the letter, add two lines, type "Sincerely," add three lines, and then type a name. Use the text in Figure 19.8 for the form letter.

16. Stop recording and save the document.

Task 5   Using a macro to create a template.

You can have a macro perform many tasks, including opening a document or a template.

1. Close all documents and click File|New.

2. Click Blank Document, click the Template option, and then close the New dialog box.

3. Insert a watermark, format and position it, then save and close the new template. Save the template to a different disk as "Watermark Page", and then close the file.

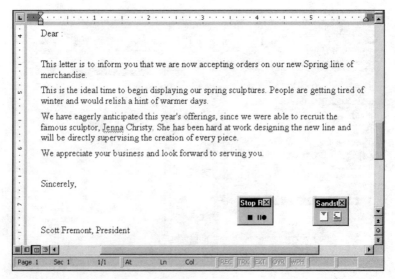

Figure 19.8   The body of the form letter.

4. Double-click the REC button and name the macro Create_Main_Doc, and then click the Store Macro In: list arrow and select the current document.

5. Assign the macro to the toolbar you created. Hide the button text and create an open folder button design in a different color than the Open button in Word.

 You can copy and paste the Open button image and then edit the colors.

6. Close the Customize dialog box to start the macro recording.

7. Click File|New, click the tab (or the disk) that contains the Watermark Page template, and then double-click the template.

8. Click Tools|Macro|Macros.

9. Select the macro that creates your letterhead, and then click Run.

10. Press the Alt+L keys to run the LetterFooter macro.

11. Stop Recording and close the document without saving.

Task 6   Deleting a macro.

1. Create and name a macro of your choice.

2. Assign it to a toolbar button with an existing button picture. (Don't design the button because you will be deleting it.)

3. Click Tools|Macro|Macros.

4. Select the macro you created, and then click the Delete button. Close the dialog box.

5. Display the Customize dialog box, and then drag the button from the toolbar and release.

The macro is deleted and so is the button. If you delete a button that you assigned to a keyboard shortcut, you'll be able to reuse the shortcut once the macro is deleted.

Task 7   Editing a macro.

Create a macro that types some text, selects it, and then places it in bold and italics. (Keep in mind that you have to use the keyboard to select text when recording a macro.) When typing the text, be sure to misspell a word or two so you can practice editing the Visual Basic code. Then, assign the macro however you like.

1. Run the macro in a new document. Deselect the Bold and Italics buttons, and then press the Enter key two times.

2. Click Tools|Macro|Macros.

3. Select the macro you just created, and then click the Edit button.

4. The Visual Basic editor opens, as shown in Figure 19.9. Correct the spelling errors in the editor.

5. Change the line that reads

```
Selection.Font.Italic = wdToggle
```

to

```
Selection.Font.ColorIndex = wdRed
```

6. Click the Save button.

7. Notice that the Visual Basic editor opens in its own window so you can test the macro before closing the editor. Click the Word button on the taskbar and run the macro again.

You can see the difference in the text, as shown in Figure 19.10. Click the Visual Basic button on the taskbar, and then click the list box that has your macro name. All the macros you've created are listed. Click one and the editor

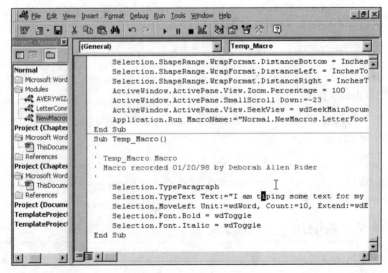

Figure 19.9 The Visual Basic editor.

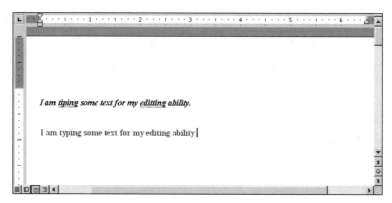

Figure 19.10   Comparing the changes in the macro code.

will take you to that macro's code. The green text at the top of all your macros are remarks. You can add comments and remarks to any code you like by beginning the line with a single quote ('). Close the editor as you would a program.

Task 8 *Copying and renaming a macro to a different file using the Organizer.*

You can copy a macro two ways: by using the Visual Basic Editor and by using the Organizer in the Macros dialog box. The Organizer will copy all macros for a template or document to another document, template, or the Normal template.

Open a new blank document and save it as CopyDoc.

1. Click File|New, click the Letters And Faxes tab, and then click the Elegant Letter option.

2. Click the Template option button, and then click OK.

3. Click Tools|Macro|Macros, and then click the Organizer button in the Macros dialog box.

4. Click the Close File button under the Normal.dot (global template) box. The button now says Open File. Click the Open File button, select the Word document (*.doc) option in the Files of type list box, display the CopyDoc document in the folder list window, and then click the Open button or double-click the CopyDoc file.

If your files are kept in My Documents, click the Look In list arrow and select the C: drive option. Then double-click the My Documents folder and open the document.

5. Click the LetterCommon macros in the In Template1 window, and then click the Copy button to copy them to CopyDoc.

6. Click the copied macros to select them, click the Rename button, and then name the macros in CopyDoc LetterMacros.

7. Click the Close button.

Task 9   Deleting a macro.

You can delete a macro (or macros) from the Macros dialog box and you can delete macros from the Organizer dialog box.

1. Open the CopyDoc document, click Tools|Macro|Macros, select the SetDate macro, and then click the Delete button.

2. Click the Organizer button in the Macros dialog box, click the LetterCommon macros in the In CopyDoc window, click the Delete button, and then click the Close button.

Task 10   Copying a macro to a different document using the Visual Basic editor.

This way of copying a macro takes a little concentration and finesse, but it can be done.

1. Open the Letterhead Document, open a new blank document, and then save it as CopyDoc.

2. Click Tools|Macro|Visual Basic Editor.

3. If your screen doesn't look like Figure 19.11, then click View|Project Editor on the Visual Basic menu bar.

HOLD That Skill!

Notice that the task bar is displaying both the Microsoft Word button and the Microsoft Visual Basic button. This allows you to move back and forth when editing between the two applications. Remember to save before quitting Visual Basic.

The pane that separates the code window from the project window is adjustable, as shown in Figure 19.11.

4. Double-click the New Macros module under the Project (Letterhead Document) Folder, and the Visual Basic code will appear in the code window.

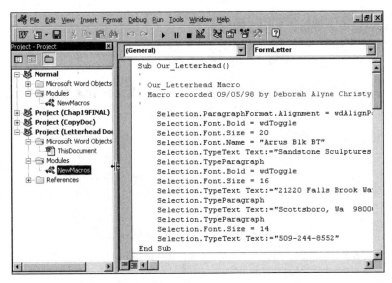

Figure 19.11   The Visual Basic editor.

5. Select all of the text for the Our_Letterhead macro, and click the Copy button on the Standard toolbar.

6. Double-click This Document under the Project (CopyDoc) folder, and then click the Paste button on the Standard toolbar.

7. Click the Save button, and then click the Close button on the title bar to close the Visual Basic editor.

8. Click Tools|Macro|Macros, and then select the CopyDoc document in the Macros In: list box. Notice the Our_Letterhead macro is now available.

Practice Projects

Perform the following projects based on what you've learned in this chapter. To do so, you'll need to open a blank document.

Project 1 Record a macro and run it from the Macros dialog box.

1. Open the file Ch19DraftDesigns from the disk that was included with your book.

2. Create a new style that's based on the following attributes: Normal, Times New Roman, 14 point, bold, justified, and 1.5 line spacing.

3. Record a macro called New_Style that applies the new style to selected text. Do not assign it to a button or keyboard shortcut.

4. Select the paragraph, but not the list, and then run the macro from the Macros dialog box.

5. Save the document as Ch19Project1.

Answer to Project 1

Click File|Open and browse to find Ch19DraftDesigns.

Click Format|Style and then click the New button in the Style Dialog box. Name the style in the Name box, and then base the new style on the Normal style. Click the Format button and then click Font. Select Times New Roman, Bold, and 14 point. Click OK. Click the Format button and then click Paragraph. Select Justified in the Alignment list box, and select 1.5 lines in the Line Spacing box. Close the Style box without applying the style.

Select some text, double-click the REC button, and then name the macro New_Style. Close the New Macro dialog box. Click the Style box on the Formatting toolbar, and select the new style you created. Stop recording.

Select some other text that you want to apply the style to, click Tools|Macro|Macros, and then select the New_Style macro. Click the Run button.

Click File|Save As, click the Save In list box, locate the folder where you want to save the document, rename it Ch19Project1, and then click the Save button. Keep the document open for the next project.

Project 2 Record a macro and assign it to a button.

Use the file Ch19Project1 you created in Project 1.

1. Record a macro called New_Style_2 and assign it to a button. Place the button on the toolbar you created in Task 4. Copy the

Bullet button image on the Formatting toolbar, and paste it to the new button. Change the button image enough to differentiate it from the original Bullet button.

2. Create a new style that's based on the following attributes: Normal, Times New Roman, 14 point, bold, left aligned, and 1.5 line spacing. Then, create a checkmark bullet that's dark blue with a bullet indent of .1" and a text indent of .35". Stop recording.

3. Apply the new style to the list but not the paragraph. Save the document as Ch19Project2.

Answer to Project 2

Double-click the REC button, and then name the macro New_Style_2. Click the Toolbar button. Drag the macro to the toolbar. Right-click the Bullet button on the Formatting toolbar, and then click the Copy command. Right-click the new macro button and click Paste. Right-click the new macro button and click Text Only (In Menus). Right-click the new macro button and click Edit. Change the image and/or color and close all dialog boxes.

Click Format|Style, and then click the New button in the Style dialog box. Name the style in the Name box, and then base the new style on the Normal style. Click the Format button and then click Font. Select Times New Roman, Bold, and 14 point. Click OK. Click the Format button and then click Paragraph. Select Left in the Alignment list box, and select 1.5 lines in the Line Spacing box. Click the Format button and then click Numbering. Click the Bullet tab and then select the checkmark style. (If this style is not available, select it from the Bullet choices in the Customized Bulleted List dialog box.) Click the Customize button, and then select the .1" bullet indent and the .35" text indent, as shown in Figure 19.12. Click the Font button and select Bold, 14 point, and Dark Blue. Close all dialog boxes without applying the style.

Select the list and then click the New_Style_2 button. Click File|Save As, click the Save In list box, locate the folder where you want to save the document, rename it Ch19Project2, and then click the Save button. Keep the document open for the next project.

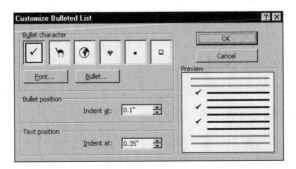

Figure 19.12 Creating a customized bulleted list with a macro.

Project 3　Create a macro to open a document.

Use the file Ch19Project2 you created in Project 2.

1. Record a macro that saves the document you're currently working on and opens a document of your choice.
2. Assign the macro to a toolbar button on the toolbar you created.
3. Run the macro.

Answer to Project 3

Double-click the REC button and name the macro.

Drag the macro to the toolbar you created. Hide the text and select a button design. Close the Customize dialog box. Click the Save button, click the Open button, and double-click the document you want opened. Stop recording.

With a document open, click the macro button and run the macro.

Project 4　Delete a macro.

1. Delete the macro you created to open a document.
2. Delete the macro button.

Answer to Project 4

Click Tools|Macro|Macros. Select the macro you created, and then click the Delete button.

Open the Customize dialog box, and then drag the button assigned to the macro from the toolbar and release. Close the Macros dialog box.

Project 5　Edit a macro.

1. Edit the macro "New_Style_2".
2. Change the dark blue bullet to red, the text position to .25", and the tab position to .25".
3. Turn on the Bold format (hint: look at a macro with bold selected).
4. Save and test the macro.

Answer to Project 5

Click Tools|Macro|Macros. Select the macro "New_Style_2" and then click the Edit button.

Change the line that reads

```
ColorIndex = wdDarkBlue
```

to

```
ColorIndex = wdRed
```

Change the line that reads

```
TextPosition = InchesToPoints(0.1) and .TabPosition
 = InchesToPoints(0.35)
```

to

```
TextPosition = InchesToPoints(0.25) and .TabPosition
 = InchesToPoints(0.25)
```

Change the line that reads

```
Bold = wdUndefined
```

to

```
Bold = wdToggle.
```

Click the Save button. Switch to the Word document and test the macro. If the macro works correctly, close the Visual Basic editor. If not, review your changes.

Project 6   Copy a macro.

1. Open the Letterhead document and copy the macros from Letterhead to CopyDoc.
2. Change the name of the macros to LetterheadMacros.
3. Save CopyDoc as CopyDocProject19.

Answer to Project 6

Click the Open button on the Standard toolbar, and then double-click the Letterhead document from the Open dialog box. Click Tools|Macro|Macros and then click the Organizer button. Click the Close File button under the Normal.dot (global template), and then click the Open File button. Double-click the CopyDoc document to open it. Select NewMacros from the In Letterhead window, and then click the Copy button.

Select NewMacros from the To CopyDoc window, click the Rename button, and name the macros LetterheadMacros. Click the Close button.

Click File|Save As and type CopyDocProject19. Click the Save button.

Project 7   Delete a macro.

1. Open CopyDocProject19, delete the LetterFooter macro, and then save the document.

Answer to Project 7

Click the Open button on the Standard toolbar, and then double-click the CopyDocProject19 document from the Open dialog box. Click Tools|Macro|Macros, select the LetterFooter macro, and then click the Delete button.

Need To Know More?

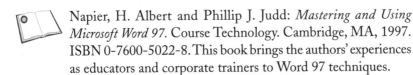
Napier, H. Albert and Phillip J. Judd: *Mastering and Using Microsoft Word 97*. Course Technology. Cambridge, MA, 1997. ISBN 0-7600-5022-8. This book brings the authors' experiences as educators and corporate trainers to Word 97 techniques.

O'Hara, Shelley and Deborah Allen Rider: *Office 97 Small Business Solutions*. IDG Books Worldwide Inc. Foster City, CA, 1997. ISBN 0-7645-3120-4. Chapter 37 discusses the use of styles.

Shelly, Gary, Thomas Cashman, and Misty Vermaat: *Microsoft Word 97: Complete Concepts and Techniques*. Course Technology. Cambridge, MA, 1997. ISBN 0-7895-1338-2. A book in the Shelly-Cashman series. Offers a step-by-step approach to learning beginning and advanced skills in Word 97.

Swanson, Marie L.: *Microsoft Word 97—Illustrated Standard Edition: A Second Course*. Course Technology. Cambridge, MA, 1997. ISBN 0-7600-5141-0. An Illustrated Series book. Covers intermediate through advanced skills.

Zimmerman, Scott and Beverly Zimmerman: *New Perspectives on Microsoft Word 97—Comprehensive*. Course Technology. Cambridge, MA, 1997. ISBN 0-7600-5256-5. Part of the New Perspectives series. Offers case-based, problem-solving approaches to learning Word 97.

Workgroup Editing

Terms you'll need to understand:

√ Versions

√ Track changes

√ Strikethrough

√ Email

√ Route

√ Master document

√ Subdocument

Skills you'll need to master:

√ Saving versions of a file

√ Tracking changes in a document

√ Adding comments to a document

√ Highlighting text

√ Routing documents via email

√ Creating a master document

Workgroup editing conjures up visions of huddling together with a team and brainstorming new changes to old ideas. Or, perhaps workgroup editing makes you think of sharing documents on a network. Although you may use the features in this chapter for document sharing on a network, you can also use them on your personal computer for your own edification.

Saving Versions Of A File

You can save a file to a different name each time the document is edited, but this can be cumbersome, confusing, and a waste of valuable disk space. A better way to save your document after making changes is to save versions of it. Each version is saved in the original document but is not visible unless you open it.

Open the file Ch20Manual from the disk that was included with your book.

Task 1   Saving versions of a document.

1. With the document open, click File|Versions.

2. The Versions In (file name) dialog box opens, as shown in Figure 20.1. The Existing Versions window is empty because you haven't saved any versions of the document. Click the Save Now button, and the Save Version dialog box will display.

3. Type a comment for your version, as shown in Figure 20.2, and then close the dialog box.

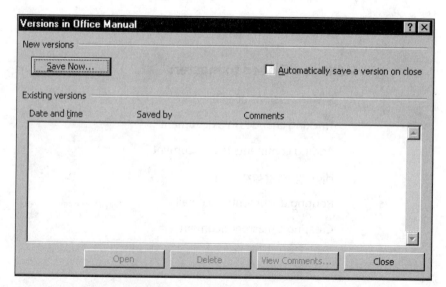

Figure 20.1   The Versions dialog box prior to saving a version of the document.

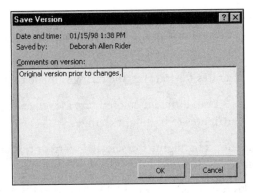

Figure 20.2   The Save Version dialog box with a version comment.

4. Save the document as Ch20.1Manual, and leave it open for the next tasks.

You've just created a version of your document that you can open and view no matter how many new changes you make to the document.

 Notice that the bottom-right side of the status bar now displays an icon. Place the mouse pointer on it, and a ScreenTip appears that reads "File Versions" (see Figure 20.3). You can double-click this icon to quickly take you to the Versions dialog box.

Tracking Changes To A Document

There are several situations in which you might want to use the Track Changes feature in Word. For example, you may be writing a professional manuscript, journal, report, or document and want to track the changes you make as you edit your work.

Tracking changes is most commonly used when someone else is editing your work. You won't want them to actually change your original work, merely

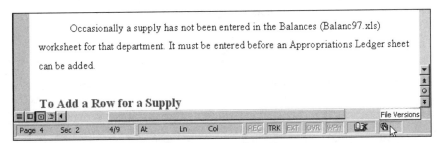

Figure 20.3   The File Versions icon in the status bar.

supply suggestions and information you can opt to accept or reject. Seeing the changes next to your text allows you to read and compare the modifications to the original.

Word offers three features for tracking the changes made to your document:

➤ **Track Changes**   Uses different colored text as well as the strikethrough and underline attributes to highlight changes.

➤ **Insert Comment**   Highlights the selected word or text and provides a note pane for typing a comment.

➤ **Highlight**   Uses selected color to highlight text but doesn't add a comment.

The Reviewing toolbar contains all the commands you'll need to track changes easily and effectively. Although the menu commands can be less efficient, the Track Changes command on the Tools menu offers a dialog box for changing the printing and viewing options. Table 20.1 describes each button on the Reviewing toolbar.

Table 20.1 The Reviewing toolbar buttons.	
Button	**Description**
Insert Comment	Highlights the selected word (or the word to the right of the insertion point), and inserts a comment.
Edit Comment	Opens the Comments pane and displays all comments for reviewing or editing.
Previous Comment	Moves the insertion point back to the previous comment.
Next Comment	Moves the insertion point forward to the next comment.
Delete Comment	Deletes the selected comment.
Track Changes	Turns the Track Changes feature on or off, using the current Track Changes setting.
Previous Change	Moves the insertion point back to the previous change.
Next Change	Moves the insertion point forward to the next change.
Accept Change	Accepts the suggested change at the insertion point, and removes the change's highlighting.
Reject Change	Rejects the suggested change at the insertion point, and removes the change's highlighting.
Highlight (Color)	Highlights the selected text in the color selected from the drop-down palette.

(continued)

Table 20.1   The Reviewing toolbar buttons *(continued)*.

Button	Description
Create Microsoft Outlook Task	Creates a shortcut to the document in Outlook as a task.
Save Version	Saves a version of a document. You can have multiple versions of a document in a single file. You can open a previous version for viewing, printing, or editing. You can also delete earlier versions.
Send To Mail Recipient	Sends the active document as an attachment to an email message.

Task 2   Tracking changes to a document.

1. Click Tools | Track Changes | Highlight Changes.

2. Click the Track Changes While Editing box, and verify that the Highlight Changes On Screen and Highlight Changes In Printed Document boxes are checked.

HOLD That Skill!

Unless you need to change the viewing or printing options for the tracked changes, you can use the Reviewing toolbar to enable the Track Changes feature. You can also start the Track Changes feature by double-clicking the TRK button in the status bar.

3. Scroll to the last paragraph on page 1 (above the heading "Adding a Sheet to the Ledger" that begins on page 2), select the text "(or by clicking Open on the File menu)", and then click the Delete button as shown in Figure 20.4. Change the word "of" to the word "on" in the previous sentence.

4. Change the sentence that begins with the words "Input the invoices" to read, "Type the information on the invoice". Notice that the text is in a different color, and a vertical line is displayed wherever you edited the text. Added text is underlined and deleted text has a line running through it (strikethrough), as shown in Figure 20.4.

 If you can't see the vertical line, switch to Normal view.

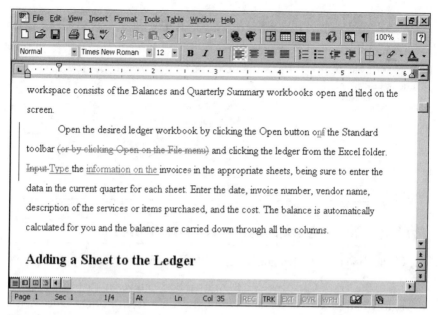

Figure 20.4 Inserted and deleted text in a document.

5. Display the Reviewing toolbar and then click the Save Version button.

6. Add comments and save the document as Ch20.2Manual.

You can use the Previous Change and Next Change buttons on the Reviewing toolbar to move from change to change in the document.

Task 3   Accepting or rejecting changes.

You can accept or reject changes to your document quickly and easily.

1. Move to the beginning of your document and click the insertion point in page 1.

HOLD That Skill!

You can use the Ctrl+Home keys to move to the beginning of the document.

2. Click the Next Change button on the Reviewing toolbar.

3. Move to each occurrence of a change in your document, accept the changes in the first two sentences, as shown in Figure 20.5, and then reject all changes in the last sentence.

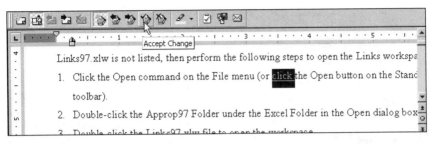

Figure 20.5 Accepting a change.

 You can also click the Accept Or Reject Changes command on the shortcut menu by right-clicking the change to display the Accept Or Reject Changes dialog box rather than using the Reviewing toolbar. You can use this dialog box to accept or reject each change individually, or you can accept or reject all changes collectively by clicking either the Accept All or Reject All button.

4. Disable the Track Changes feature by clicking the Track Changes button to deselect it. You can also double-click the TRK button on the status bar.

5. Save a new version of the document.

6. Close the Comments pane, if necessary.

Comments

Inserting comments into a document has its advantages. For example, the document is not cluttered up with strikethroughs and inserted text. When more than one person is editing a document, using comments can be a clearer alternative than seeing many colors of inserted and deleted text.

To insert a comment for a single word, you can place the insertion point to the left of the word or anywhere within the word. To insert a comment for a line of text, first select the text and then add the comment.

Task 4   Inserting a comment.

Each comment is typed into a separate pane and coded so that you know whose comment you're viewing, as shown in Figure 20.6.

1. Select the red text on page 1, and then click the Insert Comment button on the Reviewing toolbar.

2. Type the comment in the Comments pane that's displayed in Figure 20.6.

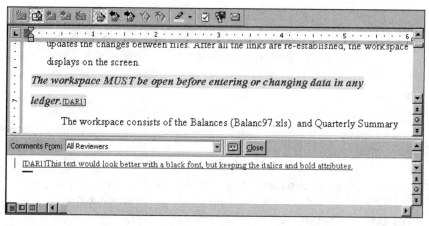

Figure 20.6 Inserting a comment.

3. Click the Close button when finished to close the Comments pane. Notice the text is now highlighted.

4. Move your mouse over the commented text and the comment will display as a ScreenTip.

5. Add several more comments to your document.

6. Save a new version of your document.

You can move through your comments by clicking the Next Comment and Previous Comment buttons on the Reviewing toolbar.

Task 5   Deleting a comment.

Deleting a comment is even easier than inserting one.

1. Click View|Comments to open the Comments pane and view all comments.

   Note: Click a comment in the Comments pane and notice how the document moves to the corresponding text.

2. Right-click the commented text in the document, and then click the Delete Comment command on the shortcut menu, as shown in Figure 20.7.

The comments will renumber themselves to accommodate the insertion or deletion of a comment.

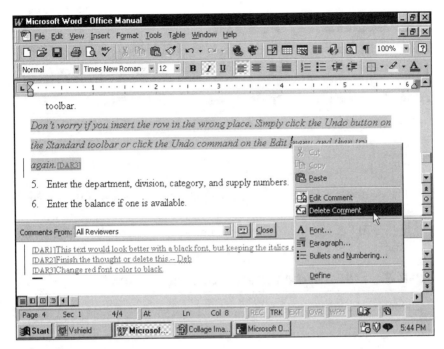

Figure 20.7   Deleting a comment.

Highlighting Text

You may want to highlight text but not add a comment to it, in which case you can use the Highlight feature. You can select a highlighting color from the fifteen shades on the Highlight palette.

Task 6   *Highlighting text.*

There are two ways to highlight text in your document:

➤   Select the text you want highlighted, and then click the Highlight button on the Reviewing toolbar.

➤   Click the Highlight button on the Reviewing toolbar, and then select the text to be highlighted.

When you click the Highlight button prior to selecting text, the Highlight feature stays enabled until you click it again to deactivate it.

You can remove highlighting by selecting the highlighted text and then clicking the Highlight button. You can change the color of your highlighter by clicking the Highlight button list arrow.

Versions Of A File

When you have saved multiple versions of a file, you can open a version and view it. You can add new comments to a saved version as well as delete a version.

Task 7 Viewing versions of a document.

1. Double-click the File Versions icon on the status bar, and then select a file version you want to view.

2. Click the Open button.

3. The current version of your document displays at the top of the screen, and the saved version displays at the bottom of the screen, as shown in Figure 20.8. Click the Close button on the saved version's title bar to close it.

Task 8 Deleting a version of a document.

1. Double-click the File Versions icon in the status bar.

2. Select the file version you want to delete.

3. Click the Delete button.

4. Click Yes when the warning box displays and the version is deleted.

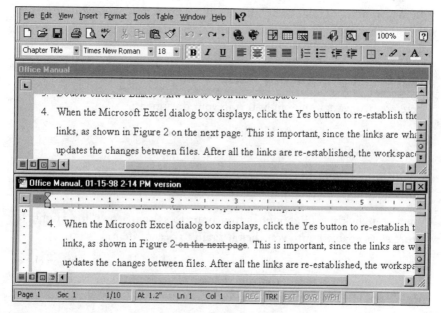

Figure 20.8 Viewing a saved version of the document.

Routing Documents

There are two ways to route a document. One is to send it via email, and the other is to post it to a Microsoft Exchange public folder.

To route a document through email, you'll need one of the following:

➤ Microsoft Exchange or any MAPI-compatible mail system. (MAPI stands for Messaging Application Programming Interface.)

➤ Lotus cc:Mail or any mail system compatible with VIM (Vendor Independent Messaging). To post a document to a public folder, you need Microsoft Exchange Server.

Task 9   *Routing a document using email.*

You can route a document through email when you want others to make revisions on a copy of the document online. To route a document, you must create a routing slip.

Author note: This section has not been on the tests, but past outlines from the Microsoft Internet site has mentioned routing documents as an expert "need to know." If you are working on a computer that is part of a network, you may not be able to access the Personal Address Book. Talk to your network administrator before proceeding.

If you are working on a personal computer and the Personal Address Book is not available, you may need to install Microsoft Mail so that you can access the postoffice. Put the postoffice in the Exchange folder under the Programs folder on the C drive.

Once you have access to the Personal Address Book, add a couple of names to it that you can use. Select the Personal Address Book from the Show Names From The: list box, click the New Entry button on the Address Book toolbar, and then select the Internet Mail Address option.

1. Click File|Send To|Routing Recipient. The Routing Slip dialog box displays, as shown in Figure 20.9.

2. Click the Address button in the Routing Slip dialog box, and then select the address book that contains your routing recipients.

3. Add each person with the To button in the Address Book dialog box.

4. To add a message to the email, type it in the Message text box.

5. Click the Route To Recipients One After Another option.

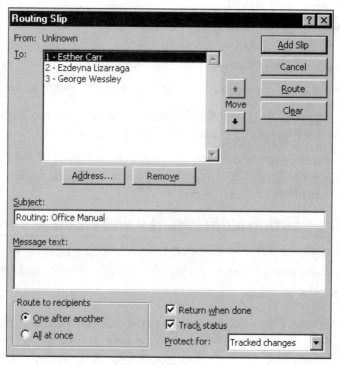

Figure 20.9 The Routing Slip dialog box.

6. Click a name in the To box. Notice the Move arrows are enabled. This allows you to change the order in which the document is sent.

7. Verify the Return When Done box is checked. This automatically returns the document to you when it has been received by all the recipients.

8. Verify the Track Status box is checked. This allows you to check on the document's status while it is en route.

9. In the Protect For list box, select Tracked Changes if you want the Track Changes feature enabled. Select Comments if you want the reviewers to insert comments but not change the contents of the document. Select Forms if you're routing a form that you want recipients to complete.

   Note: If you select (none), the reviewers' changes are not marked and you won't be able to highlight or merge them.

10. Click the Add Slip button if you want to continue editing the document. Click the Route button if you are ready to send the document.

To delete a routing slip click File|Send To|Other Routing Recipient and then click the Clear button. Close the dialog box and save the document.

Master Documents

A master document is like a folder that holds multiple files, similar to the way a book contains many chapters. Using a master document makes uniform formatting easy. You can also create a table of contents and index for a master document that includes all its documents.

 You can't convert a document with file versions to a master document. You must delete all versions before you can convert the document. If you need the file versions, save the document to another name (like [file name] Master Document), and then delete the versions in the new document only.

Task 10   *Creating a master document.*

Start with a new blank document.

1. Click View|Master Document to switch to Master Document view.

2. Type "Operating Procedures and Guidelines" as the name of the main document. This heading is assigned Heading 1 in the Style list box.

3. Press the Enter key.

4. Press the Tab key and type the title of the first subdocument, as shown in Figure 20.10. This heading is assigned Heading 2 in the Style list box.

5. Press the Enter key and type in the next subdocument name.

6. Continue adding the rest of the subdocuments' names.

7. Select all the Heading 2 titles, and then click the Create Subdocument button on the Master Document toolbar, as shown in Figure 20.10.

8. Save the master document to a different disk.

Word saves the master document with the file name you provide, but it gives each subdocument a file name based on the first characters in the subdocument's

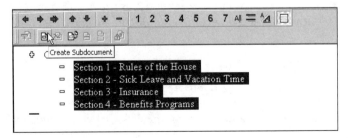

Figure 20.10   Creating subdocuments in a master document.

heading. Click the Open button and view the folder in which you saved the master document. You'll see the master document and each subdocument listed in the Open dialog box.

Task 11 Working with a master document.

You can work with a master document and its subdocuments in many ways.

1. Click the Collapse Subdocuments button. Now each subdocument is a hyperlink.

2. Click Section 1 (or the first subdocument in your master document).

3. The subdocument opens.

4. Type a few lines of text in the subdocument and then save it.

5. Click the Close button on the subdocument menu bar, and you're returned to the master document.

6. Click the Section 4 subdocument icon and then press the Delete key. The subdocument is deleted.

7. Click the Undo button on the Standard toolbar to restore the subdocument.

8. Drag the Section 4 subdocument by the subdocument icon to the second subdocument position and release. Click OK when the message box displays.

9. Click the Expand Subdocuments button (formerly the Collapse Subdocuments button).

10. Drag the subdocument by the subdocument icon to the second subdocument position and release. The subdocument is repositioned.

11. Close the Undo button, and then save and close the document.

 Be sure to drag the subdocument above the line marker that separates Section 1 and Section 2, as shown in Figure 20.11. Otherwise, it will become a subdocument within Section 2.

Task 12 Converting a document to a master document.

1. Open the file Ch20Handbook from the disk that was included with your book.

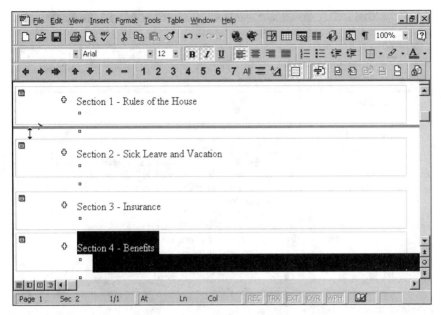

Figure 20.11   Dragging a subdocument to a new position.

2. Click View|Master Document, place the cursor in front of the word Overview, and then press the Tab key to demote it to Heading 2.

3. Click the hollow plus sign to the left of the Section 1 heading, and then click the Create Subdocument button.

4. Click the hollow plus sign in front of Harassment, and then click the Create Subdocument button. Convert Section 2 to a subdocument.

5. Save the document as Ch20.1Handbook.

Some existing documents, such as the Office Manual document, can't be converted until the headings are changed. One way to avoid changing heading styles for existing documents is to save each chapter separately as a document:

1. Copy and paste the Chapter 1 (or section, etc.) text to a new document and save it as Chapter 1. Repeat for any remaining chapters.

2. Open a blank document, type a name for the master document, and then press the Enter key.

3. Click the Insert Subdocument button and then double-click one of the chapter documents (see Figure 20.12).

4. Repeat with remaining chapters and then save the file as a master document.

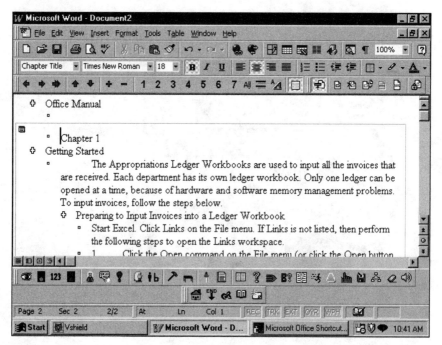

Figure 20.12 Inserting a chapter document as a subdocument.

Task 13   Merging subdocuments.

Use the Ch20.1Handbook file you created in Task 12.

1. Click the Section 1 subdocument icon.

2. Scroll to the Harassment subdocument, hold down the Shift key, and then click the Harassment subdocument icon.

3. Click the Merge Subdocument button.

4. Save the master document, collapse the subdocuments, save, and then close the file.

Practice Projects

Perform the following projects based on this chapter. Open the file Ch20Manual from the disk that was included with your book.

Project 1   Create versions of a document.

1. Open the document and save a version of it with a comment.

2. Make modifications to the document and save at least two additional versions.

3. Open one version and make changes. Save to a new version.

4. Delete a version of the document, and then save the file to a different disk as Ch20Project1.

Answer to Project 1

With a document open, click File|Versions. Click the Save Now button. Type a comment for your version.

Make changes to the document, double-click the File Versions icon, and then click the Save Now button (or display the Reviewing toolbar and then click the Save Version button). Type a comment for the version. Repeat for next version(s).

Double-click the File Versions icon on the status bar, and then select a file version you want to view. Click the Open button. Make changes to the version, and then save a new version using the File Versions icon.

Double-click the File Versions icon on the status bar. Select the file version you want to delete. Click the Delete button. Click File|Save As, click the Save In list box, locate the folder where you want to save the document, rename it Ch20Project1, and then click the Save button.

Project 2   Track changes.

1. Enable the Track Changes feature so that the changes display on the screen but do not display when printed.

2. Make several changes to the document, and then turn off the Track Changes feature using the Reviewing toolbar.

3. Turn on the Track Changes feature with the existing options without using the menu command. Make changes to the document and then turn off Track Changes.

4. Accept or reject the changes made using the Accept Or Reject Changes dialog box.

5. Save the file as Ch20Project2.

Answer to Project 2

Click Tools|Track Changes|Highlight Changes. Click the Track Changes While Editing box to enable it. Verify that the Highlight Changes On Screen box is checked, and then click the Highlight Changes In Printed Document box to remove the check.

Make the changes to the document, and then click the Track Changes button on the Reviewing toolbar to turn off the Track Changes feature.

Click the Track Changes button on the Reviewing toolbar, or double-click the TRK button on the status bar to turn on the Track Changes feature. Make changes, and then either click the Track Changes button on the Reviewing toolbar or double-click the TRK button on the status bar to turn off the Track Changes feature.

Move to the beginning of your document and click the insertion point in page 1. Click Tools|Track Changes|Accept Or Reject Changes. Move to each occurrence of a change in your document by clicking one of the Find buttons within the dialog box, and then accept or reject each change (see Figure 20.13).

Click File|Save As, click the Save In list box, locate the folder where you want to save the document, rename it Ch20Project2, and then click the Save button.

Project 3   Add comments.

1. Insert several comments into the document.
2. View a comment in the document and then view the next comment.
3. View all the comments at one time. Use the Comments pane to move around the comments in the document.
4. Delete a comment.

Answer to Project 3

Select the text you want to comment on, and then click the Insert Comment button on the Reviewing toolbar. Type the comment in the Comments pane. Click the Close button.

Move your mouse over the commented text, and the comment will display as a ScreenTip.

Figure 20.13   The Accept Or Reject Changes dialog box.

Click View|Comments to open the Comments pane and view all comments. Click the comments in the Comments pane to move from comment to comment in the document.

Right-click the commented text in the document and then click the Delete Comment command on the shortcut menu.

Project 4   Highlighting.

1. Change the Highlight color to light blue and then highlight some preselected text.

2. Highlight several noncontiguous sentences.

3. Remove the highlighting from one selection. Save the document.

Answer to Project 4

Click the Highlight button arrow and then click the light blue option. Select text to highlight and then click the Highlight button.

Click the Highlight button, select text to highlight, and then click the Highlight button to deactivate it.

Select the highlighted text and then click the Highlight button to remove the highlighting. Click the Save button.

Project 5   Route a document.

1. Route a document through email, selecting recipients from your address book.

2. Add a message to the email and send the document to all the recipients at once.

3. Have the documents return to you when the recipients are finished with it, enable the Track Status option, and allow the recipients to make comments but not changes within the document.

4. Continue working on the document before sending it.

Answer to Project 5

Click File|Send To|Routing Recipient. Click the Address button in the Routing Slip dialog box, and then select the address book that contains your routing recipients. Add each person with the To button in the Address Book dialog box.

Type a message in the Message text box, and then click the All At Once option in the Route To Recipients group.

Verify that the Return When Done box is checked and then verify that the Track Status box is checked. Select the Comments option in the Protect For list box.

Click the Add Slip button.

Project 6   Create a master document.

1. Create a separate document for each of the chapters in the document Ch20Project1 that you created in Project 1, close all open files, and then create a new master document.

2. Name the document "Office Manual", insert the chapters as subdocuments, and then save the new documents as Ch20Project6.

3. Collapse the subdocuments, click Chapter 1 to open it, and type a line of text. Save and close the subdocument. Save the master document.

4. Move the last subdocument to the first position and delete the subdocument that is now second. Close the master document without saving.

Answer to Project 6

Copy and paste each chapter in Ch20Project1 to its own document, and then save and close all documents. Open a blank document, click View|Master View, type a name for the document, and then press the Enter key.

Type "Office Manual", press the Enter key, click the Insert Subdocument button, and then double-click one of the chapter documents. Repeat with remaining chapters and then save the file as Ch20Project6.

Click the Collapse Subdocuments button. Click the Chapter 1 hyperlink subdocument name to open the subdocument for editing. Type the desired text. Save the subdocument and then click the document's Close button. Click the Save button. Click the Expand Subdocuments button.

Drag the subdocument by the subdocument icon to the first subdocument position and release. Click the second subdocument icon and then click the Delete key. Click the document's Close button and then click No in the message box.

Need To Know More?

 Napier, Albert H. and Phillip J. Judd: *Mastering and Using Microsoft Word 97*. Course Technology, Cambridge, MA, 1997. ISBN 0-7600-5022-8. This book brings the authors' experiences as educators and corporate trainers to Word 97 techniques.

 Shelly, Gary, Thomas Cashman, and Misty Vermaat: *Microsoft Word 97, Complete Concepts and Techniques*. Course Technology, Cambridge, MA, 1997. ISBN 0-7895-1338-2. A book in the Shelly Cashman series. Offers a step-by-step approach to learning beginning and advanced skills in Word 97.

 Swanson, Marie L.: *Microsoft Word 97—Illustrated Standard Edition: A Second Course*. Course Technology, Cambridge, MA, 1997. ISBN 0-7600-5141-0. An Illustrated Series book. Covers intermediate through advanced skills.

 Zimmerman, Scott and Beverly Zimmerman: *New Perspectives on Microsoft Word 97—Comprehensive*. Course Technology, Cambridge, MA, 1997. ISBN 0-7600-5256-5. Part of the New Perspectives series. Offers case-based, problem-solving approaches to learning Word 97.

Lists, Forms, And Mail Merges

Terms you'll need to understand:

√ Bullets

√ Forms

√ Online form

√ Form field

√ Mail merge

√ Data source

√ Merge fields

√ Catalogs

Skills you'll need to master:

√ Creating a list

√ Using bullets with a list

√ Creating a printable form

√ Creating an online form

√ Opening a data source

√ Creating a data source

√ Inserting merge fields

√ Merging documents

√ Creating a catalog

Lists

You can create different types of lists in Word. For example, you can have a list of figures, a list of text, and a list of paragraphs. A list can consist of bulleted or numbered text, a table of information, a list of figures (such as the figures in this book), and numbered paragraphs.

Lists can be a separate document or part of a document with other types of text. A list can be used in conjunction with other documents, like a mail merge.

Task 1   Creating a list of names.

Start with a new blank document for this task.

1. Click Table|Insert Table, and select six columns and four rows in the Insert Table dialog box.

   Note: You can use the Insert Table button on the Standard toolbar to create up to a 4x5 table.

2. Click in the first cell and type the first heading name. Use the data in Figure 21.1 for your table. Press the Tab key and enter the next heading name. Continue until all the headings are added.

3. Press the Tab key and enter the first name. Press the Tab key and enter the company name. Continue until all of the information is added for all contacts.

Contact	Company	Address	City	State	Zip
Jeff Orion	Warner Classics, Inc.	121 Caste Pl.	New York	NY	10020
Ben Storm	Palms to Sea Gifts	1540 Rodeo dr.	Beverly Hills	CA	94802
Benjamin Scott	Allen Rider Co.	6657 Lone Star Way	Dallas	TX	63225
Rebecca Book	Pressman's Originals	10-665 5th Ave.	New York	NY	10001
Jennifer Starr	Design Concepts	798 York St.	Seattle	WA	98002
Christy Stone	Nova Gifts	112 Hanley Dr.	Sandpoint	ID	87852
Debora Windsome	Geranium Rose	8581 Bridgeport	Orlando	FL	25605

Figure 21.1   A list of clients' names.

When you get to the end of the table, pressing the Tab key will add another row for you.

4. Select row 1 (with the headings), and make the font bold and centered. Then, increase the font to 14 points for all the titles.

5. Select column 2, as shown in Figure 21.2, and then move the mouse to the line between column 1 and column 2.

6. When the mouse becomes a two-headed arrow, double-click and the column will automatically resize to fit the longest entry (see Figure 21.3). Start with the smallest columns first.

Contact	Company	Address	City	State	Zip Code
Jeff Orlon	Warner Classics, Inc.	121 Caste Pl.	New York	NY	10020
Ben Storm	Palms to Sea Gifts	1540 Rodeo dr.	Beverly Hills	CA	94802
Benjamin Scott	Allen Rider Co.	6657 Lone Star Way	Dallas	TX	63225
Rebecca Book	Pressman's Originals	10-665 5ª Ave.	New York	NY	10001
Jennifer Starr	Design Concepts	798 York St.	Seattle	WA	98002
Christy Stone	Nova Gifts	112 Hanley Dr.	Sandpoint	ID	87852
Debora Windsome	Geranium Rose	8581 Bridgeport	Orlando	FL	25605

Figure 21.2   Selecting a column.

Contact	Company	Address	City	State	Zip Code
Jeff Orlon	Warner Classics, Inc.	121 Caste Pl.	New York	NY	10020
Ben Storm	Palms to Sea Gifts	1540 Rodeo dr.	Beverly Hills	CA	94802
Benjamin Scott	Allen Rider Co.	6657 Lone Star Way	Dallas	TX	63225
Rebecca Book	Pressman's Originals	10-665 5ª Ave.	New York	NY	10001
Jennifer Starr	Design Concepts	798 York St.	Seattle	WA	98002
Christy Stone	Nova Gifts	112 Hanley Dr.	Sandpoint	ID	87852
Debora Windsome	Geranium Rose	8581 Bridgeport	Orlando	FL	25605

Figure 21.3   Automatically resizing the column to the longest entry.

Note: If the entry is not completely on one line, such as Design Concepts in Figure 21.3, then you do not have enough page width to enlarge the column any farther.

7. Resize the rest of the columns and then select the rows you want to enlarge. Drag the bottom line down to the desired height.

8. When you have finished formatting the table, save it with the name Ch21.1Client, and then close the document.

Task 2   Creating a bulleted list.

You can customize an existing bullet or select and customize the bullet of your choice.

1. Open the file Ch21DraftFoot from the disk that is included with this book.

2. Beginning with elephant, select all the items in the list, and then click Format|Bullets And Numbering.

3. Click the Bulleted tab, if necessary. Click the bullet window you want to replace and then click the Customize button.

4. Click the Bullet button and then click the Font list arrow in the Symbol dialog box. Click the Animals font (select another if Animals isn't available), select the camel (see Figure 21.4), and then click the OK button.

5. Click the Font button, click Bold, and select the 18 point font size and the Dark Blue color.

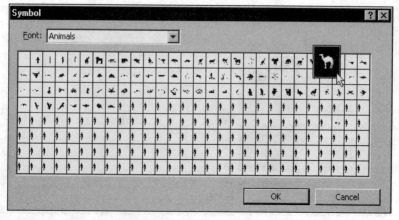

Figure 21.4   Choosing symbols.

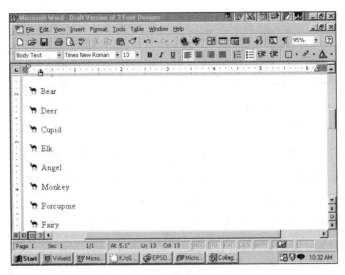

Figure 21.5   The completed bullet list.

6. Click OK to close the Bullets And Numbering dialog box. The bullets are automatically applied to the selected text, as shown in Figure 21.5.

7. Place the cursor at the end of the last item. Press the Enter key. A new bullet will appear, ready for the next item on the list. To deselect the bullet option, click the Bullets button on the Formatting toolbar.

 You can also press the Enter key twice to deselect the bullet option and create a blank line.

8. Save the file as Ch21.1DraftFoot and then close the document.

Forms

You don't need a complex database to input information into a form. You can create a data form right in Word. You can create the following types of forms:

➤ A blank form that you print and then fill out.

➤ A simple online form that can be used through email or a local area network.

➤ A customized online form that uses the Visual Basic programming language.

Task 3 Creating a printed form.

Before creating your form, it's a good idea to sketch out a basic guide for your form. For example, what fields do you want to include? How do you want to separate similar fields? How do you want to group your fields?

1. Open a new, blank document. Right-click a toolbar and display the Forms toolbar.

2. Type the company header information, as shown in Figure 21.6.

3. Type the Date heading and use the underscore to add the line.

4. Create a text box by clicking the Insert Frame button on the Forms toolbar and then dragging the mouse to the desired size (see Figure 21.7).

5. Fill in the text box with the recipient's information in Figure 21.8 and add write-in lines.

6. Widen the text box, if needed, by dragging one of the sizing handles, as shown in Figure 21.8.

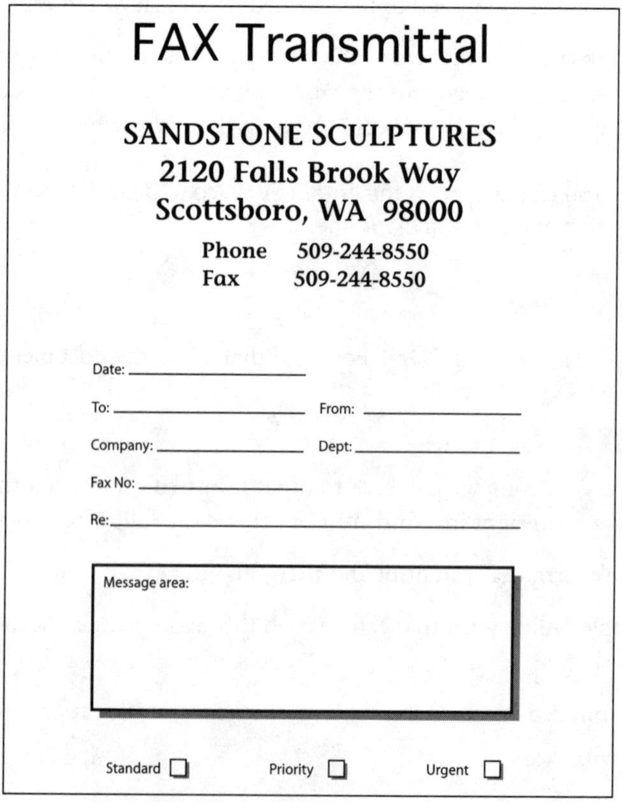

FAX Transmittal

SANDSTONE SCULPTURES
2120 Falls Brook Way
Scottsboro, WA 98000

Phone   509-244-8550
Fax   509-244-8550

Date: _____

To: _____   From: _____

Company: _____   Dept: _____

Fax No: _____

Re:_____

Message area:

Standard ☐   Priority ☐   Urgent ☐

Figure 21.6 The completed form.

Figure 21.7   Drawing a text box on the form.

Figure 21.8   Dragging the sizing handles to enlarge the box.

7. Select the text within the text box, right-click the text box, and then click the Paragraph command on the shortcut menu.

8. Click the Indents And Spacing tab, if necessary, and then select the 1.5 lines option in the Line Spacing list box in the Spacing group (see Figure 21.9).

9. Make the titles in the list box bold.

10. Create another text box adjacent to the first one. Type in the sender's information (From: and Dept:) and add write-in lines.

11. Click the recipient's box (the sizing handles will appear), click the Format Painter button on the Standard toolbar, and then click and drag the mouse pointer across all data in the sender's text box.

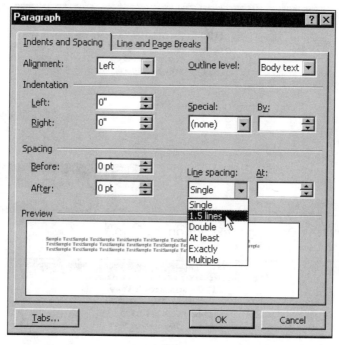

Figure 21.9 The Paragraph dialog box.

12. Right-click the border of one of the text boxes (when the mouse pointer becomes a four-headed arrow), and then click the Borders And Shading command on the shortcut menu.

13. On the Borders tab, click the None box to remove the border. Repeat this step for the other text box.

14. Create a large text box and add the text "Message area" with bold formatting.

15. Right-click the text box and then click the Borders And Shading command.

16. Add a border and a shadow to the box.

17. Place the cursor between the smaller text box and the larger text box. Type "Re:" and add a write-in line to the end of the page.

18. Press the Enter key until the cursor is halfway between the bottom of the large text box and the bottom of the page.

19. Type "Standard", press the spacebar twice, and then click the Check Box Form Field button on the Forms toolbar.

20. Press the Tab key, type "Priority", press the spacebar twice, and then click the Check Box Form Field button on the Forms toolbar.

21. Press the Tab key, type "Urgent", press the spacebar twice, and then click the Check Box Form Field button on the Forms toolbar.

22. Center the entire line you just created. Use the Tab key to space the items evenly across the page, as shown back in Figure 21.6.

23. Save the form as Ch21.1Fax.

Task 4   Creating an online form.

Before creating your form, decide what types of options you want to include. For example, are you going to include a drop-down form field? Are you going to limit the size of text form fields? Are you going to include Help text?

An online form must be created and saved as a template. The user will open the template, fill it in, and then save the current form as a document.

1. For the sake of ease, open Ch21.1Fax and click Edit|Select All. Click the Copy button and then close the fax form.

HOLD That Skill!
You can press Ctrl+A to select all the text in a document.

2. Click File|New, click the General tab in the New dialog box, click the Blank Document icon, click the Template option, and then click OK.

3. When the new Template 1 file opens click the Paste button. You now have a basic form design that you'll modify for online use.

4. Select the write-in line after the Date heading and press the Delete key.

5. With the cursor still to the right of the Date heading, click the Text Form Field button on the Forms toolbar.

6. Double-click the form field, and select the Date type format and the MMMM d, yyyy style in the Text Form Field Options dialog box, as shown in Figure 21.10.

7. Delete the write-in line for the "To:" heading, and then click the Drop-Down Form Field button on the Forms toolbar.

8. Double-click the drop-down form field, and type the first name (Jeff Orion) in the Drop-Down Item text box (you can print the data source file to use the Contact names).

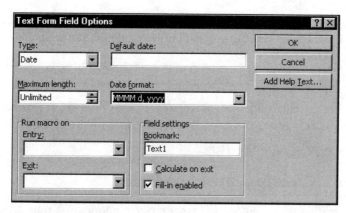

Figure 21.10 The Text Form Field Options dialog box with the date format and style.

9. Press the Enter key and type the next name. Continue until you have entered all the names that will appear in the drop-down box.

10. Click on a name and use the Move arrows to put the names in alphabetical order.

11. Click the Add Help Text button, click the Status Bar tab, and then click the Type Your Own option. Type in the Help text, as shown in Figure 21.11.

12. Close the dialog boxes and repeat steps 7 through 11 for the Company field.

13. Add a text form field box for the fax number and the "From:" field, making no changes in the Form Field Options dialog box.

14. Add a text form field box for the "RE:" field. In the Form Field Options dialog box, click the Title Case option in the Text Format list box, then close the dialog box.

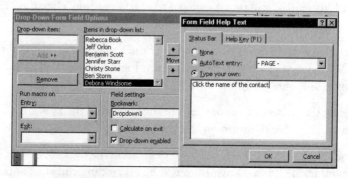

Figure 21.11 The Drop-Down Form Field Options and Form Field Help Text dialog boxes.

15. Click the form field box and then press the left arrow key. Click the Underline button on the Formatting toolbar, hold down the Ctrl and Shift keys, and then press the right-arrow key. This will underline all the text entered in this box.

16. Click to the right of the Message Area text, press the Enter key twice, and then add a form field box.

17. Add a text form field box for the "Dept.:" field. In the Form Field Options dialog box, select Number in the Type list box, the maximum length 4, the default number 123, and the number format 0.

18. Click the Protect Form button on the Forms toolbar, close the Forms toolbar, save the form as Ch21.2Fax, and close it.

Now you get to see if your form works. Click File|New and then select your fax template, opening it as a document. Type in a date in number format, click a drop-down field, select a name, type in a remark in the RE: box, and select a number for the Dept. code. Notice the Help text in the status bar when you click the Name or Company drop-down arrow.

Watch how each field will automatically perform the formatting you created. You can choose to not have the form field shading in each field by deselecting the Form Field Shading button on the Forms toolbar.

Mail Merge

Mail merge—the very name conjures goose bumps and chills for many people. But take heart, because gone are the days when a mail merge required a Master's degree in computing software. Word 97 offers a mail merge feature that is easy and fun (really).

A *mail merge* consists of two parts: the main document in which the field codes and any repeating text are entered, and a secondary document (called a data source) that contains the list or information that will be inserted into the main document. When the merge is initiated, the data source replaces the field codes with the correlating information.

You can create the main document by scratch, or you can use one of the many templates provided with Word 97.

You've already created a macro to help you create documents, so you can use it here. If you didn't create the template or macro in Chapter 19, start with a blank document and type in your own text when you are directed to run a macro.

Task 5   Creating the main document.

1. Click the Create_Main_Doc button on your toolbar. This should create a page with a letterhead and a watermark.

2. Select Tools|Mail Merge.

3. Click the Create button, and then click the Form Letters option in the Mail Merge Helper dialog box.

4. Click the Active Window button in the Message dialog box.

5. Click the Get Data button in the Mail Merge Helper dialog box, as shown in Figure 21.12, and then click the Open Data Source option.

6. Select Ch21.1Client, created earlier in this chapter.

7. A message box displays informing you that there are no merge fields in the main document. Click the Edit Main Document button in the message box.

8. The main document is displayed with the Mail Merge toolbar. Create the body of the letter with the FormLetter button you created in Chapter 19.

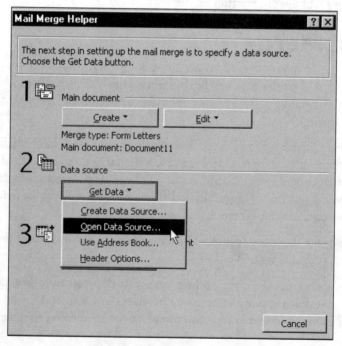

Figure 21.12 The Mail Merge Helper dialog box.

Task 6   *Inserting merge fields.*

1. Use the mouse or arrow keys to place the cursor two lines below the date (don't use the Enter key).

2. Click the Insert Merge Field button on the Mail Merge toolbar, and select the Contact option, as shown in Figure 21.13.

3. The Contact merge field is added to the document. Press the down arrow key (not the Enter key), click the Insert Merge Field button, and then select the Company merge field. Repeat this for the Address field.

4. Press the down arrow key, click the Insert Merge Field button, and then select the City merge field. Type a comma and then press the spacebar.

5. Click the Insert Merge Field button and then select the State merge field. Press the spacebar twice, and then insert the Zip merge field (see Figure 21.14).

Task 7   *Editing the data source.*

1. Click the Edit Data Source button on the Mail Merge toolbar, and then click the View Source button on the data form.

2. When you move the mouse pointer above the columns, the pointer becomes a black column-selection arrow. Point to the area to the right of the last column and then click the mouse button. Select Table| Insert Columns.

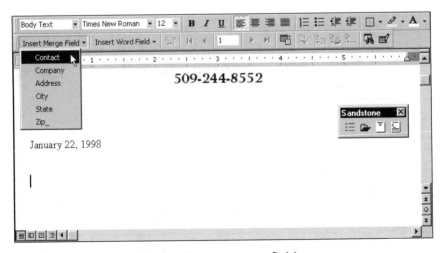

Figure 21.13   Inserting the Contact merge field.

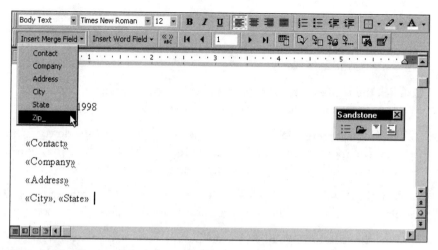

Figure 21.14 Inserting the Zip merge field.

 When you are viewing the data source you can also click the Manage Fields button on the Database toolbar to add a column header.

3. Type the Salutation heading and then add the salutation to each record, as shown in Figure 21.15.

4. Remove the bold formatting from the headings and resize the columns to best fit all the data.

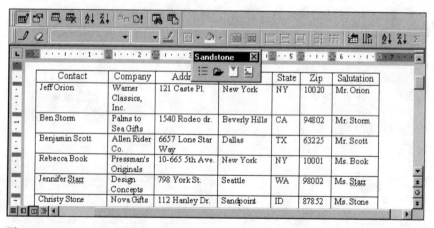

Figure 21.15 Adding a column to the data source and filling in the new fields.

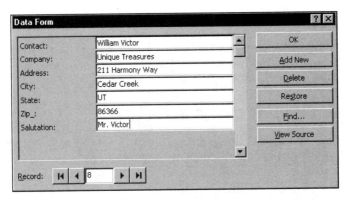

Figure 21.16   A new record in the data form.

5. Click the Data Form button on the Mail Merge toolbar and then click the Add New button on the data form. Enter the new record, as shown in Figure 21.16, and then click the OK button.

6. Click the Mail Merge Main Document button on the Mail Merge toolbar.

7. Place the cursor to the right of the word "Dear" and to the left of the colon in the main document, click the Insert Merge Field button, and select the new Salutation option.

Task 8   Merging the two documents.

Now you're ready to perform a mail merge.

1. Click the Merge To New Document button on the Mail Merge toolbar.

2. You now have a letter to each person in your data source in a document called Form Letters 1.

3. Close Form Letters 1 without saving.

> You don't need to save form letters once you have printed them. It's a waste of disk space; new merges are easy once you have created and saved a main document and a data source.
>
> You can create new main documents, such as a different form letter, a flier, mailing labels, or a catalog, and use the same data source each time.

4. Save the main document as Ch21.1Merged and save the Client data source as Ch21.2Client. Close both documents.

Catalogs

A *catalog* is a type of main document where all the merged data is placed in one merged document. You can use a catalog main document to create a list or directory with ease.

Task 9   Creating a catalog.

You can start with a blank document, or you can create a main document with your watermark by opening the Watermark Page template as a document.

1. Select Tools|Mail Merge.

2. Click the Create button and then click the Catalog option.

3. Click the Active Window button in the message box.

4. Click the Get Data button in the Mail Merge Helper dialog box, and then click the Open Data Source option.

5. Select the file Ch21.2.

6. Click the Edit Main Document button in the message box to merge fields in the main document.

7. Place the merge field codes across the page, separating each with a tab, and then press the Enter key after the Zip field, as shown in Figure 21.17.

8. Click the Merge To New Document button.

9. Change the page orientation to landscape, select all the data, change the line spacing to 1.5 lines, increase the font to 12 point bold, and click a

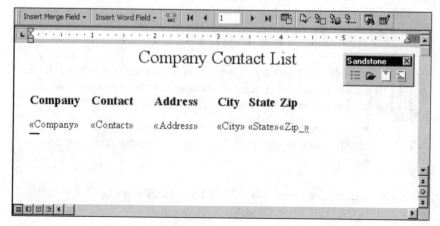

Figure 21.17   Placing the merge field codes.

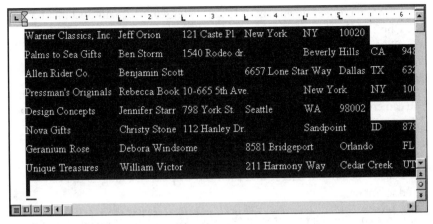

Figure 21.18   All the text is selected while making changes.

left-aligned tab on the horizontal ruler at the beginning of each column (see Figure 21.18).

10. Don't worry if the data looks messed up. Once you have adjusted the tab placements, all the fields will line up. With all the data still selected, drag the tabs on the ruler at least one inch to the right, starting with the Zip field.

11. Work with the tabs until the data looks right to you. Figure 21.19 shows the completed catalog in Print Preview mode.

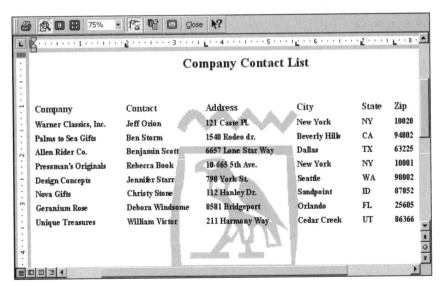

Figure 21.19   The completed catalog in Print Preview mode.

12. Save the merged document as Ch21.2Merged, the main document as Chp21.1Catalog, and then save the Client Data Source as Ch21.3Client. Close all the documents.

Task 10   Creating a data source.

You can create a catalog by creating a new data source. Create a catalog of your debtors.

1. Open Chp21.1Catalog , which you created in Task 9.

2. Select Tools|Mail Merge and then use Chp21.1Catalog as the active document.

3. Click the Get Data button in the Mail Merge Helper dialog box and then click the Create Data Source option.

4. When the Create Data Source dialog box displays, click the Remove button to remove all unnecessary fields.

5. Add a Contact field, a ZIP code field, and then rename the Address1 field to Address.

6. Enter the data on the data form. Save the data source as Chp21.2Catalog.

7. Click the Mail Merge Helper button and then click the Setup button for the main document. Insert the merge fields and then merge the documents to a new document.

8. Save the merged document as Chp21.3Catalog.

Practice Projects

Perform the following projects based on this chapter.

Project 1   Create a list in a table.

Begin with a blank document.

1. Create a two-column list of your household belongings. Name the items in column 1 and list their value in column 2.

2. Increase the heading sizes, and adjust the columns and rows as necessary.

3. Save the list as Chp21.1Datasource.

Answer to Project 1

Click the Insert Table button on the Standard toolbar, and select a two-column table with the amount of rows of your choice. Create headings and type the data into the columns.

Select the row containing the headings and increase the font size by about two points. Move the mouse to the right-hand column boundaries. When the mouse becomes a two-headed arrow, double-click or drag the boundary to the right. Adjust the rows as needed by double-clicking or dragging the bottom row boundary for each row.

Save the document, calling it Chp21.1Datasource.

Project 2   Create a bulleted list.

1. Use a 12-point font to create a numbered, 20-item list. Create two columns so there are 10 items per side.

2. Change the numbering in the second list to bullets. Select a new bullet and change the shape, size, and color of the bullet.

3. Turn off the Columns feature and type a sentence after the lists.

4. Save as Chp21.1List and then close the document.

Answer to Project 2

Click the Font Size window and select 12 points. Click the Numbering button and create the list of items. Place a continuous section break at the bottom of the list.

Select the list on the right and click Format|Bullets And Numbering. Click the Bulleted tab and select a bullet to replace. Click the Bullets button, select a bullet, and then close the Bullets dialog box. Click the Font button and select a font size of 12 points to match the text size. Select a color for the bullets.

Press the Enter key, click the Columns button, and select 1 column. Type the sentence. Your screen should have the same elements as Figure 21.20.

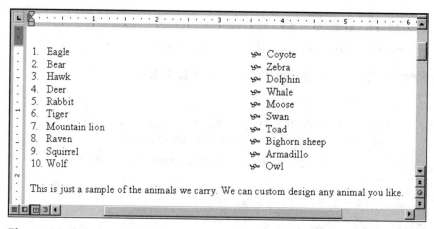

1. Eagle
2. Bear
3. Hawk
4. Deer
5. Rabbit
6. Tiger
7. Mountain lion
8. Raven
9. Squirrel
10. Wolf

- Coyote
- Zebra
- Dolphin
- Whale
- Moose
- Swan
- Toad
- Bighorn sheep
- Armadillo
- Owl

This is just a sample of the animals we carry. We can custom design any animal you like.

Figure 21.20   A sample of a twenty-item list.

Select File|Save As, name the file Chp21.1List, click the disk drive from the Save In list box, and then click the Save button.

Project 3   Create a form from a table.

1. Create a company form that has a letterhead, a Date write-in line, a page footer, and a four-by-four cell table for the items purchased, cost, unit, and total.

2. Use the Draw Table feature to create a two-by-three cell addition to the table below the total column for the subtotal, tax, and grand total.

3. Save the document as Ch21Project3.

Answer to Project 3

Right-click a toolbar and display the Forms toolbar. Type the Company header informa-tion or use your macro. Use the LetterFooter macro to add a page footer. Type the Date heading and use the underscore to add the write-in line. Use the Insert Table button on the Standard toolbar to create a four-by-four cell table. Type the headings in the first row.

Move down to the bottom of the table, and click Table|Draw Table to draw a two-by-three cell addition to the table directly below the total column (see Figure 21.21).

Click the Save button on the Standard toolbar and then save the document as Ch21Project3.

Type "Subtotal", "Tax", and "Grand Total". See Figure 21.22 for an example of the form.

Project 4   Create an online form from a table.

Use the form you created in Project 3, Ch21Project3.

1. Create an online form from a table. Format the columns as follows (*Hint:* you can copy and paste redundant fields).

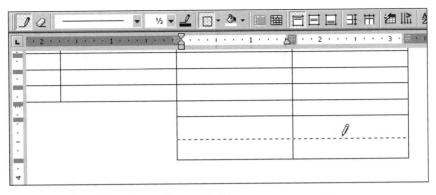

Figure 21.21 Drawing cells on a table.

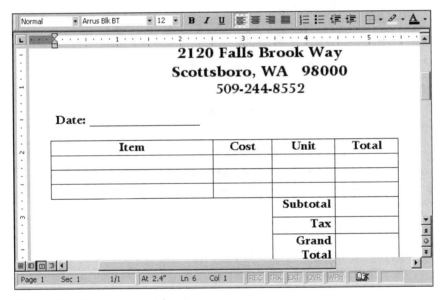

Figure 21.22 A printed form.

2. Format the Date as a date with a M/dd/yy format.

3. Format Cost as a number with a decimal format.

4. Format Unit as a number with an integer format.

5. Format Total as a number with a currency format.

Answer to Project 4

Click Edit|Select All (or Ctrl+A) with your table form open. Click the Copy button and then close the table form. Click File|New, click the General tab in the New dialog box, click the Blank Document icon, select the Template option, and then click OK. When the new Template 1 file opens, click the Paste button.

Select the write-in line after the Date heading and press the Delete key. With the cursor still to the right of the Date heading, click the Text Form Field button. Double-click the form field, and select the Date format and the M/dd/yy date style in the Text Form Fields Options dialog box.

Select the first Cost cell and then click the Text Form Field button. Double-click the form field, and select the number type and format with the 0.00 option. Copy this field and paste it to the other Cost fields.

Select the first Unit cell and then click the Text Form Field button. Double-click the form field, and select the number type and format with the 0 option. Copy this field and paste it to the other Unit fields.

Select the first Total cell and then click the Text Form Field button. Double-click the form field. Select the number type and format with the $#,##0.00;($#,##.00) option. Copy this field and paste it to the other Total fields.

Project 5 Create a mail merge.

Use a blank document to begin.

1. Start a mail merge with the form letter option as your main document.

2. Create a data source using six family members as your data.

3. Set up the page format as a personal letter, insert the merge fields, and then merge the documents into one document called Ch21.1Letter.

Answer to Project 5

Select Tools|Mail Merge. Click the Create button and then click the Form Letter option. Click the Active Window button in the message box.

Click the Get Data button in the Mail Merge Helper dialog box, and then click the Create Data Source option. The Create Data Source dialog box displays, as shown in Figure 21.23. Click the Remove button for all unnecessary fields, and add a Name field and a Zip field. Enter the data on the data form. Save the data source.

Click the Mail Merge Helper button and then click the Setup button for the main document. Insert the merge fields and then merge the documents to a new document. Save the merged document as Ch21.1Letter.

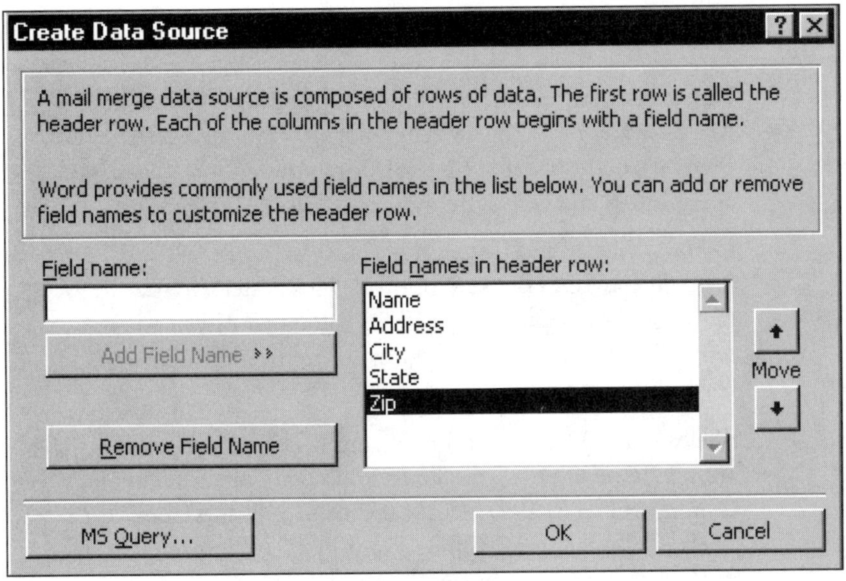

Figure 21.23 The Create Data Source dialog box with field names selected.

Need To Know More?

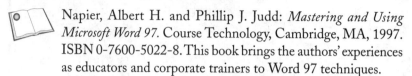

Napier, Albert H. and Phillip J. Judd: *Mastering and Using Microsoft Word 97*. Course Technology, Cambridge, MA, 1997. ISBN 0-7600-5022-8. This book brings the authors' experiences as educators and corporate trainers to Word 97 techniques.

O'Hara, Shelley and Deborah Allen Rider: *Office 97 Small Business Solutions*. IDG Books Worldwide Inc., Foster City, CA, 1997. ISBN 0-7645-3120-4. Chapters 5 through 7 offer basic to intermediate techniques for creating a letterhead, mail merge, fax cover sheet, and more.

Shelly, Gary, Thomas Cashman, and Misty Vermaat: *Microsoft Word 97 Complete Concepts and Techniques*. Course Technology, Cambridge, MA, 1997. ISBN 0-7895-1338-2. A book in the Shelly Cashman series. Offers a step-by-step approach to learning beginning and advanced skills in Word 97.

Swanson, Marie L.: *Microsoft Word 97—Illustrated Standard Edition: A Second Course*. Course Technology, Cambridge, MA, 1997. ISBN 0-7600-5141-0. An Illustrated Series book. Covers intermediate through advanced skills.

Zimmerman, Scott and Beverly Zimmerman: *New Perspectives on Microsoft Word 97—Comprehensive*. Course Technology, Cambridge, MA, 1997. ISBN 0-7600-5256-5. Part of the New Perspectives series. Offers case-based, problem-solving approaches to learning Word 97.

Sorting

Terms you'll need to understand:

√ Sort

√ Catalog

√ Query

Skills you'll need to master:

√ Sorting a list

√ Sorting a paragraph

√ Sorting a table

√ Sorting records to be merged

Although sorting on a word processor isn't the same as sorting your socks, it does turn out to be just as easy (okay, almost as easy).

You can sort just about anything in Word 97: lists, mail merge data, tables, and paragraphs to name a few. You can sort in ascending or descending order, and in some cases you can sort by columns, rows, or fields.

You can use the documents you created in previous chapters, or you can create new documents to sort.

Sorting A List

Sorting a list is probably the most common use of the sort feature in Word.

Task 1 Sorting a bulleted list.

Open the bulleted list document, Chap21.1List, you created in Chapter 21 for this task.

1. Select the bulleted items and then click Table|Sort.

2. Verify that you're sorting by paragraph in ascending order with no header rows, and then click the OK button in the Sort Text dialog box, as shown in Figure 22.1.

3. Save the file as Ch22.1List and close it.

Task 2 Sorting a catalog.

Open the merged catalog document, Ch21.1Merged, you created in Chapter 21 for this task.

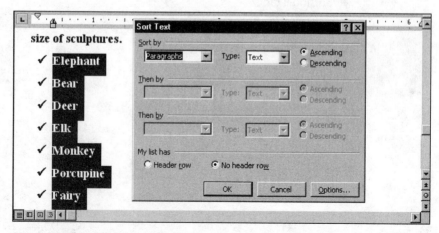

Figure 22.1 The Sort Text dialog box and the selected text.

1. Select the headings and catalog list information (but not the title), and then click Table|Sort.

2. Verify that you're sorting by paragraph in ascending order.

3. Select the Header Row option, as shown in Figure 22.2, and then click OK.

4. Save the file as Ch22.1Catalog and then close the file.

Sorting Paragraphs

You may think it's impossible to sort paragraphs. On what would you base the sort criteria? Well, here's a simple strategy for sorting paragraphs to your heart's content.

Task 3   Sorting paragraphs.

Open Ch14Say.doc on the disk that was included with your book.

1. Place the number 4 and a space in front of the first paragraph, as shown in Figure 22.3.

2. Place the number 3 in the second paragraph, the number 1 in the third paragraph, and the number 2 in the fourth paragraph.

3. Select the four paragraphs, click Table|Sort, and then click OK.

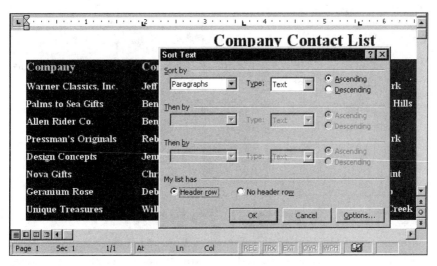

Figure 22.2   Sorting a catalog with a header row.

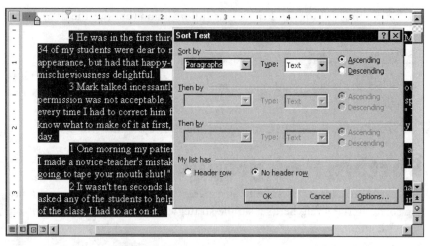

Figure 22.3 Sorting paragraphs.

4. Remove the numbers and extra spaces.

5. Close without saving.

Sorting A Table

Sorting a table is as easy in Word as it is in Excel. You can sort any kind of table—from a Word table to an imported table.

Task 4 Sorting a table.

Use the Word table, Ch16.3Books, you created in Chapter 16 for this task.

1. Select all the cells in the first column (Book Types) except for the Totals cell. Then click Table|Sort.

2. Verify that the Header Row option is selected and the Sort By box states the name of the first column, as shown in Figure 22.4.

3. Click OK.

4. Save the file as Ch22.1TableSort and close it.

Sorting Records To Be Merged

Sorting records prior to a mail merge can be very convenient. Your data source doesn't have to be in alphabetical order to have alphabetized form letters, labels, and so on.

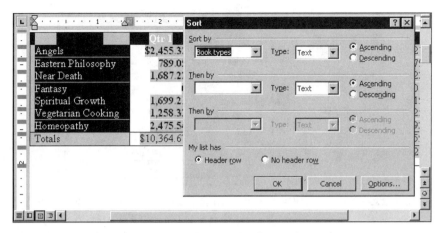

Figure 22.4 Sorting a Word table by the first column.

Task 5   Sorting records to be merged.

Use the Ch21.1Merged and Ch21.1Client documents you created in Chapter 21 for this task.

1. Open Ch21.1Merged and then select Tools|Mail Merge.

2. Click the Create button, and then click the Form Letters option in the Mail Merge Helper dialog box.

3. Click the Active Window button in the message box.

4. Click the Get Data button in the Mail Merge Helper dialog box, and then click the Open Data Source option.

5. Select the data source document you want to use, Ch21.1Client.

6. Click the Edit Main Document button in the message box if you haven't entered the merge fields.

7. Click the Insert Merge Field button on the Mail Merge toolbar and enter the merge fields.

8. Click the Mail Merge Helper button and then click the Query Options button.

9. Click the Sort Records tab and then click the first Sort By list arrow.

10. Click the Company option, as shown in Figure 22.5.

11. Click the second Sort By list arrow and then click the State option.

12. Return to the Mail Merge Helper dialog box and then click the Merge button.

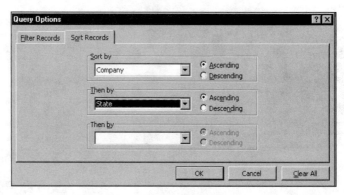

Figure 22.5　The Sort Records tab in the Query Options dialog box.

Practice Projects

Perform the following projects based on this chapter. You'll need to open or create documents as needed.

Project 1   Sort a numbered list.

1. Open or create a document with a twenty-item list, as you created with Chp21.1List in Project 2 of Chapter 21. Balance the numbered items evenly between two columns. Create a title above the columns and a short paragraph below the columns.

2. Sort the 20 items in descending order.

3. Save the document as Ch22.1List.

Answer to Project 1

Format the title in 1 Column format. Type a paragraph below the items. Select the 20 items, click the Numbering button, and then click the 2 Column option.

With the list still selected, click Table|Sort and then click the Descending Order option. The list should resemble the list shown in Figure 22.6.

Click the Save As button and save file as Ch22.1List.

Project 2   Sort a simple list.

Use the Ch22.1List document from the previous project. Remove the title, the ending paragraph, and the number and column formatting.

1. Sort the simple, unformatted list in ascending order.

2. Save the file as Ch22.1SimpleList and then close the file.

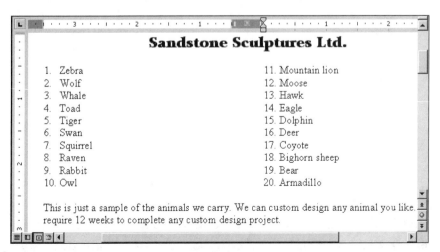

Figure 22.6   A two-column list sorted in descending order.

Answer to Project 2

With a simple list of items entered, select Table|Sort (without selecting the text). Verify that the Ascending Order option is selected and then click OK.

Select File|Save As, change the name to Ch22.1SimpleList, click the disk drive from the Save In list box, and then click the Save button.

Your document should resemble Figure 22.7.

Project 3   Sort a list of columns.

1. Open the file, Client List, from the disk that was included with your book.

2. Sort by State in ascending order, then by City in descending order, and then by Company in ascending order.

Answer to Project 3

Open Client List from the disk.

Select the headings and catalog list information, and then click Table|Sort. Verify the Header Row option is selected. Click the first Sort By list arrow and select the State option. Verify that the Ascending Order option is selected. Click the second Sort By list arrow, select the City option, and then click the Descending Order option. Click the third Sort By list arrow and select the Company option. Verify that the Ascending Order option is selected. Click OK.

The list should now resemble Figure 22.8.

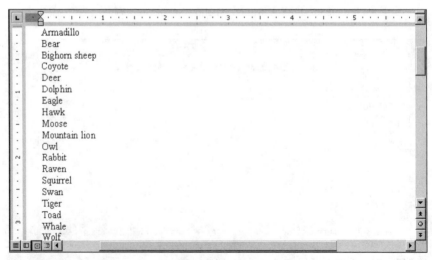

Figure 22.7 A simple list after being sorted in ascending order.

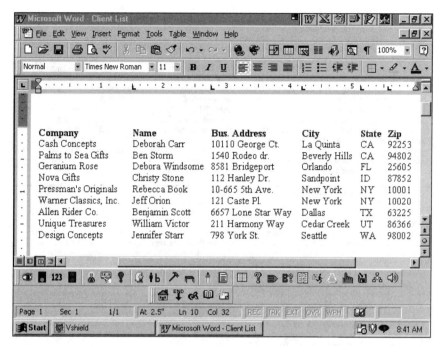

Figure 22.8   A list after sorting by three columns.

Project 4   Sort paragraphs.

Open the file SomethingGood from the disk that is included with this book.

1. Sort the first five paragraphs so that paragraph three is first, paragraph five is second, paragraph one is third, paragraph four is fourth, and paragraph two is fifth.

2. Close the document without saving.

Answer to Project 4

Place the number 3 and a space in the first paragraph, the number 5 in the second paragraph, the number 1 in front of the third paragraph, the number 4 in the fourth paragraph, and the number 2 in the fifth paragraph. Click Table|Sort; then click OK. Remove the numbers and extra spaces.

Click the Close button on the document's title bar and then click the No button in the Message box.

Figure 22. 9 shows the paragraphs before and after the sort.

Project 5   Sort a table.

Use the Ch16.3Books document you created in Chapter 16 for this project.

> 3 He was in the first third-grade class I taught at Saint Mary's School in Morris, Minn. All 34 of my students were dear to me, but Mark Eklund was one in a million. Very neat in appearance, but had that happy-to-be-alive attitude that made even his occasional mischievousness delightful.
>
> 5 Mark talked incessantly. I had to remind him again and again that talking without permission was not acceptable. What impressed me so much, though, was his sincere response every time I had to correct him for misbehaving - "Thank you for correcting me, Sister!" I didn't know what to make of it at first, but before long I became accustomed to hearing it many times a day.
>
> 1 One morning my patience was growing thin when Mark talked once too often, and then I made a novice-teacher's mistake. I looked at him and said, "If you say one more word, I am going to tape your mouth shut!"
>
> 4 It wasn't ten seconds later when Chuck blurted out, "Mark is talking again." I hadn't asked any of the students to help me watch Mark, but since I had stated the punishment in front of the class, I had to act on it.
>
> 2 I remember the scene as if it had occurred this morning. I walked to my desk, very deliberately opened my drawer and took out a roll of masking tape. Without saying a word, I proceeded to Mark's desk, tore off two pieces of tape and made a big X with them over his mouth. I then returned to the front of the room. As I glanced at Mark to see how he was doing he winked at me. That did it! I started laughing. The class cheered as I walked back to Mark's desk, removed the tape and shrugged my shoulders. His first words were, "Thank you for correcting me, Sister."

> One morning my patience was growing thin when Mark talked once too often, and then I made a novice-teacher's mistake. I looked at him and said, "If you say one more word, I am going to tape your mouth shut!"
>
> I remember the scene as if it had occurred this morning. I walked to my desk, very deliberately opened my drawer and took out a roll of masking tape. Without saying a word, I proceeded to Mark's desk, tore off two pieces of tape and made a big X with them over his mouth. I then returned to the front of the room. As I glanced at Mark to see how he was doing he winked at me. That did it! I started laughing. The class cheered as I walked back to Mark's desk, removed the tape and shrugged my shoulders. His first words were, "Thank you for correcting me, Sister."
>
> He was in the first third-grade class I taught at Saint Mary's School in Morris, Minn. All 34 of my students were dear to me, but Mark Eklund was one in a million. Very neat in appearance, but had that happy-to-be-alive attitude that made even his occasional mischievousness delightful.
>
> It wasn't ten seconds later when Chuck blurted out, "Mark is talking again." I hadn't asked any of the students to help me watch Mark, but since I had stated the punishment in front of the class, I had to act on it.
>
> Mark talked incessantly. I had to remind him again and again that talking without permission was not acceptable. What impressed me so much, though, was his sincere response every time I had to correct him for misbehaving - "Thank you for correcting me, Sister!" I didn't know what to make of it at first, but before long I became accustomed to hearing it many times a day.

Figure 22.9   Five paragraphs, before and after sorting.

1. Sort all fields of the table by the Qtr 1 column in ascending order.

2. Close the document without saving.

Answer to Project 5

Select all the cells of the second column (Qtr 1) except for the total cell and then click Table|Sort. Verify that the Header Row option is selected and that the Sort By box states the name of the second column; then click the Descending Order option.

Click the Close button on the document's title bar and then click the No button in the Message box.

Figure 22.10 shows the table before and after the sort.

Project 6   Sort records prior to a merge.

1. Open Chp21.1Catalog, which you created in Chapter 21, and use the Ch21.1Client file.

2. Before merging the documents, sort the catalog in ascending order by the Contact name.

3. Save the merged document as Ch22Project6.

Book types	Qtr 1	Qtr 2	Qtr 3	Qtr 4	Total
Angels	$2,455.32	$1,504.65	$1,785.99	$3,587.25	$9,333.21
Eastern Philosophy	789.05	454.00	575.99	855.75	2,674.79
Near Death	1,687.22	1,200.58	908.77	1,574.65	5,371.22
Fantasy	0	0	0	455.01	455.01
Spiritual Growth	1,699.21	1,474.12	1,569.50	1,875.36	6,618.19
Vegetarian Cooking	1,258.33	1,587.99	1,758.05	2,105.88	6,710.25
Homeopathy	2,475.54	1,999.52	2,005.36	2,677.50	9,157.92
Totals	$10,364.67	$8,220.86	$8,603.66	$12,676.39	$40,320.59

Book types	Qtr 1	Qtr 2	Qtr 3	Qtr 4	Total
Homeopathy	2,475.54	1,999.52	2,005.36	2,677.50	9,157.92
Angels	$2,455.32	$1,504.65	$1,785.99	$3,587.25	$9,333.21
Spiritual Growth	1,699.21	1,474.12	1,569.50	1,875.36	6,618.19
Near Death	1,687.22	1,200.58	908.77	1,574.65	5,371.22
Vegetarian Cooking	1,258.33	1,587.99	1,758.05	2,105.88	6,710.25
Eastern Philosophy	789.05	454.00	575.99	855.75	2,674.79
Fantasy	0	0	0	455.01	455.01
Totals	$10,364.67	$8,220.86	$8,603.66	$12,676.39	$40,320.59

Figure 22.10   A table before and after sorting by the second column.

Answer to Project 6

Open Catalog Main Document and then select Tools|Mail Merge. If necessary, click the Get Data button in the Mail Merge Helper dialog box and then click the Open Data Source option. Click the Query Options button on the Mail Merge Helper dialog box.

Click the Sort tab and then click the first Sort By list arrow. Click the Company option. Return to the Mail Merge Helper dialog box and then click the Merge button.

Click the Save button on the Standard toolbar and then name the file Ch22Project6.

Your sorted document should resemble Figure 22.11.

Allen Rider Co.	Benjamin Scott	6657 Lone Star Way	Dallas	TX	63225
Design Concepts	Jennifer Starr	798 York St.	Seattle	WA	98002
Geranium Rose	Debora Windsome	8581 Bridgeport	Orlando	FL	25605
Nova Gifts	Christy Stone	112 Hanley Dr.	Sandpoint	ID	87852
Palms to Sea Gifts	Ben Storm	1540 Rodeo dr.	Beverly Hills	CA	94802
Pressman's Originals	Rebecca Book	10-665 5th Ave.	New York	NY	10001
Unique Treasures	William Victor	211 Harmony Way	Cedar Creek	UT	86366
Warner Classics, Inc.	Jeff Orion	121 Caste Pl.	New York	NY	10020

Figure 22.11   A catalog that was sorted before a merge.

Need To Know More?

 Napier, Albert H. and Phillip J. Judd: *Mastering and Using Microsoft Word 97.* Course Technology, Cambridge, MA, 1997. ISBN 0-7600-5022-8. This book brings the authors' experiences as educators and corporate trainers to Word 97 techniques.

 O'Hara, Shelley and Deborah Allen Rider: *Office 97 Small Business Solutions.* IDG Books Worldwide Inc., Foster City, CA, 1997. ISBN 0-7645-3120-4. Chapter 15 offers basic to intermediate techniques for creating a mail merge.

 Shelly, Gary, Thomas Cashman, and Misty Vermaat: *Microsoft Word 97: Complete Concepts and Techniques.* Course Technology, Cambridge, MA, 1997. ISBN 0-7895-1338-2. A book in the Shelly Cashman series. Offers a step-by-step approach to learning beginning and advanced skills in Word 97.

 Swanson, Marie L.: *Microsoft Word 97—Illustrated Standard Edition: A Second Course.* Course Technology, Cambridge, MA, 1997. ISBN 0-7600-5141-0. An Illustrated Series book. Covers intermediate through advanced skills.

 Zimmerman, Scott and Beverly Zimmerman: *New Perspectives on Microsoft Word 97—Comprehensive.* Course Technology, Cambridge, MA, 1997. ISBN 0-7600-5256-5. Part of the New Perspectives series. Offers case-based, problem-solving approaches to learning Word 97.

Advanced File Management

Terms you'll need to understand:

√ Protect

√ Unprotect

√ End of protected section

√ File properties

√ Preview

√ Compare documents

Skills you'll need to master:

√ Protecting an entire document

√ Protecting a document while tracking changes

√ Protecting a document with sections

√ Unprotecting a document

√ Viewing file properties before opening a document

√ Previewing a file

√ Saving a picture preview

√ Modifying file properties

√ Comparing documents for tracked changes

Protecting Documents

If you're the only person accessing your documents, there's usually little reason to protect them. However, if others have access to your computer and/or your documents, whether it's the kids at home or your co-workers on the network, you may want to protect your documents (or at least parts of them).

Another time when you'll want to protect a document (or sections of a document) is when filling in an online form. You cannot use the form fields unless the fields are *locked*, or *protected*.

Table 23.1 describes the options in the Protect Document dialog box on the Tools menu.

Task 1   Protecting a document.

1. Open the Ch21.1Merged file you created in Chapter 21 and then click Tools|Protect Document.

2. Click the Forms option and then click the OK button.

Notice that the entire document is protected and no changes can be made.

Task 2   Unprotecting a document.

1. Click Tools|Unprotect Document.

Now you can modify the document again.

Task 3   Protecting a document during tracked changes.

1. Using the Ch21.1Merged file that you created in Chapter 21, click Tools|Protect document.

Table 23.1 Options for protecting a document.	
Option	**Action**
Tracked Changes	When the Tracked Changes option is selected, you can't turn off change tracking, and you can't accept or reject tracked changes.
Comments	Allows comments to be inserted. Also allows reviewers to change the body of the document.
Forms	Protects a document except in form fields or sections that are unprotected. You can turn protection on or off for a section by clicking the Sections button.

2. Select the Tracked Changes option.

3. Make modifications to the document, as shown in Figure 23.1, and then click Tools|Track Changes|Accept Or Reject Changes.

4. When the Accept Or Reject Changes dialog box displays (see Figure 23.1), click one of the Find buttons until the change is highlighted.

5. Click the Accept, Accept All, Reject, or Reject All button, and then click the Yes button if a dialog box displays asking you if you want to accept (or reject) all changes before viewing them.

> Notice that there's no change to the status of the tracked changes. When the document is protected, you cannot accept or reject changes, but you can continue to edit the document.

6. Close the document without saving.

Task 4   *Protecting a document with sections.*

1. Open the Ch14.1Office document you created in Chapter 14 and then click Tools|Protect Document.

2. Click the Forms option and then click the Sections button.

3. Click all but sections 1 and 2 to deselect the sections you want to be unprotected in the Section Protection dialog box (see Figure 23.2). Then return to the document.

4. Try to make changes to the first two chapters and then try to make changes to the remaining chapters. The Section Break line becomes the End Of Protected Section line, as shown in Figure 23.3.

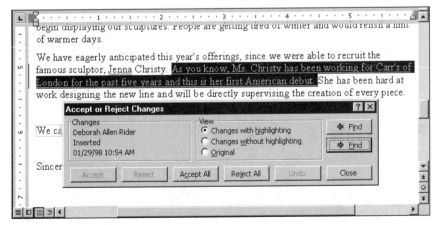

Figure 23.1   The Accept Or Reject Changes dialog box.

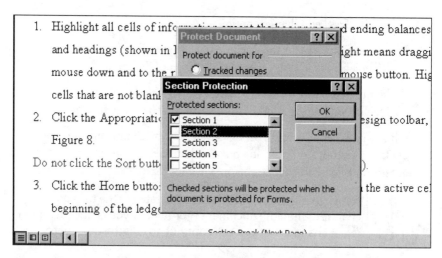

Figure 23.2 Protecting sections in a document.

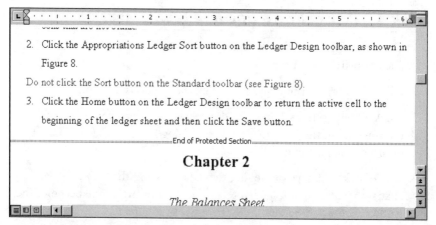

Figure 23.3 The End Of Protected Section line.

Note: If you can't see the section break, click the Normal View button on the horizontal scroll bar.

5. Close the document without saving.

File Properties

Every document you create has file properties that you can access and customize. In fact, you use file properties when you open a document. The Open dialog box contains file names, file sizes, and the dates the files were last modified. These are all file properties.

Now you have the opportunity to take the use of file properties to a new level. You can use them to locate a document, to preview a document, to change the name of the document's author, to add comments, and more.

The Open Dialog Box

You can use the Open dialog box to view file properties and to preview a document before opening it. Refer to Table 23.2 for explanations of the Properties fields.

Task 5   Using the Open dialog box to view properties and preview a document.

1. Click the Open button on the Standard toolbar.

2. Open the Client List.doc from the chapter 22 folder on the disk included with this book, and then click the Properties button on the dialog box toolbar, as shown in Figure 23.4.

3. Scroll the Properties window.

4. Click the Preview button to view the document in the Preview window.

Table 23.2 The Properties fields in the Open dialog box.	
Field	**Description**
Revision	Describes how many times the document has been modified
Application	The program used to create the document
Edited	The total number of hours and minutes spent on modifying the document
Created	The original date the document was created
Modified	The last time the document was modified
Pages	Total number of pages in the document
Words	The total number of words in the document
Characters	The total number of characters (letters, numbers, and special characters), not including spaces
Company	The company that registered the software program
Size	The total number of bytes
Lines	The total number of lines
Paragraphs	The total number of paragraphs
Characters With Spaces	The total number of characters including spaces

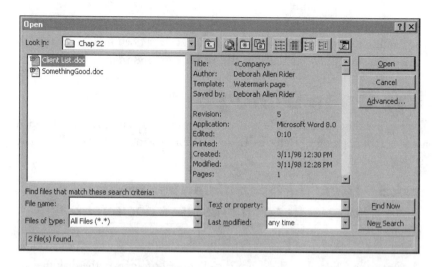

Figure 23.4 Viewing a document's properties in the Open dialog box.

 You can easily locate a document with a particular property by typing or selecting the property information in the Text or property list box in the Open dialog box.

The Properties Dialog Box

When a document is open, you can make modifications to the properties. You can change the author's name, add comments, add custom fields, and more.

Task 6   Creating a page preview for your document.

1. Click the Open button, change to the 3 1/2 Floppy (A:) drive, and then click the Ch15 Designs document.

2. Click the Preview button. Notice how the document is previewed.

3. Open the document and then click File|Properties.

4. Click the Summary tab in the Properties dialog box, and then click the Save Preview Picture option.

5. Save and close the document.

6. Preview the document again in the Open dialog box.

Figure 23.5 displays the difference between previewing a document with and without the Save Preview Picture option selected.

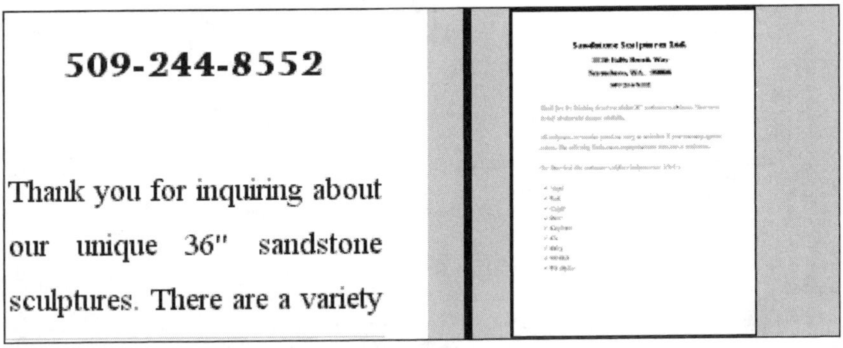

Figure 23.5   The preview of a document before and after the Save Preview Picture option.

Task 7   *Adding comments to file properties.*

1. Open the Ch15Designs document.

2. Select File|Properties.

3. Click the Summary tab in the Properties dialog box, click the Author text box, and then type your name.

4. Click the Comments text box and type "This document has been modified to include new author's name."

5. Close and save the document to a diskette.

Task 8   *Comparing documents.*

Comparing documents is a handy way of seeing changes made to a document. You may have a document on a floppy disk or storage device, and you want to know how it differs from the copy you have on your computer (or on another type of storage device).

Another reason to compare documents is if you use My Briefcase and/or a laptop computer. You may need to compare recent changes to the original document.

1. Open the Ch21.1Merge document, make changes to the document, and save it to another folder or a different drive.

2. With only one of the documents open, click Tools|Track Changes|Compare Documents.

3. The open document will show the differences as tracked changes, as shown in Figure 23.6.

4. Save a version of the document with the changes.

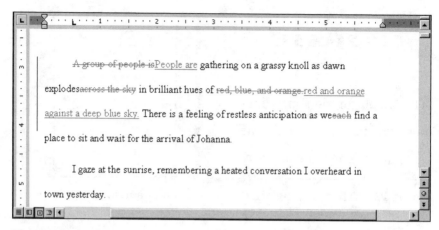

Figure 23.6 Comparing two documents for changes.

Practice Projects

Perform the following projects based on this chapter. You'll need to open the specified document from the disk included with this book.

Project 1   Protect an entire document.

1. Open the Ch21.1 Fax document you created in Chapter 21 and protect it from all changes.

2. Unprotect the document. Close without saving.

Answer to Project 1

Double-click the Ch21.1Fax. Click Tools|Protect, click the Forms option, and then click OK.

Click Tools|Unprotect. Click the Close button, and then click the No button when asked if you want to save the changes.

Project 2   Track changes in a protected document.

1. Open the Ch21.1Merged file you created in Chapter 21, protect the document, and then add the following information to the bottom of the list:

   Critters n' Things, Julie Albert, 2122 West 3rd Avenue, Denver, CO 88002

2. Accept the changes, then save and close the document.

Answer to Project 2

Double-click the Ch21.1Merged file. Click Tools|Protect, click the Tracked Changes option, and then click OK. Type the new company information.

Click Tools|Unprotect, click Tools|Track Changes|Accept Or Reject Changes, and then click the Accept All button. Click the Save button and then click the Close button.

Project 3   Protect a document with sections.

1. Use the Ch21.1Merged file.

2. Create a drop-down form field between the last paragraph and the word "Sincerely"; then use Figure 23.6 to fill in the field items. (Hint: Use the spacebar to create a blank field item.)

3. Insert a section break above and below the form field.

4. Protect only the section containing the form field. Attempt to modify section 1; then select an item from the drop-down list box.

5. Save the document to a new name and close it.

Answer to Project 3

Double-click the Ch21.1Merged file and insert three extra lines above "Sincerely". Place the cursor halfway between the last paragraph and "Sincerely".

Display the Forms toolbar, click the Drop-Down Form Field button, click the Properties button, and then fill in the field items, as shown in Figure 23.7.

Move the cursor to the line above the form field and then click InsertIBreak. Select the continuous section break. Repeat this for the line below the form field.

Click ToolsIProtect, click the Forms option, and then click the Sections button. Protect only section 2. Click section 1 and try to modify the letter. Click the drop-down list box and select an item from the list.

Click FileISave As and give the file a new name, saving to a diskette.

Project 4 Open a file using the Properties button.

1. Open the file on the disk that was included with this book that has the comment "Taken from the Internet".

2. Open the Properties dialog box and save the picture preview.

3. Save the document with the same name.

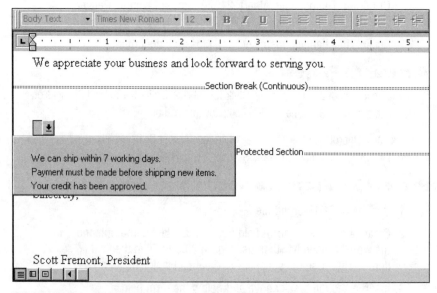

Figure 23.7   The field items for a drop-down list box.

Answer to Project 4

Click the Open button, click the Properties button on the Open dialog box, type "Taken from the Internet" in the Text or property text box. Double-click the file in the File list box.

Click File|Properties, click the Summary tab, and then click the Save Picture Preview option. Close the dialog box.

Click File|Save As, and then save the document on a diskette with the same file name.

Project 5   Open a file using the Preview button.

1. Open the file that you created in Chapter 21 that has the preview shown in Figure 23.8.

2. Add the comment "Need to add new customer data as of July 1, 1998."

3. Save the document with the same name.

Answer to Project 5

Click the Open button, click the Preview button in the Open dialog box, scroll the documents, and then double-click the Client data source file.

Click File|Properties, click the Summary tab, click the Comment text box, and then type the comment. Close the dialog box.

Click File|Save As, and then save the document on a diskette with the same file name.

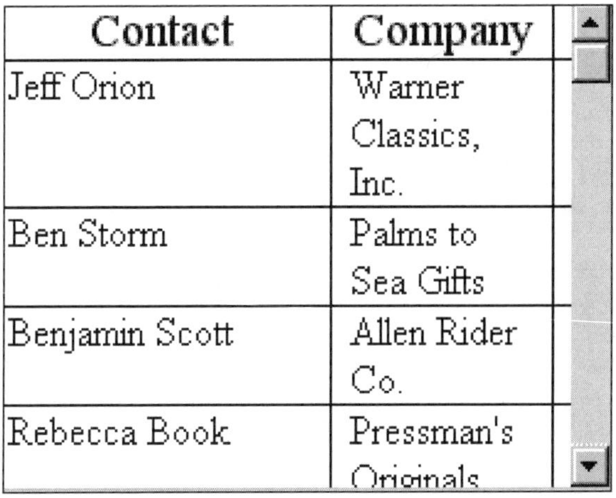

Contact	Company	
Jeff Orion	Warner Classics, Inc.	
Ben Storm	Palms to Sea Gifts	
Benjamin Scott	Allen Rider Co.	
Rebecca Book	Pressman's Originals	

Figure 23.8   Preview of a document created in Chapter 21.

Project 6   Compare two documents.

1. Open an existing document, make changes to the document, and then save it to another disk.

2. Compare the two documents, and close without saving.

Answer to Project 6

Open the document of your choice, and modify it. Save the document to a different drive, to a floppy or other disk storage type, or to a different folder.

With one of the documents open, click Tools|Track Changes|Compare Documents. View for changes, and then close the document, clicking No when asked if you want to save the changes.

Need To Know More?

 Napier, Albert H. and Phillip J. Judd: *Mastering and Using Microsoft Word 97*. Course Technology, Cambridge, MA, 1997. ISBN 0-7600-5022-8. This book brings the authors' experiences as educators and corporate trainers to Word 97 techniques.

 Shelly, Gary, Thomas Cashman, and Misty Vermaat: *Microsoft Word 97: Complete Concepts and Techniques*. Course Technology, Cambridge, MA, 1997. ISBN 0-7895-1338-2. A book in the Shelly Cashman series. Offers a step-by-step approach to learning beginning and advanced skills in Word 97.

 Swanson, Marie L.: *Microsoft Word 97—Illustrated Standard Edition: A Second Course*. Course Technology, Cambridge, MA, 1997. ISBN: 0-7600-5141-0. An Illustrated Series book. Covers intermediate through advanced skills.

 Zimmerman, Scott and Beverly Zimmerman: *New Perspectives on Microsoft Word 97—Comprehensive*. Course Technology, Cambridge, MA, 1997. ISBN 0-7600-5256-5. Part of the New Perspectives series. Offers case-based, problem-solving approaches to learning Word 97.

24

Sample Expert Level Test

The following sample test is designed to approximate the actual test.

The test comprises exercises or steps that you must complete correctly.

Chapter 25 contains the solutions to the sample test.

Information, Please

You'll be given approximately 41 tasks to complete. Each task will contain from one to five steps. The actual test has a 60-minute time limit, so you should time yourself as you practice these exercises.

If at any time the computer freezes, tell the test administrator. Occasional difficulties may occur at some test sites.

Testing, Testing

When you first sit down to take the test, you will read several windows of instruction. Take your time and read the instructions carefully, because the timer doesn't begin until you start the test. You'll have something to write on (some sites offer paper, and others offer a washable board and marker), so take notes if you need to. You can also write down things you want to remember before beginning the test.

A Tip To Help Test Stress

The biggest mistake you can make is to get too stressed about the test. Relax and don't let yourself feel rushed. Pretend you're completing a project for your employer. You want to do it efficiently and you want to do it right.

Taking The Test

Once you have checked out all the instructions, take a deep breath, and get comfortable while the test is loading.

Read the instructions in the window carefully. Once you move the mouse or use the keyboard the instructions will minimize to the bottom of the screen but will remain visible throughout the task. Occasionally, a dialog box may cover the instructions, but you can drag it out of the way.

What To Memorize

You don't need to memorize everything about Word to pass this test. Just make sure you know where to find toolbar buttons and menu items. You won't have time to search Help if you have a memory lapse, so the best plan is to memorize the menu items and buttons with which you're the least familiar. Also, committing the Cram Sheet to memory will give you a big start.

Last But Not Least

You're not allowed to go back to previous tasks, so try to complete each task and read the instructions carefully. This can't be stressed enough, because a spelling error, punctuation difference, or even a case difference will count the entire task wrong. So, if they tell you to type in all uppercase, do so!

Test Exercises

We've provided you with some practice exercises in the following pages. You may remember some of these tasks from previous chapters. Only this time, we've presented the exercises more closely to how you would perform them during the test. For answers to these practice exercises, read Chapter 25.

Exercise 1

1. Open the Ch14Say document from the disk that was included with this book, and insert a watermark on the first page using the clip art image of your choice. Resize and align the watermark to the center of the page.

2. Create a header on the odd pages with the title of the document on the left and the date on the right. On the even pages, create a header with the author's name (Sister Helen Mrosia) on the left.

3. Create a footer with the word "Page" and the page number in the center of the footer.

4. Create a style called Title_Case that will change selected text to a Brush Script (or equivalent), Teal, 22-point, bold, and italic font that's centered with 12-point spacing after the styled text. Apply the style to the title Say Something Good.

5. Save the document as Excercise1 and close it.

6. Open the file Ch24Books.

7. Add all the totals (Qtr 1 through Total), and then calculate the maximum annual sales total.

8. Save the document as Exercise1.1 and close it.

Exercise 2

1. Open the Ch24Design document from the disk.

2. Create a style called Bullet_Organizer that is based on the Normal style and applies a style with the following attributes:

   ➤ A 13-point, bold, Times New Roman font.

   ➤ A dark blue ◆ bullet, with the bullet position at .1 and the text position at .35.

3. Select the text from Angel through Porcupine and apply the style.

4. Insert an angel clip art of your choice, sizing and positioning it at the right margin in the center of the bulleted text. The top and bottom text should be .2 inches away from the image, and the clip art should move with the surrounding text.

5. Add one of the two-tone page borders using the color Blue. Size the border to 4 1/2 points, and position it 6 points away from the text on all four sides. Save the document as Exercise2 and close it.

6. Create a form letter mail merge using the Exercise2 document and the Ch24Data document that was included with this book.

7. Add the following record to the data source: Jamaica My Day, Leo Cransville, 12 W. Key Lime St., Miami, FL 01221.

8. Perform the merge, sorting the records in ascending order first by the company and then by the state.

9. Save the merged document as Exercise2Merge, save the Ch24Data document as Ch24.2Data, and then save the Exercise 2 document as Exercise2.2.

10. Close all of the documents.

Exercise 3

1. Open the Ch14Newsletter document from the disk.

2. Create three columns on page 1 of the newsletter, from "Help Is On The Way" through "we will work something out together". Make the column widths 2.1", 1.8", 1.8", and the spacing .4" each. Place a line in between each column.

3. On page 2 of the newsletter, change the last paragraph of column 1 that begins with "Being a single mom" so that it starts in the second column.

4. Save the document as Exercise3 and close it.

5. Open the file called Ch24Manual.

6. Make each chapter a subdocument.

7. Create a table of contents using the Classic style, showing four levels and dot style tab leaders.

8. Save the document as Exercise3.1.

9. Collapse the subdocuments, save as the same name, lock the document, and then close the master document.

Exercise 4

1. Open the Ch24Skis document from the disk.

2. Shade only page 1 with a light trellis pattern and turquoise background color.

3. Remove the border from only page 1 and then add a shadow box border.

4. Save the document as Exercise4 and close it.

5. Open the Ch18Income document.

6. Shade the heading row Violet with White text.

7. Shade the Totals and Average Annual Sales rows Violet with White text.

8. Save the document as Exercise4.1 and close it.

Exercise 5

1. Open a new blank document, and insert Ch24Skis and Ch24Books as subdocuments.

2. Switch to Page Layout view, and change the Category axis font to Times New Roman.

3. Delete the Fantasy row in the table and then save the document as Exercise5Master. Close the document.

4. Change the projected income for the year 2000 to $500,000.00, and then change all of the 1997s to 1998s.

5. Save the document as Exercise5a.

6. Compare documents Exercise5a and Ch24Skis. Save the compared document as Exercise5b.

Answers To Sample Expert Level Test

25

This chapter contains the answers to the Chapter 24 test exercises.

Exercise 1

1. Open the file Ch14Say from the disk included with this book. Click View|Headers And Footers, click Insert|Picture|Clip Art, select an image, and then click the Insert button. Reduce the size of the image, drag it to the center of the page, right-click the image, and then click the Format Picture command. Set the Color option on the Picture tab to Watermark, select the None option on the Wrapping tab, click the Position tab, select the Lock Anchor option, and then deselect the Move Object With Text option. Click OK to close the dialog box and accept the changes.

2. Click the Page Setup button on the Header And Footer toolbar, click the Different Odd And Even option, and then deselect the Different First Page option on the Layout tab. Type "Say Something Good" on the left side of the header, tab twice, and then click the Insert Date button. Click the Show Next button and type "Sister Helen Mrosla" on the left side of the Header.

3. Click the Show Previous button, click the Switch Between Header And Footer button, type "Page", press the spacebar, click the Insert Page Number button, and then click the Close button.

4. Click Format|Style, click the New button, type "Title_Case" in the Name box, and then select Normal in the Based On list box. Click the Format button and then select the Font option. Select the Brush Script font (or equivalent) from the Font list box, select the Bold Italic option in the Font Style list box, select the 22 point size option in the Size list box, and select the Teal option in the Color list box. Click the OK button. Click the Format button and then select the Paragraph option. Verify that the Indents And Spacing tab is active, select the Center option in the Alignment list box, and then type or select 12 points in the After spin box in the Spacing group. Click the OK button to accept the changes, and then click the OK button in the Style dialog box to return to the document. Select the title, click the Style box list arrow on the Formatting toolbar, and then select the Title_Case style (see Figure 25.1).

5. Click File|Versions, click the Save Now button, type any comments, and then close the Versions dialog boxes. Click File|Save As, click the Save In list box, locate the folder where you want to save the document, rename it Exercise1, and then click the Save button.

6. Open the file New Ch24Books from the disk included with this book.

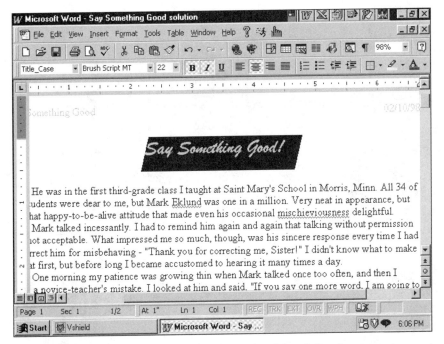

Figure 25.1 Applying the new style to the title of the document.

7. Click the cell below the Qtr 1 totals, click Table|Formula, verify that the formula in the Formula box says =SUM(ABOVE), replace above with the cell locations (b2:b8), and then click OK. Repeat this for Qtr 2 through Qtr 4, adjusting the column location for each new column (c2:c8 for Qtr 2, d2:d8 for Qtr 3, and e2:e8 for Qtr 4). Click in the cell to the right of the Maximum Annual Sale heading, click Table|Formula, delete the SUM(ABOVE) formula in the Formula box (leaving the equal sign), click the Paste function list arrow and select the MAX function, type "f2:f8" inside the parentheses, and then click OK (see Figure 25.2).

In real life table calculations you can use SUM(ABOVE) and MAX(ABOVE) functions. But for the test, go ahead and use the cell references to make sure the task is scored correctly.

8. Click File|Save As, click the Save In list box, locate the folder where you want to save the document, rename it Exercise1.1, and then click the Save button.

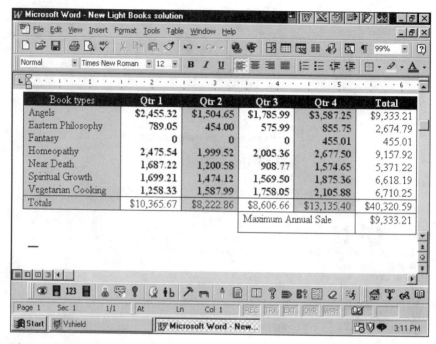

Figure 25.2 The table with the columns totaled and the maximum annual sales found.

Exercise 2

1. Open the file Ch24Design from the disk included with this book.

2. Click Format|Style, click the New button in the Style dialog box, type Bullet_Organizer in the Name box, and then select Normal in the Based On list box. Click the Format button and then select the Font option. Select the Times New Roman font from the Font list box, select the Bold option in the Font Style list box, type 13 in the Size list box, and then click the OK button. Click the Format button and then select the Numbering option. Click the diamond-shaped bullet and then click the Customize button. Click the Font button, type 13 in the Size list box, select the dark blue color from the Color list box, and then click the OK button. Type or select .1 in the Bullet Position Indent At spin box, and then type or select .35 in the Text Position Indent At spin box. Close the Style dialog box.

3. Drag the mouse from the text that begins with Angel and ends with Porcupine to select it. Click the Style list box down arrow on the Formatting toolbar, and then click the Bullet_Organizer style.

4. Click at the end of a word in the list, click Insert|Picture|Clip Art, click the Find button, type the word "angel" in the Keywords text box, and then click the Find Now button. Select an angel clip art and then click the Insert button. If you don't have an angel, then select a clip of your choice. Reduce its size and drag it to the right margin, centering it with the bulleted text. Right-click the image and then select the Format Picture option. Click the Wrapping tab, select the Square wrapping option and the Left option in the Wrap To group, and then type or select .2 in the Top and Bottom spin boxes in the Distance From text group. Click the Position tab, and then verify that the Move Object With Text option is selected and that the Lock Anchor option is deselected (see Figure 25.3).

5. Click Format|Borders And Shading, click the Page Border tab, scroll down the Style list box and select one of the two-tone borders, click Blue in the Color list box, and then click 4 1/2 points in the Width list box. Click the Options button, select the Text option in the Measure From list box, and then type or select 6 points in the Top, Bottom, Left, and Right spin boxes (see Figure 25.4). Close the dialog box and then click File|Save As, click the Save In list box, locate the folder where you want to

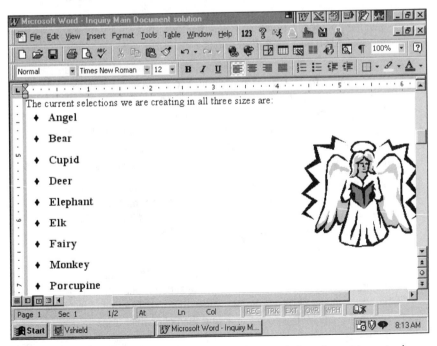

Figure 25.3 Bullet style applied to the list, and the clip art inserted and formatted.

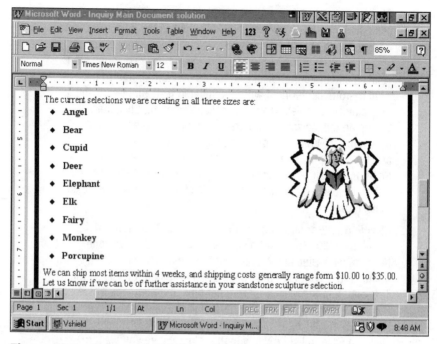

Figure 25.4   The Inquiry Main Document with a page border.

save the document, rename it Exercise2, and then click the Save button. Click the Close button to close the document.

6. Click Tools|Mail Merge, click the Create button on the Mail Merge Helper, select the Form Letters option, and then click the Active Window button in the message box. Click the Get Data button on the Mail Merge Helper, click the Open data source option, and then select the Ch24Data document from the disk included with this book. Click the Edit Main Document button in the message box, and then insert the merge fields in Exercise2 (see Figure 25.5).

7. Click the Mail Merge Helper button, click the Edit button in the Data Source group, click the Add New button on the data form, add the record, Jamaica My Day, Leo Cransville, 12 W. Key Lime St., Miami, FL 01221, and then click the OK button.

8. Click the Mail Merge Helper button, click the Query Options button, click the Sort Records tab, and then select Company in the first Sort By list box and State in the second. Click the Merge button on the Mail Merge Helper, verify that New Document is selected in the Merge To list box, and then click the Merge button.

9. Click File|Save As, click the Save In list box, locate the folder where you want to save the document, rename it Exercise2Merge,

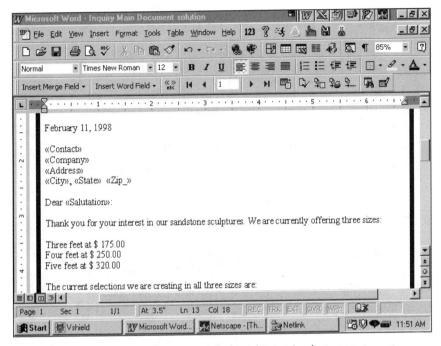

Figure 25.5 The merge fields added to the main document.

and then click the Save button. Click File|Save As, click the Save In list box, locate the folder where you want to save the document, rename it Ch24.2Data, and then click the Save button. Click File|Save As, click the Save In list box, locate the folder where you want to save the document, rename it Exercise2.2, and then click the Save button.

10. A quick way to close all active documents is to hold down the Shift key while clicking the File menu command. The Close command becomes the Close All command. Click Close All to close all open documents.

Exercise 3

1. Open the file Ch14Newsletter from the disk included with this book.

2. Select the text from "Help Is On The Way" through "we will work something out together". Click Format|Columns, click the three-column option (three in the Presets group), and then deselect the Equal Column Width option. Click the Width spin box for column 1 and enter 2.1"; click the Spacing spin box and enter .4". Click the Width spin box for column 2 and enter 1.8"; click the Spacing spin box and enter .4". Then, verify that the Width spin box for

column 3 is 1.8". Click the Line Between option and then click the OK button.

3. Place the cursor in front of the line *Being a single mom*, click Insert|Break, and then click the Column Break option.

4. Click File|Save As, click the Save In list box, locate the folder where you want to save the document, rename it Exercise3, and then click the Save button.

5. Open the file Ch24Manual from the disk included with this book.

6. Click View|Master Document, click the hollow plus sign next to Chapter 1, and then click the Create Subdocument button. Repeat this for Chapters 2 and 3.

7. Place the cursor to the left of the Chapter 1 title, click Insert|Index And Tables, and then click the Table Of Contents tab. Select Classic in the Formats list box, select 4 in the Show Levels spin box, and then select the dot option in the Tab Leaders list box.

8. Click File|Save As, click the Save In list box, locate the folder where you want to save the document, rename it Exercise3.1, and then click the Save button.

9. Click the Collapse Subdocuments button, save the document when prompted by the message box, click the Lock Document button, and then click the Close button.

Exercise 4

1. Open the Ch24Skis document from the disk that was included with this book.

2. Switch to Normal view, if necessary, add a continuous section break just above the page break, delete any space between the breaks as necessary, and then select all the text on page 1. Click Format|Borders And Shading, click the Shading tab, click the Patterns list arrow, and then click the Lt Trellis selection. Click the Turquoise color option from the Color list box (not the Color palette), and then verify the Paragraph option is showing in the Apply To list box. Click OK to close the dialog box, click to the right of 1997, and then press the Enter key until the trellis background shading covers the entire page.

3. Click Format|Borders And Shading, click the Page Border tab, click the Shadow option, click the This Section option in the Apply To list box, and then close the dialog box.

4. Click File|Save As, click the Save In list box, locate the folder where you want to save the document, rename it Exercise4, and

click the Save button. Click the Close button on the document menu bar.

5. Open the Ch18Income document from the disk that was included with this book.

6. Click to the left of the table's heading row (when the mouse pointer becomes a hollow arrow that faces to the right), right-click a toolbar, click the Tables And Borders toolbar, click the Shading Color list arrow, and then click the Violet option. Click the Font Color list arrow on the Formatting toolbar and then select the White option.

7. Click to the left of the Totals row (when the mouse pointer becomes a hollow arrow that faces to the right) to select it, click the Shading Color button, and then click the Font Color button on the Formatting toolbar. Repeat for the Average Annual Sales row.

8. Click File|Save As, click the Save In list box, locate the folder where you want to save the document, rename it Exercise4.1, and then click the Save button. Click the Close button on the document menu bar.

Exercise 5

1. Click the New button on the Standard toolbar. Click View|Master Document, click the Insert Subdocument button, double-click the Ch24Skis document on the disk that was included with this book, and then repeat for Ch24Books. Click the Save button on the Standard toolbar, name the document Exercise5a, and then click the OK button on the Save dialog box.

Note: If a message box displays asking you if you want to rename any styles that are duplicated, click the No To All button.

2. Click the Page Layout View button on the scroll bar, double-click the chart to activate it, and then click the Category axis text to select it. Select the Times New Roman option in the Font list box on the Chart Formatting toolbar to change the font. Click outside of the chart area to deselect it.

3. Scroll to the table, click to the left of the Fantasy row to select it, and then click Table|Delete Rows.

4. Scroll to the last sentence on page 3, and change $175,000.00 to $500,000.00. Scroll to the top of the document, click the Browse button on the Vertical scroll bar (see Figure 25.6), and then click

Skis n' Things

Sales Report

Select Browse Object

2/4 | At 1" | Ln 1 | Col 1 | REC | TRK | EXT | OVR | WPH

Figure 25.6 The Browse button tool tip will say Select Browse Object.

the Find option (the binoculars). Click the Replace tab, type "1997" in the Find What box, type "1998" in the Replace With What box, and then click the Replace All button.

5. Close the Find dialog box, click File|Save As, type Exercise5b in the File Name text box, and then click the Save button.

6. Click Tools|Track Changes|Compare Documents.

Glossary

3-D Effects—Word's tools for making two-dimensional shapes look like three-dimensional shapes.

Alignment—How text, graphics, and other elements line up with other items on the page.

Alternating headers and footers—Headers and footers that differ on even and odd pages.

Arrow style—Effects that you can apply to drawn arrows with the Drawing toolbar.

Art border—A decorative page border.

AutoCorrect entries—Items that you can specify in AutoCorrect so that word automatically can change abbreviations or misspellings when you type them. For example, you can enter your initials as an AutoCorrect entry so that Word spells out your name whenever you type your initials.

AutoCorrect Exceptions—Words, abbreviations, and other items of text that you can specify so Word doesn't automatically correct them.

AutoCorrect—A Word feature that corrects misspellings and specified items while you type.

AutoShapes—A set of pre-set shapes that you can draw in your documents with Word's drawing features.

AutoText—Boilerplate text items stored in Word so you can apply them to documents without having to type them from scratch.

Bitmap—A clip art or other graphic object that cannot be ungrouped and edited.

Bookmark—An item that you can create to mark a location in a document, an entry for an index, or a cross-reference. When working with HTML documents, you can use bookmarks to create hyperlinks to areas within the current document. You can also use bookmarks to jump to a particular location in your document.

Border—A line that bounds an object. Borders for tables can be specified in the Borders And Lines dialog box. Borders for drawn objects can be specified with the Drawing toolbar.

Browsing—To search for a file by clicking folders and selecting available servers and computers in the Open dialog box.

Bullet style—Bullets can appear as circles, squares, and a variety of characters (see also Number style).

Bullet—A typographic character or symbol used to separate and list text elements.

Callouts—A type of AutoShape (see AutoShapes) that lets you point to an item on a picture and enter explanatory text. These look similar to comic strip balloons.

Catalog—A mail merge that displays all on one page.

Character effects—Settings that you can apply to text characters through the Font dialog box, such as superscript, subscript, engraving, and shadows.

Chart—A graphical representation of a data series.

Column break—Marks the end of a column and stores the column's formatting.

Column spacing—The amount of space between columns.

Column width—The width of a column.

Columns—A Word layout feature that enables you to lay out text in columns similar to how text is formatted in magazines and newspapers.

Compare—Viewing changes to a document that is either saved in two locations or is saved by two different names.

Copy—To copy text or an object to the system's clipboard without removing the text or object from the original location.

Cross-reference—Suggests an alternate index location for a word or phrase in a document.

Current document—The file that is displayed in your document window.

Cut—To copy text or an object onto the system's clipboard while removing the text or object from the original location.

Dashed line style—Effects that you can apply to a drawn line or border through the Drawing toolbar or the Borders And Lines dialog box.

Data source—A collection of data records that contains the data fields used in a mail merge.

Datasheet—A worksheet containing sample data that is provided by Word.

Demote—To assign an outline item a lower-level heading and move it down in priority in an outline.

Directory—A folder. Folders on a server are often referred to as "directories."

Document Map—An option that you can select from the View menu in order to display a frame that lists all of the headings in the current document.

Document window—The area of the Word application window that displays the document.

Document—A file created or readable using Microsoft Word.

Downloading—Retrieving files from a remote server using Word, a Web browser, or an FTP program.

Email—Sending a document as mail via the Internet.

Embedding—Placing an entire copy of another document within another, so that the data can be edited by double-clicking the embedded object.

Endnotes—A comment or explanation of referenced text. It generally appears at the end of the document.

Even and Odd headers and footers—*See* Alternating headers and footers.

File management—The set of skills associated with locating, opening, creating, and saving files.

File properties—Information about a document that includes file names, file sizes, the dates the files were last modified, and more.

File Transfer Protocol (FTP)—A set of standard procedures for getting files from a remote server and saving them to a remote server. This is also called *downloading* and *uploading* files.

Fill—The color and shading that fills a drawing or table cell.

Find And Replace—Displays a dialog box so you can search for a symbol, a word, or group of words within a document and replace them with different text.

Find—An operation that enables you to search for a symbol, a word, or group of words within a document.

Fonts—Typefaces that you can select from the Font dialog box or Font list and apply to selected text.

Footer—A section at the bottom of a page with information that repeats on each page, like page numbers, an author's name, or today's date.

Footers—Customize a document. Footers display at the bottom of each page.

Footnotes—A comment or explanation of referenced text. It appears at the bottom of the page that contains the text reference.

Form Field—A field that inserts a checkbox, drop-down list, or text box in an *online form.*

Format Painter—A toolbar button that allows you to select a paragraph and apply its character and paragraph formatting to another paragraph.

GoTo—An operation that enables you to locate page elements, including sections, headings, bookmarks, graphics, and tables.

Grammar—Word's feature for checking grammar in a document.

Graphic—A picture, clip art, chart, drawing, or other image that can be inserted in a document.

Hanging indent—The first line begins to the left and the lines below wrap to a tab stop.

Header—A section at the top of a page with information that repeats on each page, like page numbers, an author's name, or today's date.

Headers—Customize a document. Headers display at the top of each page.

HTML document—A document that is formatted by special HTML tags so it can be viewed in a Web browser. When Word converts documents to HTML, it automatically adds the tags.

Hyperlinks—In HTML documents, hyperlinks enable you to click on text or images to display another file or jump to a different area within a document.

Hypertext Transfer Protocol (HTTP)—The set of standards and procedures for viewing and distributing Web pages.

Hyphenation—A Word feature that helps you determine how words that are too long to fit on the current line should be split by hyphens.

Importing data—Inserts data into a table, which maintains all the Word table formatting.

Indent—To force the right or left margin of a paragraph inward to set it apart from other paragraphs in a document.

Index—Text that usually appears at the end of a document. It lists words or phrases in a document, including the page numbers where they appear.

Intranet—An private office network that offers services—such as Web pages and FTP—that are similar to the Internet.

Landscape orientation—Specifies that the document will be viewed and printed with the long edge of the paper at the top.

Line spacing—The amount of space between paragraphs.

Line style—The appearance and width of a drawn line. Line styles can be applied with the Drawing toolbar.

Linking—Placing a connection to another file within one file, so that the original file can be edited by double-clicking the linked object.

Macro—A string of commands and keystrokes that you record and use to automatically accomplish a task.

Mail Merge—Combining a primary document and a data source to create form letters, labels, parts lists, and catalogs.

Margins—The space at the top, bottom, right, and left of a page that offsets the text from the edges of the page.

Master document—Holds a set of separate files or subdocuments that are related, such as the chapters of a book.

Merge Fields—A set of codes that instruct Word to automatically insert text, graphics, page numbers, or other material into a document at a specified location.

Metafiles—clip art objects that can be ungrouped and edited.

Nonbreaking space—A nonbreaking special character keeps two words together, not allowing them to be broken across a page or an end of a line.

Normal view—Word's default view for a document. The Normal view hides layout elements (such as graphics, headers, and footers) so you can type and make edits more quickly.

Number style—The number formatting options that can be applied to page numbers and numbered lists (*see also,* Bullet style).

Online form—A form that can be filled out on the computer and then printed.

Orphan—The first line of a paragraph that is printed at the bottom of the current page.

Outline view—Displays documents organized by headings, subheadings, and subordinate text, so you can quickly arrange and prioritize headings and text.

OverType—A Word feature that enables you to replace text by typing over it.

Page break—Ends the current page and begins a new page.

Page Layout view—Displays documents with layout elements, such as graphics, columns, headers, and footers, so you can precisely position page elements.

Page numbering—A Word feature that allows you to automatically number pages by placing a page number in the headers or footers of a document.

Page orientation—How the document will be viewed and printed. There are two types of orientation: *portrait* and *landscape*.

Page Setup—A dialog box for specifying basic page layout settings, such as margins and alternating headers and footers.

Paste—To place text or other elements from the system's clipboard into the place where you've inserted your cursor.

Point size—The height of the printed characters. The width of one character equals 10 1/2 points.

Portrait orientation—Word's default print orientation. It specifies that the document will be viewed and printed with the short edge of the paper at the top.

Print Preview—Displays a document as it will appear when printed.

Promote—To move an item in an outline up one level and to assign a higher-level heading to it.

Protect—Adds protection to a document, which keeps others from altering data.

Query—Asks a question of the document with particular parameters. Is a means of finding all the records stored in a data source that fit a set of criteria you name.

Replace—An operation that enables you to locate and replace words and groups of words.

Rotate Text—*See* Text Direction.

Route—Sending a document through the Internet or intranet for editing.

Save as HTML—Displays the Save as HTML dialog box so you can save the current document as a Web page.

Save As—Displays the Save As dialog box, so you can save the current document with a different name, or save it to a different folder.

Save—Saves the current document.

Section break—Specifies a new section for a document so you can format the new section differently than the rest of the document.

Shading—Background coloring for text and text boxes.

Sort Ascending/Descending—A Tables And Borders toolbar option that enables you to sort items in a table in numerical or alphabetical order. The Ascending option lists items from 1-100 or A-Z, and the Descending option lists items from 100-1 or Z-A.

Sorting—Places text, lists, paragraphs, and other text into alphabetical order.

Special characters—Special characters can be international characters, typographic characters, and symbols like an arrow or happy face.

Spelling And Grammar—You can check just spelling, or grammar and spelling, by displaying the Spelling And Grammar dialog box.

Strikethrough—A line through deleted text in Track Changes mode.

Styles—Stored text and paragraph formatting attributes that you can create, edit, and apply automatically to text in a document from the Style list or Style dialog box.

Subdocument—A separate document within a master document.

Subfolder—A folder inside the current folder.

Tab alignment—Tabs can align left, to the center, as a decimal, or to the right. You can apply tab alignment options from the Tabs dialog box.

Tab leader—A line that connects items of tabbed text. You can apply tab leaders from the Tabs dialog box.

Table of contents—Appears at the beginning of a document. It lists the headings of each chapter, and any sections within each chapter and their corresponding page numbers.

Template—A document that stores boilerplate text, graphics, headers, footers, and other standard document elements so you can use the formatting over and over again. You can create templates and select them from the New dialog box.

Text Direction—An option that allows you to rotate text in 90 degree increments.

Thesaurus—A Word feature that lets you select a word, and select from and substitute alternative words.

Track Changes—A command that visually marks additions or deletions to a document.

Underline styles—Effects that you can apply to underlines through the Font dialog box.

Uploading—Copying files to a remote server using Word, a Web browser, or an FTP program.

Versions—Multiple versions, or "snapshots," of a document saved within the same document.

Vertical alignment—How text and other objects line up in relation to the top and bottom of the page.

Visual Basic—The programming language that uses macros to automate redundant tasks.

Watermark—A graphic, WordArt, AutoShape, logo, or drawing that appears behind existing text in your document. It appears lightly in the background of each printed page.

Web page—*See* HTML document.

Widow—A widow is the last line of a paragraph that is printed at the top of a new page.

Index

What's On The Companion Disk?

The companion disk contains the Word documents needed to perform all tasks, practice exercises, and practice tests discussed in the book. These files are compressed in a zip format.

See the readme file located on the disk for more information about using these files.

Software Requirements:

➤ Word 97

➤ Excel 97

➤ WinZip or other file compression program

Hardware Requirements:

➤ Platform—Intel and compatible 486/66

➤ Microsoft Windows 95, Windows 98, or Windows NT

➤ 8MB of RAM minimum (16MB recommended)